THE CHINA
YEARS

THE CHINA YEARS

The Life and Letters
of the Rev & Mrs Clifford V. Cook
China Missionaries 1925-52

EDITED BY

RAYMOND COOK

MARION BOYARS
LONDON • NEW YORK

Published in Great Britain and the United States in 2005 by
MARION BOYARS PUBLISHERS LTD
24 Lacy Road
London SW15 1NL

www.marionboyars.co.uk

Distributed in Australia and New Zealand by
Peribo Pty Ltd
58 Beaumont Road
Kuring-gai, NSW 2080

Printed in 2005
10 9 8 7 6 5 4 3 2 1

A CIP catalogue record for this book is available from the British Library.
A CIP catalog record for this book is available from the Library of Congress.

ISBN 0-7145-3112-X
13 digit ISBN 9780-7145-3112-0

Set in Sabon 11.5/14pt
Printed in England by Bookmarque Ltd

CONTENTS

List of Illustrations

Introduction

序

As modern day China builds itself into an increasingly
formidable world power, the romantic images of
mysticism and intrigue that the West once associated with
the country are being swiftly corroded. In the wake of
Communism, the 21st century will see such immense
commercial developments as the Three Gorges project on
the banks of the Yangtze River change the face of China
irrevocably. And so it seems that the publication of this
account of my parents' time as country missionaries is
particularly timely. Creating a microcosm of life in China
in the 20s, 30s and 40s – a life that was was often brutal
but never dull – this first-hand account provides an
invaluable glimpse of the country as it was before the vast
social and political upheaval of recent years. My hope is
that perhaps this will also help us understand China's
impending role in the international political arena.

The account largely speaks for itself, through the
letters they wrote home during those turbulent years.
My father wrote regularly to his parents, while my
mother corresponded with her sister in Australia. While
it is disappointing that the record is far from complete,
more than one hundred and eighty letters written by
them have survived until today. These form the
backbone of this book.

To help set the social and political context in which
the letters were written, I have drawn on additional
information from other sources, as well as adding my
own commentary. The most important single source of

filling in the gaps is my mother's book *China as I Remember It* (privately published in 1994).

On occasion, letters by both my parents have been included describing the same event, since my parents' style of reporting is very different – my mother's more personal and generally with greater feeling, while my father's is more factual and with more mention of political developments and other background information.

In a number of places, such as descriptions of photos and in the title of letters, indicating the author and the recipient, I have used my parents' initials – CVC (Clifford Vallance Cook) for my father and EMC (Elsie May Cuthbertson/Cook) for my mother – by way of abbreviation. In letter headings I have also used the abbreviation AIC (Alice Isabel Cook) for my grandmother.

My mother, who was seven years older than my father, arrived in China in 1925, having left England on New Year's Day that year. My father sailed for China in late 1929, aged just twenty-three. Apart from the occasional furlough, my parents remained there until a few months before the Communists completed their conquest of the country in 1949.

My father returned to Hong Kong eighteen months later, leaving my mother, my brother and me in Bristol, to work with the flood of refugees who had fled into Hong Kong to escape the retribution of the new Communist government. My father worked among them for two years before returning to England and entering the home circuit where he worked until his death in 1972.

Raymond Cook, 2005

Chapter 1
China: The Early Years - EMC

Her calling

My mother, Elsie May Cuthbertson, was born in Stanley in County Durham, on 27th August 1899, in the final months of the 19th century. She was the fifth and last child of her parents Ralph and Jane Cuthbertson.

The family was a religious one, but not deeply so. Ralph was an Anglican, while Jane was a Methodist. It seems as a compromise neither attended church regularly after their marriage.

On leaving school my mother secured a post as a 'pupil-teacher', in the expectation that teaching would be her lifetime career. However, a few years later, largely as a result of reading David Livingstone's *In Darkest Africa*, she became convinced that her duty lay in becoming a missionary. She spoke to her mother about her dream. Her mother was not opposed to the idea, but persuaded her to wait a few years to see how things developed, presumably expecting her enthusiasm to wane. But it didn't. From that time onward my mother never wavered in her conviction that her destiny was to be a missionary. She prayed every day that this might come to pass.

About four years later, following the death of her mother, she spoke to a visiting preacher, who had formerly been a missionary, and he suggested that my mother got in touch with the Wesley Deaconess Order, offering to write to the Deaconess College in Ilkley on her behalf. Within a few weeks my mother was at Ilkley starting her training.

Before she had completed the course my mother wrote to the Methodist Missionary Society offering her services and after attending the usual interviews in London she was accepted. She wrote to the committee telling them that she wanted to go to Africa, the continent of David Livingstone. If they wished she was prepared to go to India or Ceylon, but did not want to go to China. But after posting the letter she thought about what she had written and felt unhappy that after having prayed so fervently to be able to be a missionary she was now trying to dictate the terms. So she wrote again, withdrawing her previous stipulations, asking them to send her wherever they wished...and they sent her to China.

As none of her family had been missionaries, nor had she ever met anyone who had been one, my mother's decision to become a missionary was entirely her own. None of her friends or contemporaries ever aspired to such things. It must have taken considerable determination, self-belief and courage for her to break from the narrow confines of her upbringing and set sail for far-off China in 1925.

Sailing for China

My mother sailed from England on New Year's Day 1925 aboard the SS Rawalpindi. After a six week voyage via the Suez Canal, Ceylon and Singapore she arrived in Shanghai. Spending a few days in Shanghai she then travelled down the Yangtze by river steamer to Hankow, a journey of six hundred miles, which took four days, then took a crowded launch to Changsha, the capital of

Hunan Province. In Changsha she met the Chairman of the district, Mr Gibson, along with some of her new colleagues, and learned at first hand about the work she was to undertake and the life she was to live. She then travelled back down the Hsiang River, Hunan's longest river, on another crowded launch, retracing much of the route she had taken from Hankow to the Tung T'ing Lake. From there a short way up the Tze River to Yiyang, a busy river port on the Tze River in the north of Hunan, lying just south of the Tung T'ing Lake, the second largest lake in China. This was to be her first home in China.

Early days in China

Before my mother could carry out any useful work it was necessary for her to learn some Chinese. So her first task was to get to grips with the language. Her teacher was an old Chinese gentleman who knew no English and with her knowing almost no Chinese the possibilities for confusion were rife. She described these lessons in a letter she wrote to her sister Jean in Australia.

Letter of 3rd March 1925 from Yiyang

We arrived here in Yiyang a week yesterday, and what a busy time we have had since then. The whole of the first day was spent unpacking and making our introductory bows to visitors. Of course we cannot understand a word they say but we bow and smile and sit and try and look intelligent, while they talk away fifty to the dozen.

We got fixed up with a teacher and began our Chinese lessons on Wednesday morning and now every day finds me with a pile of unfinished work. You have to put in such a tremendous

11

amount of work to get the smallest result in Chinese.

Chinese lessons are very funny. Our teacher cannot speak a word of English and in spite of work on board ship my Chinese vocabulary, to say the very best of it, is limited. It is a blessing that smiles don't need translating because it is the only language I have at present.

The teacher is always in the room waiting for me. Please don't think it is my old habit of being late. It isn't, but I have just come over from morning prayers at that time. He puts his hands up his sleeves and bows and smiles. I bow and smile. We both mutter something, then we look at our chairs and smile, then I sit down and he does the same. First we do what is called tone drill. He says, 'Ma, ma, ma, ma, ma', in the five tones and like a lost lamb I go, 'Ma, ma, ma, ma, ma', after him. Then he 'moos' and I 'moo'. Then he 'mews' and I 'mew'. It is a wonder I don't get indigestion with all the laughter I swallow.

After that we read from 'An Idiom a Lesson', more commonly known as 'An Idiot a Lesson'. Once more, like a very meek little parrot I pipe along after him. Then I decide I want to ask a question. With about one Chinese word and a dozen English ones I ask it and he replies in fifty Chinese words. We gaze at each other in amazement for a minute, then we smile to show there is no ill feeling, wonder whatever the other was talking about, then continue with the lesson.

Very occasionally we do understand each other, for example this morning I said something which sounds something like 'Ngo boo lun shway dsun kuo hwa', which means 'I am not able to speak Chinese', and we both most heartily agreed.

After I have worried the dear man for an hour my new colleague Maud Millican has him for an hour, then the two of us have what is left of him for another hour. In the last hour we have writing and 'conversation'. Some conversation! The only way to get to know what the Chinese for something *is, is to do the action, so behold Maudie and me walking around the room, opening the window or door, or shutting them, putting coal on the fire etc.*

Maudie runs a little dispensary for the school girls and she goes there from nine to ten in the morning and in the evening from five to six. I go in the evening to help her and we practice our Chinese, while those of the scholars who are learning English practice their English. We do make some howlers. I am still almost too afraid to open my mouth. The other night Maudie meant to say 'sit down'; instead of that she said 'chicken, chicken'. Lillian (Grand) asked her at supper to ask the servant for some cheese, but she said 'I want a wife', and wondered why the poor man looked puzzled. One night when the teachers were over I tried to be polite and asked them to 'sit down' – at least I meant to – but it happens I told them to 'get out', in the sense of 'hop it quick'... The trouble with Chinese is the slightest difference in tone, ie the pitch of your voice or the sound, doesn't merely mean a mistake, it gives a totally different meaning.

For six months my mother followed this routine, spending three hours a day with her teacher and six studying on her own. Then when the heat of the Hunan summer became too intense she went up to the beautiful hill station of Kuling for several weeks. This was the normal practice for Europeans in China at the time, especially in the case of women. The death rate of Europeans in Hunan and the neighbouring province of Hupeh – from malaria, dysentery, sprue, typhus, cholera etc – was as high as 'the white man's grave' of West Africa and it was considered essential for the women and children to spend most of the summer up in the hills, their husbands joining them for a shorter period. Kuling was the most popular hill station in China and was widely used by the British and other foreign communities.

The summer season in Kuling was a wonderful time for renewing acquaintances and meeting new people. In the inter-war years there was a British school there and a number of expatriates lived there permanently. There were swimming pools, tennis courts, concerts etc.

While in Kuling during her first summer of 1925 my mother joined in many of the activities and met many new people, but continued to spend much of her time trying to improve her Chinese.

On returning to Yiyang, much refreshed, she continued with her language training, but at the same time went out on several trips into the countryside, to visit the country chapels run by Chinese ministers. The only means of transport for these journeys was by foot, which either meant walking or being carried by chair (very often it was a combination of the two). The chair was a seat with a canopy overhead suspended on two long wooden poles, held at either end by a coolie. Often a third coolie was employed to carry luggage. After the relative luxury of the Yangtze river steamers and the clean, cool air of Kuling this was a return to real missionary life.

One such country visit, which my mother made with fellow missionaries Lillian Grand and Maud Millican, is described in the following letter.

A Country Journey, 1925

We set off at 8.30 am on the Saturday. The cavalcade consisted of first Lillian striding ahead clearing the way, then Maud and I in the chairs being carried in state by two men each. Behind us came the cook and behind him the baggage coolie. It was a glorious sunny morning, so it was a joy either to walk or ride. The road ran through beautiful scenery – slightly hilly. Most of the trees out here do not turn our lovely brown, but a vivid red, which stands out in striking contrast to the light feathery green of the bamboos...

The road is about three feet wide, sometimes a little less and sometimes a little more. In the centre runs − at least for part of the way − a stone path, made of slabs of stone about a foot broad, placed end to end. On each side of this is either hard earth, or, in wet weather, mud. We only had stone for the first mile or so, after that it was all mud, so you can imagine what it was like travelling back on the Monday after a day's rain. But that comes at the end of the story and not the beginning. (I forgot to mention this was a main road!)

Our first stop was at Hsin Tze T'ou. Here Lillian Grand took a service in the packed chapel and jolly hard work it was too. There was such a crowd of people and some of them, who were just there out of curiosity, persisted in walking about to have a good look at the foreigners. After the service Maud vaccinated some children and after they had finished howling we sat down to a Chinese meal, which the members had provided for us. I daren't tell you how much I ate!

We left Hsin Tze T'ou at 2 pm and arrived at Lan Pa about 6 pm. In all this time we had only travelled twenty miles... The scenery was really wonderful, every turn of the road had something different to show, and when I say every turn it means a lot, for Chinese roads wind in and out like a snake in a fit.

We were staying at a very highly respectable inn. It was so different from the usual Chinese inn... This inn was kept by one of our members and the good lady pressed upon us her own bedroom. One result of this was every time anyone came to buy some oil or pickles the dear lady had to come to our room to get them. It doesn't sound very exciting, but you have never smelt Chinese pickles!

About 8.30 pm we dispersed the audience which had surrounded us from the time of our arrival, and decided to go to bed. There was one bed for the three of us. I was put in the middle. It wasn't a case of 'When father says turn, we all turn', it was more like turn if you can. Sometimes I could lie flat and sometimes I couldn't. I went up the bed and down it seeking air, but I found it not – neither did the others. At last Lillian got up and made a lot of holes in the window. Don't be alarmed, it was paper, not glass. After that breathing became possible. We were very fortunate in having only one rat to keep us company – luckily there was not room for him in the bed!

On Sunday morning we had a Chinese breakfast, then set off for Ku Hsi T'ou, about five miles further on. It is a most interesting congregation. It was one of those places where the people do not die, they just fade away. One old man, who looked about a hundred, sat and smoked all through the service (his pipe was so long it was resting on the ground), another old man was totally blind, another had three big bits of sticking plaster on his forehead. Maud had just 'doctored him up'. By the side of these, the rest of the congregation were very ordinary. There were several women and twice as many babies. Two of the babies stood up in the middle of the floor and had a fight… When the howls became too loud they were separated.

Although I cannot help laughing about some of the people, and the singing was just impossible, I do admire them. They have had to suffer an awful lot of persecution this last year and have stood firm through it all. They haven't a proper chapel or preacher. The only help they get is from the preacher of the next station ten miles away. He is a faithful soul. Last summer when the persecution was so bad and their lives were threatened, he came and lived with them for three months until the worst was over…

Later in the day there was another service in Lan Pa, then we dismissed our audience once more and prepared for bed. This night I decided to go to the bottom of the bed, and so became the guardian of the toes. It was an adventurous night, but I was able *to breathe. It poured with rain all night, so the next morning we had to hire another chair. Our foreign shoes are no use on these roads when they are wet. The coolies were wearing straw sandals and even then they did a lot of skidding. I was quite sure I would have to be fished out of a rice field before the journey was over!...*

In this letter I have emphasised the funny side of things. I am almost afraid to speak of the other. The only way to keep sane out here is to see the funny side of the situation, otherwise you would become so saddened and depressed you would lose heart and the work would suffer. To see the funny side doesn't mean shirking the facts — you are too often brought up against them to miss them — the awful poverty of the ordinary people, the terrible diseases from which they suffer. The little children in particular make my heart ache and so little of their suffering is necessary. If only they were properly cared for they wouldn't have half the diseases and some of the ones they have could easily be cured, if only they could be sent to hospital. In some cases it is because their parents don't understand the importance of sending them, but in many cases it is because they cannot afford to...

That is all on the physical side, the mental and spiritual is even more appalling. They are so bound by cruel superstitions. They live in perpetual fear of evil spirits. Once they do become Christians it changes their whole lives... Tradition means such a terrible lot to them and they do mistrust us foreigners so...it is so hard to realise what their background is and therefore what interpretation they put on our words.

Pingkiang

The following year with her proficiency in Chinese much improved my mother was appointed to Pingkiang. Pingkiang is a medium-sized town in the north-east corner of Hunan. The mission compound was situated on higher ground just outside the town, giving it beautiful views of the surrounding countryside on three sides and overlooking the town on the fourth. It was the site of one of the three hospitals the Methodist Church had in Hunan[1]. There was also a large boys' school and a smaller girls' school. My mother, who was, of course, a trained teacher, was placed in charge of the latter. While in Pingkiang she lived with the hospital matron, Gladys Wentworth. The Rev John Stanfield was the minister in charge.

A visit to the barber

My mother, in her book *China As I Remember It*, tells the following amusing story from that time:

> One event I can clearly remember from that period was the day the street barber cut off all my hair. I needed a trim, so I asked one of the street barbers we regularly used to come and do it. I tried to explain in my faltering Chinese how I wanted him to do it, but no luck. He had not the faintest idea what I was trying to say. Then suddenly I had an inspiration. 'Like Tan Shi Mu (Mrs Stanfield)', I said, for she too had short hair. Sadly however I got it the wrong way round and said, 'Like Tan Mu Shi (Mr Stanfield)'. And he was bald! At last the barber appeared to understand what was required of him. Quickly the shears snipped away and within moments all the hair from one side of my face was gone. It was only then that I realised what was happening. It was too late. I decided I would look even more ridiculous going around with hair on only one side of my head, so I had to ask him to shear off the other side as well. This he willingly did. For several weeks afterwards I went around wearing a hat!

While living in Pingkiang my mother had on several occasions reason to travel the seventy miles to the provincial capital and Church headquarters of Changsha. There was no railway or motor road, nor was one able to travel by river. The only route was the typical Chinese 'road', with stone slabs placed end to end, winding between the paddy fields.

In the following circular letter my mother describes the return journey from Changsha to Pingkiang she made in the company of Rev William Gibson, the Chairman of the district.

Letter of March 1926:
Travelling from Changsha to Pingkiang

I feel when I attempt to describe a road journey I am attempting the impossible. It is quite impossible to give you an accurate picture of a Chinese inn, the scenery or passers by. Never mind, I will make an attempt and leave the rest to your imagination...

Mr Gibson and I set off from Changsha at about 1.30 pm on Thursday, February 25th. It was beautifully warm indoors and horribly cold outside! Still, I hardly felt it at all, I was so well wrapped up. When they had finished tucking me into my chair it was a job to find me again, and in addition to all my wrappings I had a foot warmer and was nursing a hot water bottle.

We did about thirty li (three li is equivalent to one mile), then I thought I had better get out and find an appetite for supper. The roads were in an awful condition. There was so much mud we could hardly find the narrow stone path. We did another fifteen li and then stopped for the night. The first inn we went to I walked in after Mr Gibson and wanted to see the room where I was to spend the night. I was politely, but firmly, put out, but not before I had had a peep — and that was enough.

Mr Gibson walked around like a bloodhound on the scent, but it did not seem to agree with his nose either. So we said we would try elsewhere.

We then found what Mr Gibson called 'a home from home'. Again I tried to see my room and was politely told to admire the scenery. After various curtains in strange hues had been removed – the strangeness having been acquired during their years of use – along with two or three questionable looking bed mats, and after the lady of the inn had wandered around with a brush, I was allowed to enter and inspect the room. I am sure Mr Gibson wondered what the joke was when I came out laughing, but the idea of my sleeping there was certainly amusing. Under the window, which was, of course, covered with paper in place of glass and had one or two peepholes, was a dirty table. On either side of the room was a Chinese bed covered with straw and at the end a trestle to sit on. The walls were of mud, dirty and damp looking. The ceiling, I suppose, was wood, but it was so black I could not make anything of it, and the floor was earth. Still I was very thankful for it, as it seemed private. I did discover an eye looking at me the next morning, but when looked at it disappeared, which is more than eyes usually do. The fact that I could hear when anyone else in the inn turned over, and that two or three people were snoring didn't matter.

I do wish I could give you some idea of the rest of the inn. There were several small rooms such as mine, opening out from the main hall or courtyard, which without the handicap of any wall or doorway opened straight onto the road. To say it looked like a barn is not quite accurate. No self-respecting farmer would have such a dirty roof, or such filthy smoke-grimed walls. He would certainly white-wash them, but these inn walls would never see white-wash from the day they were put up to the day they tumble down… I am not drawing a picture of an exceptionally bad inn, this is just the average of what I saw and the inns on the Pingkiang Road are supposed to be good!

We were up at 5.30 am the next morning. Everything looks strange in the early morning mist, and so did those two figures walking behind the chair, Mr Gibson with a dirty face, filthy boots and no collar, and me with a dirty face, mud to the top of my wellingtons and a wooden helmet. We walked fifteen li, then stopped for a wash and breakfast.

Shortly after breakfast we got onto a sandy road and travelling was very much easier. We were now getting into the hilly country and the scenery was becoming more and more beautiful. I walked another fifteen li after breakfast and then got into the chair for a while. Very soon after this we caught up with a batch of soldiers with all their baggage and couldn't get past until they stopped at an inn for their meal, then we made a dash for the next village. When first we arrived at the inn there was hardly anyone visible, but before long two or three men and some women appeared. They had heard that some soldiers were on the way and when we came along thought it was the soldiers arriving, so had hidden themselves. It is always the same when you are on the road where soldiers are. They are dreaded everywhere, for wherever they go they take just what they want without paying and force men to come along with them and carry their baggage. Before we had finished our meal the soldiers had caught up with us again and seeing us there came in to watch us eat. Needless to say we soon finished our meal and got on to the road as quickly as possible. After that we made sure we kept ahead of them…

The next morning we were off again before dawn. This time with our faces washed… It was a lovely day's journey and I enjoyed it very much. The sun was shining brightly and the scenery through the hills was simply wonderful, particularly at one place when we went along by the riverside for a few miles. I have never seen anything quite so wonderful. We did eighty li that day and did it in splendid time considering how heavy the going was. We crossed the river by boat bridge into Pingkiang and arrived on the compound just after 4 pm...

In the summer of that year there was serious flooding, which my mother described as follows:

It had rained incessantly and torrentially for several days. The river became dangerously high then broke its banks. Throughout the night the waters roared down the narrow gorges sweeping away a large part of the city. As I lay in bed I heard the sound of houses crashing to the ground knowing that each held within it a story of human tragedy. A few days afterwards I left for Changsha, and then on to Kuling, with Mr Stanfield. We travelled by boat as Mr Stanfield wanted to visit some of the out-stations on the way. One or two villages we could not find at all. They had been completely swept away by the flood. Others had only the odd house standing. We little knew what had happened to their inhabitants. Many must have perished.

The death of Lillian Grand

During that summer Lillian Grand contracted cholera and died shortly afterwards. My mother was asked to return to Yiyang to take charge of the school where she had been headmistress, which was a larger one than the one she had been in charge of in Pingkiang.

Anglo-Chinese relations

My mother's arrival in Yiyang coincided with a period of a virulent anti-foreign feeling in China. This was something which erupted from time to time, fuelled by the deep underlying resentment by the Chinese people of the manner in which they had been treated by the

European powers, in particular the British, over the previous century. When walking along the street it was common occurrence to have the children, and sometimes even the adults, calling after you 'Yang kuei tsi' – 'foreign devil'.

To understand better the reasons for this resentment, and thus to put events into some context, it is useful to recall how relations between Britain and China had developed since the first British traders made contact with China in the middle of the 18th century. In those early days the three products the British traders were primarily interested in buying from the Chinese were silk, tea and porcelain, but they soon found it difficult to purchase these products because of a relative lack of interest from the Chinese in what Britain had to offer in return. So in 1773 a group of enterprising British merchants started selling opium[2], which was grown in India, in territory under the control of the East India Company. As addiction grew so did the demand for the drug, thereby boosting British exports. But as the problems of addiction increased the Chinese government banned the import of the product into the country.

In 1839, twenty thousand chests of opium were seized as illegal goods by government officials in Canton. For Britain, already much annoyed by constant Chinese interference in what she regarded as her legitimate trading interests, this was the last straw and led to the British Navy being sent to the China Seas. The Chinese government, being aware that it was no match for the British naval power, quickly backed down and agreed to the resumption of trade in this invidious product and to pay the British a large indemnity for having destroyed their stocks. Not satisfied with this humiliating victory, in a triumphant

23

ceremony in Nanking the British forced the Chinese to sign the first of the infamous 'unequal treaties'. In this treaty the Chinese agreed to cede Hong Kong to the British in perpetuity and to the opening up of five trading ports, including Shanghai, Canton and Hankow, for the use of British and other European traders. The terms effectively meant the surrendering of Chinese sovereignty in large areas of these cities. These concessions were governed by the laws of the countries concerned, each of which had its own police force and armed forces. No Chinese were allowed in these areas, except on authorised business, although on occasions they served as a refuge for people wanted by the Chinese government.

The Chinese have throughout their history been suspicious of foreigners and have generally shunned contact with them. This humiliating treatment at the hands of the British gave rise to recurring explosions of anti-foreign feeling erupting from time to time. The most serious occasion was the 'Boxer Uprising' of 1900. The Boxers were a Chinese secret society, which called itself 'The Fists of Righteous Harmony'. Foreigners called members of this society 'Boxers' because they practiced martial arts. The Boxers were initially opposed to the ruling Manchu Dynasty[3] but through skilful manipulation by the Empress Dowager Tze Hsi, their anger was redirected towards the foreigners living in their midst. During this bloody episode one hundred and eighty-six missionaries across the country were butchered and thousands of Chinese Christians were slaughtered. The Boxers then entered Peking and surrounded the foreign legation.[4]

Following the revolution of October 1911, led by Sun Yat Sen, which overthrew the Manchu Dynasty, centralised control of the country ceased and China broke up into a number of fiefdoms ruled over by several warlords. In the north the most powerful was the former Manchu general Yuan Shih-kai, to whom Sun Yat Sen had ceded authority to avoid a civil war. Perhaps surprisingly this was a good period for missionary work in China. Most of the warlords were aware how much China had fallen behind the Western nations technologically and they regarded the missionaries as a conduit for modern ideas and attitudes.

Sun Yat Sen, after being forced to leave Peking by Yuan Shih-kai, set up a revolutionary government in Canton, but once again was evicted from office and forced to flee to Shanghai. There he established the National Party, or Kuomintang. Believing China not to be ready for multiparty democracy, and being wary of the self-seeking divisiveness that was characteristic of it, he thought it necessary for the country to go through a transition period of one-party rule, as was happening in Turkey under Kemal Attaturk, and in Russia under Lenin. Following Lenin's vision of the role of the Communist party in Russia, he intended that the Kuomintang should infiltrate all aspects of Chinese life, acting as a vehicle to push forward reforms and modernisation throughout society. The Kuomintang was at that stage strongly anti-foreign, Sun Yat Sen believing that many of China's problems resulted from the policies of countries such as Britain, who had so shamelessly abused and plundered China for her own ends.

After Sun Yat Sen's death from cancer in Peking in 1925 Chiang Kai-shek, by virtue of his position as head of the armed forces, effectively became his successor. His first priority was to reunite the country by defeating all the warlords who were not prepared to submit to his authority, in particular the 'Old Marshal', Chang Tso-lin and the 'Christian General', Feng Yu-Hsiang. In alliance with the recently formed Chinese Communist Party and with the assistance of his Russian advisers, led by Michael Borodin, Chiang Kai-shek marched from his base in Canton in a campaign to reunite the country. In 1926 his forces took Hankow and a combination of Communists and left-wing Kuomintang supporters took control of the city.

The Kuomintang's attacks on 'the foreign powers that exploited China', along with the growing influence of the Communist Party in many parts of the country, gave rise to a climate of anti-foreign feeling which many of the Chinese were happy to exploit.

Such was the situation my mother encountered on arriving in Yiyang. The school she was put in charge of had its fair share of troublemakers and despite the loyal support of the staff, after weeks of struggling and countless meetings with the students they were obliged to close the school.

Trouble flared up again at the end of December 1926, with rioting in Hankow and elsewhere. The British Embassy ordered all British subjects to withdraw to the foreign concessions on the coast for their own safety. This was not, however, always easy. On receiving the instruction in Yiyang my mother, Maud Millican and Kitty Pickles (another missionary colleague) hastily packed their most valued possessions, hired two small boats to take them and their luggage to Hankow, and prepared to leave the next day. Boat was the only safe mode of transport, for it was the only way one could travel without being seen. As my mother reports in her book:

The following morning…[we] were sitting having our farewell breakfast when suddenly a great horde of people came swarming into the compound waving sticks and rifles and shouting 'Down with the foreigners!' We were told much later that the rifles were dummies, but they looked frighteningly real and there was certainly nothing phoney about the sticks and knives. We immediately barred the doors and closed the shutters, but the crowd continued to howl outside. Any glimpse of us (and some of the windows had no shutters) turned them to even greater frenzy. So we retreated upstairs out of sight and sat down to await events.

A few hours later we saw our old Chinese minister the Rev Wu I Tang going round among the crowd trying to quieten them. They were very agitated and he must have known that he was in great danger, but all that day he wandered among the mob telling anyone prepared to listen that we were good people and were only there to help. He tried in vain to persuade them to let us go.

Immediately the rioting began we sent a message to the office of the governor (known as the 'Yamen'), asking for help, but it was about 10 pm before their answer came. Eventually a group of soldiers appeared and ordered the crowd to disperse. But the mob were unwilling to give up their prey and turned their anger on the soldiers. At one stage they were threatening to kill the officer in charge. That was the time when I was really frightened. I could hear the crowd yelling 'sa ta, sa ta', 'kill him, kill him'. If they killed him I knew it would be our turn next. But the officer stood firm and eventually the crowd reluctantly drifted away.

At about midnight we got a message that we could go

so we started to get our things ready for a departure under the cover of darkness. Shortly afterwards Mr Wu appeared again imploring us to stay put for the moment. He had been warned that an ambush had been prepared for us. Outside the town a group was waiting to seize us as we passed by. So there we waited. Some of the women members also crept in under cover of darkness and told us that, led by Mrs Wu, they were praying and fasting for us. They would neither eat nor drink, but would continue to pray incessantly until we were released.

When the sun rose on the compound the next morning the scene was quiet. A few soldiers were there and a small crowd, but thankfully there was no shouting of slogans or brandishing of weapons. We were told by the soldiers that if we were prepared to pay for their food – and they did not ask an unreasonable sum – they would stay and guard us. We willingly paid!

All that day Mr Wu and the elders of the Church tried to negotiate our release, while the crowd stood waiting for their instructions. It was only some time later we discovered they were waiting to see what happened in Hankow, where the British concession was under siege. The British marines had been sent on shore to guard all the approaches. They had strict orders not to open fire or retaliate in any way. They had an awful time. They were spat at, had rotten fruit thrown at them, and were insulted in every possible way, but they just stood firm and took it. Had one of them fired or injured a Chinese, serious rioting would certainly have broken out and we folk up-country would most probably have been massacred…

Late in the day news came through that there had been no fighting in Hankow and the British government had announced that it was prepared to negotiate the ceding of the concession to China. We were saved!

About midnight two bedraggled officials came and told us we could go, but asked us to walk quietly lest we awaken the people and rioting start again. It was with much relief that we reached the boats we had hired. There to our great surprise we found two other boats tied up alongside. They were both occupied by missionaries from Paoking. The boatmen had refused to go on until they had heard what they should do with us.

We then set off down the river and across the Tung T'ing Lake. In a launch we could have done it in just over a day, but with our old sailing boats it took ten long days. One day the wind was with us and we actually made good progress, but then had to come back again because there was no safe place to tie up, since bandits were believed to be about.

Whenever we came near a village or small town we had to lie down in the bottom of the boat and remain silent. To put it mildly foreigners were not popular at that time and the less we were seen the safer we would be. Eventually we arrived at the far side of the lake and there we found another two boatloads of fleeing missionaries, one from Pingkiang and the other from Paoking. Dr Pearson[5], who was in one of the boats, negotiated with the owner of a small launch to tow us all to Hankow, and travelling at a much more respectable rate we arrived the following evening.

There the situation was still tense and we were advised not to go ashore. Shortly after our arrival, a group of British marines arrived and transferred us to a river steamer bound for Shanghai, which had delayed its departure especially to take us on board.

A few days after my mother's arrival in Shanghai the mob over-ran the British concession in Hankow, with the few remaining foreigners escaping in gunboats. Soon afterwards the British government surrendered its concessions in Hankow, along with the one in Kiukiang, to the Chinese government.

Shanghai

Shanghai was full of British and other European subjects who had fled from inland China. Many returned to England, while others waited, hoping the situation inland would soon improve. My mother fitted into the latter group, taking work as a shorthand typist with the British and Foreign Bible Society. She continued in this work for more than a year, waiting for life to return to normal.

While she was in Shanghai the power struggle for control of China continued, with Chiang Kai-shek and his Communist allies striving to reunite the country. Early in 1927 Chiang Kai-shek inflicted a resounding defeat on the northern warlord, the 'Old Marshal', Chang Tso-lin, in a hard fought battle near Hangchow. Chang Tso-lin then took Nanking, but Kuomintang forces soon arrived at the city, forcing Chang Tso-lin to withdraw northwards. Some of the Kuomintang troops then indulged in a wave of lawlessness – looting foreign property and attacking foreigners, some of whom were killed. This rampage was only brought to an end by British and American naval vessels evacuating all foreigners and shelling the city. Chiang Kai-shek, who was in Shanghai at the time, on receiving the news hurried to Nanking to restore order, investigate what had happened and try and repair relations with the foreign powers.

Differences between Chiang Kai-shek and his Communist allies were becoming more prominent, caused in part by the Communist Party's policy of assisting trade unions in taking over factories and encouraging peasants to take over the land they worked. The crucial break between the erstwhile allies occurred in Shanghai, while my mother was living in the international settlement there. But the settlement, being effectively a country of its own, was shielded from what was happening elsewhere in the city.

The Communists reached Shanghai before the Kuomintang and on taking the city immediately placed the civic organisations and many of the factories in the city in the hands of Communist trade unions, peasants' associations and revolutionary students. Chiang Kai-shek, who had never trusted the Communists as Sun Yat Sen had, regarded these actions as a direct challenge to his leadership. On 12th April 1927, a few days after the Kuomintang troops entered the city, they turned on the Communists and their supporters, massacring large numbers of them. After a few bloody days of battle the Communists were routed and the Kuomintang took charge of the city. Chiang Kai-shek promptly expelled Borodin and the other Russian advisers and soon after banned the Communist Party.

Despite this altercation Chiang Kai-shek was able to take Peking in the following year, in what became known as the Northern Expedition, and the remaining warlords, including the 'Old Marshal', Chang Tso-lin and the 'Christian General', Feng Yu-Hsiang, ceded their power to him. China was thus united for the first time since the overthrow of the Manchus and Chiang Kai-shek was its undisputed ruler. He transferred the capital from Peking to Nanking.

Return to Hunan

In the summer of 1928, with the Communists in retreat and Chiang Kai-shek's forces involved in action further north, the situation became much calmer and foreigners started to return to Hunan. My mother was appointed to Paoking, in the south of Hunan, as a deaconess, along with Maud Millican (her former colleague in Yiyang who was to be matron of the hospital), Stanley Lamming and Douglas Thompson (who were to be the ministers there). Stanley, Douglas and Maud had all evacuated Hunan at the same time as my mother, but spent the intervening time 'on loan' to India and elsewhere. They had now returned to Shanghai and with my mother set off on the long trek from Shanghai to Paoking.

Although the four of them were relatively young and inexperienced they were able to rely on the advice of Dr Pearson, who was already in Paoking when they arrived. He was in charge of the Methodist hospital, which he had played such an important part in establishing. With the arrival of Maud Millican he extended the work of the hospital by setting up a training programme for nurses, which, during the following couple of decades trained large numbers of nurses, to serve both in the Paoking hospital and elsewhere in China.

My mother recalls the night before they left Shanghai talking to Mr Gibson, who was Chairman of the district. It was her first proper appointment as a deaconess and she felt in need of a bit of guidance from such an experienced missionary.

So, perhaps a bit naively, I asked him, 'What am I supposed to do?' He looked at me helplessly for a few moments as though he were thinking 'What a daft question', then shrugging his shoulders he replied, 'Oh, see what needs doing, and do it'. It was advice I never forgot.

Paoking (Shaoyang)

Paoking, or Shaoyang as it was later known, was set at the junction of two valleys, where the rivers Tze and Shao met, with hills all round. The compound, where the hospital was situated, and Methodist missionary staff lived, was outside the city proper, on the other side of the Shao river. The hospital, which was much the largest of the three missionary hospitals in Hunan, was built in the shape of a Chinese temple, with a farm on the hillside behind.

There was a small hospital when Dr Pearson arrived in 1920, situated in the heart of the city. The location made expansion impossible so Dr Pearson bought some land across the river and in 1923 he started to build a new hospital. In the following year, before it was completed, there were very severe floods and Dr Pearson had the sorrow of seeing most of his new hospital destroyed. The floods of 1924 were particularly bad, but flooding was a common occurrence in Paoking. In 1924 the river level rose fifty feet above normal. Undaunted, Dr Pearson rebuilt the hospital, this time ensuring that the foundations and material could withstand even the worst of floods. In 1949 a similar level of flooding occurred and the hospital survived. It remains an important hospital today.

Travelling around the circuit

As soon as my mother was settled in Paoking she thought of Mr Gibson's advice and asked herself, 'What needs doing?' Soon she found herself teaching English in the mission school to both staff and students, running a bible class in the hospital for nurses, as well as starting a Sunday school for whoever could be persuaded to attend.

Once these ventures were up and running she decided it was time to visit some of the out-stations in the surrounding countryside, where solitary Chinese preachers supervised little country chapels. However, she was advised by her Chinese colleagues that it was too dangerous for a foreign women to travel on her own, because of the number of bandits operating in the area. A cumbersome plan was hatched, whereby one preacher should deliver her over to the next, somewhere near the mid-point between their two chapels. But this soon revealed its drawbacks and before long my mother and her assistant, Mrs Tsao, were travelling around on their own.

Mrs Tsao was what was generally described as a 'Bible Woman' − the title by which Chinese women evangelists, or lay preachers, were generally known. In her book my mother describes her as:

> ...a dear old lady, tireless, willing and faithful. More a chaperone than a helper. She had bound feet, but this never prevented her from tramping around with me. She was a woman of no formal education and quite illiterate.

In a letter she wrote to her sister Jean in May 1929 she describes such a trip she made around the circuit with Mrs Tsao.

A letter of May 1929 to Jean

For several months now I have been wanting to go around the circuit, but there always seemed to be some good reason why I couldn't go. First it was the severe weather, then it was the bandits…next I caught a cold and lost my voice and although you can do without many things while you are travelling you cannot do without a voice. After I had recovered my voice there were too many troops about, but at last it seemed safe to attempt it. So on Saturday May 18th Mrs Tsao, our Bible Woman, and I set out.

The first stop was Chiu Kong Chiao, a three and a half hours' walk from Paoking. The walk out was uneventful, but interesting – because the people were busy in the fields ploughing, planting rice, working the water wheels and so forth. Late afternoon Mrs Tsao and I went on to the street and visited the members and talked to all those who were willing to listen to us. The next morning I met all the members at morning service and listened to a sermon which lasted one hour. I was so scared I would disgrace myself by falling asleep, but I had to keep awake because the preacher kept appealing to me to substantiate what he was saying. I wore foreign dress between the various places while I was walking, but changed into Chinese dress immediately I arrived anywhere. It attracted a little less attention and I think made the people feel more at ease.

On Monday morning it was very wet so I hired a chair, but only used it for about one hour, and the other four hours I walked. The road that day was very wild and mountainous, which made me remember every bandit story I had ever heard, but never a bandit did we see. We passed one dead one who had been killed by soldiers a day or two before, but, although invited to, I preferred not to look at him. It may be strange, but I have no desire to see bandits, neither dead nor alive…

We arrived at Tan Tu Ko… During the afternoon we visited all the members the preacher could imagine they had… The evening was spent receiving members and all the folk who came to see the foreign 'Hsiao Chieh'[6]. *Mrs Tsao was in her element and preached to all who came. She is a great woman for preaching to non-believers, but I do wish she would not get up at dawn to chant her prayers! We had so many visitors it was always about 11 pm before we got to bed and Mrs Tsao was up two or three times a night chasing mosquitoes, rats or something else. Then she would get up at 4.30 am to pray! I did not love our Bible Woman much at that hour!*

On Tuesday morning we set off for Pe Tsan Shih. What a lovely walk, but what a hot road and what a wild place to arrive at. It took us about four hours and I arrived very hot and as usual thirsty. Half the population of Pe Tsan Shih crowded around and almost stood on top of me until I could hardly breathe. One of the members, a nice wee body, took us to visit the other members. I am not very big myself, but this little lady was even smaller. She clutched my hand, tucked me under her arm and set off with a most determined look on her face. Mrs Tsao, who was scared of being left behind in the mob, grasped the other hand and thus I walked the street in the middle of about a hundred folk. But we visited the members…and so did the mob. In one place they put me behind the shop counter lest I should be smothered. The children soon came over the top, but at least I could breathe. In that wee shop I counted seventy people.

Pe Tsan Shih to Ta Sheng Chiao I was told was fifteen li. It is certainly the longest five miles I have ever tramped! It took us just over four hours to do it. The coolies were opium eaters and just crawled along. At one place I lost them altogether and had to storm a village before I could get them on the road again. Even in the midst of the pouring rain I enjoyed the scenery, but what terrible poverty-stricken villages and dirty looking people. The people in all the villages around there are heavy opium smokers and they look it. It is not only their poverty. They look so degraded and the places smell of evil.

I do not wonder crowds of people came to see me at Ta Sheng Chiao… It isn't every day you see a foreign Hsiao Chieh dripping wet with mud up to the eyebrows; but I do wish they would not be so persistent. We had to barricade the windows and Mr Mao (the preacher) mounted guard at one door and Mrs Tsao at the other…while I got into some clean dry clothes. Then they just poured in and kept it up until we left on Thursday morning…

Thursday morning we set off for Liu Chi Ping. It was lovely scenery, but it was hot tramping and the coolies were at first very difficult to manage. At Liu Chi Ping we met the members, held a service for about thirty people, had tsung fan *(midday rice) and then we pushed on to Wu Feng Pu, but it was cruelly hot. I was nearly dead when I arrived. Needless to say I revived after a few pots of tea and a bath (of a sort).*

I was afraid I could not manage the tramp to Paoking — thirty miles — so called an extra chair, but they were poor carrying coolies… I was only in the chair twenty li (seven miles) at the most and in that time they toppled the chair over twice. Quite a good way to get rid of a passenger! So I decided I would prefer to walk and see the countryside. So home I tramped through the rain and arrived covered in mud in the midst of a compound of aggressively clean and tidy foreigners. The houses were so sweet and clean after living in dirty little rooms for a week. And that first bath…! And clean fresh clothes that had not been carried around in a box for days. And that first meal…! What a little pig I made of myself, but I had not had a bit of foreign food, or tea, for over a week…

Getting engaged

After eighteen months in Paoking my mother was due for furlough. However, one momentous event occurred about six weeks before her departure. A new missionary arrived in Paoking. He was Clifford Cook. Before she left for furlough they were engaged. Although no letters survive by either of my parents about this memorable event we have the following account my mother wrote many years later.

Cliff came to Paoking, a new missionary just out from England, about six weeks before I was due to leave for my first furlough. It wasn't love at first sight. I think it took two days! We had known each other about a month when Cliff proposed to me. I wouldn't answer at once, although my heart said 'yes'. I loved my work and wanted to continue with it; but I knew if I married it would be different. Would I still be able to undertake journeys out into the countryside by myself and run training programmes for rural women?

That night I had little sleep; but prayed and thought about what I ought to do. By morning I had decided the answer must be 'yes'. And so we got engaged.

Shortly after this I left for furlough. I sailed to Australia from Shanghai, where I stayed with my sister Jean and her husband Percy. I spent three happy months there, with Cliff never far from my thoughts. However, on the way back to England, at Port Said, I received a cable from him suggesting we break off our engagement. I was bitterly disappointed and rather confused. What had made him change his mind? When I arrived in England there was a letter explaining his decision.

After I left China there had been a lot of fighting in Hunan between the Communists and Nationalists and supporters of dissident generals opposed to both groups. The province was very unsettled and no one knew how things would develop. Cliff was new to it all and considered it was no place to bring up a family. He thus decided he ought to be a celibate missionary

Furlough

My mother then spent a year's furlough in England, Despite having broken their engagement my father invited my mother to stay at his parent's home in Weston-super-Mare. My father's parents made her very welcome and took to my mother immediately. They asked her to write to them when she returned to China and tell them about the work she was doing. This she did. Several years later when my parents eventually decided to marry they were delighted.

Endnotes

1. The other two being at Paoking — much the largest — and Lingling.
2. The Chinese word for opium means 'foreign dirt'.
3. Alternatively known as the Qing dynasty.
4. Where the foreign embassies were built and their staff lived. Prior to the 1911 revolution the legation was surrounded by a wall and guarded by the British, French, the other foreign troops. It was within these walls that the western diplomats, businessmen and missionaries were beseiged during the Boxer Rebellion of 1900.
5. Dr George Pearson, the veteran missionary doctor, who built and ran the Methodist hospital in Shaoyang.
6. Chinese title of respect, roughly translated as 'Madam'.

Chapter Two
China: The Early Years – CVC

My father was born in Bristol on 24th September 1906. His father, the Rev Vallance Cook, was a Methodist minister and Connexional evangelist, who held evangelical missions all over Britain, as well as in Australia and New Zealand. He wrote many books on popular theology and while minister at Mildmay Park, London was elected a member of the Hackney Borough Council for the Labour Party.

My father's mother was a local preacher and a devoted evangelist, and like her husband a prolific writer of books on popular religion. She was the first women delegate to the Methodist Conference and was at one time president of the British Women's Temperance Association. My father's great grandfather, the Rev Richard Griffith, was a missionary in India and Ceylon in the middle of the 19th century and his great, great grandfather, the Rev Joseph Roberts, was one of Methodism's pioneering missionaries to Asia.

With such a background, which was so very different from my mother's, it is perhaps not surprising that he should decide to give himself to missionary work. He went to Handsworth College in Birmingham for theological training.

When he went out to China in 1929 he was only twenty-three years old. He arrived in Shanghai in December of that year, then travelled to Hunan, via Hankow. On arriving in Hunan he spent a very short period in Paoking, where he first met my mother, before

ARE you kidding?

going to Yungchow for language training. Learning Chinese is a formidable task for anyone, but it wasn't long before he acquired reasonable proficiency in the language.

He wrote the following circular letter soon after his arrival in China, while he was still undertaking language tuition, describing a tour of the Yungchow circuit he made with fellow missionary Cyril Baker.

Letter of March 1930:
A Country Tour of Yungchow Circuit

Friday March 21st
Baker and I start a tour of the Tung-An section of the Yungchow circuit. Leave Yungchow at 10.30 am. Walk some ten miles before grubbing at an inn. As usual crowds gathered to see the foreigners eat, and they became intensely interested when, after eating some Chinese food, the foreigners produced some jam tarts and drank foreign tea. After tiffin[1] we walked about five more miles and arrived at a place called Shih Chi Chan, a beautiful little town situated on the juncture of two rivers. We have a church there and a resident Chinese preacher. No service had been arranged, but the members hearing of our arrival turned up, so we had one. We slept in a little room on the church premises.

Saturday March 22nd
Walk fifteen miles to Tung An, a small town, in which we have a church, school, resident preacher and a resident school master. We are to stop here for the weekend. Our home is another little room on the church premises, the best room we have stayed in on this tour. It is built of mud bricks and has a dried mud floor... The walls are white-washed, and the beds — straw on wooden boards — are clean, so we lived luxuriously. Prayer

41

meeting followed by the eating of Chinese sweets in honour of our visit.

Sunday March 23rd
Baker takes morning service. Walk through town together, and to a Confucian temple in the afternoon. Baker giving words of wisdom to groups and individuals. Baker takes evening service, but I give short address in English, which he translates. Communion afterwards.

Monday March 24th
Walk about six miles to Pai Ya Shih, where we have about six members, but no church. It is market day, so we go into the market place and give out literature and Baker speaks to the crowds. The evening service is held in the inn where we stay, the owner of which is a member. The inn is fairly full of guests — mainly coolies — and these swell the congregation. The owner hasn't yet learnt that cleanliness is next to godliness, for his inn is a foul place. In the main room all the lodgers sleep — in a row on a wooden board on the floor — and eat. All sorts of animals walk about and rub against you when you are having a meal. They hang about with the hope of getting a morsel. Dogs, a cat, several fowls and several small pigs were present. Imagine my eating rice with a pig or two at my feet!

Baker and I managed to get a private room — that is we were separated from the main room by some filthy partitions. Within these partitions we slept, though we had two meals in the main room. Our private enclosure had two windows — one looking into a neighbouring room as dirty as ours, the other looking indirectly onto a back yard, where the pigs — many little ones and a few older ones — and the poultry slept, and where evil smelling enclosures are to be found. I use the word 'indirectly' because we looked onto the yard through a kind of wooden structure, where lodgers bathed – if they did bathe – in small tubs. The windows were supposed to give light, but not sight, with penetrating paper over them, but this was so torn as to be almost non-existent...

Tuesday March 25th
Walk about seven miles to Ching Tou Shu. We have no members here, but there are a number of interested people in the place, so we may have before long. Here we stayed at the 'Grub & Maggot Hotel', which belongs in the same category as the one mentioned above. We visit many houses and yarn with the people. I'd like you to have seen the picture of Baker sitting at the inn table in the evening by the light of a storm lantern, talking to enquiring Chinese. People kept coming and going, and some were seriously and intelligently concerned.

Wednesday March 26th
Walk about ten miles to Shih Chi Chan. We are now on the way home. The weather is very warm and we have a bathe in the river en route. At Shih Chi Chan we hold a baptismal service, baptising several children and three adults. I speak in English and Cyril interprets...

Thursday March 27th
Walk fifteen miles to Yungchow, preaching in a country house on the way. Arrive at home about 2 pm, tired and weary. It is great to get back home again after a country tour – not that such a tour is unenjoyable – that is certainly not the case. Have a hot bath, change all my clothes and go to Baker's for a welcome meal. Nice big pile of mail awaiting our arrival.

In the last chapter we heard of the anti-foreign riots of December 1926, which my mother was caught up in in Yiyang, and how this led to all missionaries withdrawing to the foreign concessions on the coast. About a year later missionaries started to return to inland stations and some time in 1928 my mother left Shanghai to work in Paoking.

In the same year Chiang Kai-shek turned on his former allies, the Communists, in Shanghai, massacring large numbers of them. The Communists then withdrew into the Kiangsi province to regroup themselves. Two years later they tried to seize a number of major cities in central China. On 28th July 1930 their forces, under the command of Peng Teh-huai, took control of Changsha.

As a result of these military operations missionaries were once again evacuated from Hunan. We know that my father went initially to Wuchang[2], where he carried on with his language training. We also know from photographs that he spent some time in Hankow and Shanghai. Otherwise we have little information about where he lived, or what he did during this period of enforced exile. The following letter to his parents suggests that he seems to have spent some time in Teian, an ancient provincial capital, about twenty-five miles north of the Hankow on the Hankow to Peking railway line. What we do know for certain is that he returned to Yungchow in February 1931.

Letter of 24th February 1931 from Wuchang

Tomorrow afternoon I take the train for Changsha and so start on the first part of my journey back to Yungchow…

I had an interesting journey back from Teian. I left last Thursday. The snow was far too deep for motors to run so I had to walk the twenty miles to the railway station… The walk was not too stiff and I enjoyed it. I got to the railway at two-thirty in the afternoon, and immediately went to an inn to await the arrival of the coolies with my boxes and the train for Hankow. The coolies didn't turn up until seven the next morning! They talked so quickly when making excuses that I only half understood what they were saying. Apparently they'd found carrying boxes in the snow very difficult (and I'm not surprised) and on reaching the outskirts of the village where I was waiting, towards evening they were afraid of the military sentries.

Anyhow they left me with nothing to change into or sleep in. My socks, boots etc were sopping when I'd finished the journey, but fortunately one of the inn people was very obliging and lent me a pair of his socks and shoes, and brought me a big fire, so I was quite ok. I slept in my clothes...

The following letter describes the latter part of the journey from Wuchang to Yungchow, via Changsha.

Circular Letter of 1931:
Travelling from Wuchang to Yungchow

On Wednesday February 25th at 4 pm I left Wuchang on the Changsha 'express' train and yesterday afternoon, about five-thirty, arrived at Yungchow. Just six days! Quite good travelling for China. Of course, I did not come all the way by train. I had one night on the train during which I slept on the rack. I shared a compartment with a German CIM⁵ missionary and his wife. The next morning, early, I arrived at Changsha... Thursday night was spent in Changsha, and then at seven-thirty on Friday morning I left on the Paoking bus. The bus journey was quick, and without the long waits that often characterise this route, and at 4 pm I was in Paoking.

I made my way to our mission premises and spent the night in Stanley Lamming's house. The place, both the hospital and church compounds, looked very deserted and strange without anyone living in the foreigners' houses. No foreigners have returned to the country circuits yet, except Miss Simpson to Yiyang. The Chinese in Paoking were very thrilled to see a foreigner arrive and made anxious enquiries about the return of the others. On Saturday morning I paid a hasty visit to the Germans at the CIM and then started on the road to Yungchow.

I purposely was not carrying very much so it was only necessary to hire one coolie. The rest of my things are coming from Changsha by boat. That day we walked about twenty-five miles and finished up at a village inn. The only event of the night was when I heard a scratching sound on the table near where I was lying and switched on my torch and saw a nice fat rat scratching away at a tin of milk. The next day there was much rain with thunder and lightning and we only walked fifteen miles… This night was spent in one of the village churches in the Paoking circuit. I was in time to join in the evening service, it being Sunday.

The next day we did about twenty-three miles and finished up at one of the churches in the Yungchow circuit. The man in charge here is very full of zeal and on my arrival summoned together members and interested folks, and when they had met me I gave them an address. This place is about seventeen miles from Yungchow. I was told there was a good north wind so I ought to travel the rest of the journey by boat. Foolishly I took this advice and consequently spent eight hours cramped in a cold little river boat. The north wind was not very strong and, as we were going against the current, progress was very slow. A great part of the way we were moving slowly in shallow water by the river bank with the boatman poling the ground to make us move at all. China does need good communications! At one point the current against us was so strong that the boatman had to get out on to the river bank and pull the boat with a rope.

On arrival at Yungchow I found my house closed up and my servant gone to the country to visit a relative. The letter telling of my coming had arrived only a few hours before I did myself. However, the house was soon opened and the Bakers' cook is looking after me for the time being... Today I have had visits from the leading Church officials and really it is awfully cheering to see how glad they are to welcome you back... At the moment I am the only Protestant foreigner in Yungchow...

The next news we have of my father comes from some notes made by his missionary colleague the Rev Robert Harrison. These tell how Harrison arrived in China in 1930 and travelled to Hankow, where he stayed because of the uncertain political situation, learning Chinese.

...in the spring of 1931, I was sent to Lingling (Yungchow). I travelled overland to Shaoyang – by bus! ...Cliff was with me, having also been appointed to Lingling. We intended to start on our three days' walk of about eighty miles from Shaoyang on a Monday in May at 5.30 am, but it was raining so heavily that it was quite impossible to make a start until half eleven. As we left the town by its south gate we saw men digging trenches and repairing the fortifications in preparation for an expected advance against the place by the troops of the Kwangsi warlord Peh Chung-hsi. Had we met his troops we should have been in no danger: they weren't Communists, just anti-Chiang Kai-shek. On the Thursday we reached Leng Hsui T'an, an outpost of the Lingling circuit. It was Ascension Day and the members were preparing to hold a special service. Cliff's unexpected arrival delighted them and they insisted that he take the service. The chapel was packed with people standing at the back and crowding the street at the door. They gave Cliff intent attention – remember he had been in Hunan barely eighteen months, but already had sufficient grasp of the language to keep the attention of that crowd mostly of strangers to the Gospel.

The Kwangsi warlord Peh Chung-hsi that Harrison refers to in the above notes and my father in the following letter, was generally known as Pai Chung-hsi. He and Li Tsung-jen, another Kwangsi warlord, raised a rebellion against Chiang Kai-shek, partly in protest at Chiang's authoritarian style of government, but primarily because of his lack of action in the face of repeated acts of aggression from the Japanese. Rather than prepare the country to defend itself against a dangerous and ruthless enemy, Chiang was putting all his energy into his dispute with the Communists.

However, before significant military contact had been made between the two armies the Japanese invasion of Manchuria started. In the face of this unprovoked attack on Chinese sovereignty a compromise was reached between the two groups, which led to the Kwangsi troops being absorbed into the Kuomintang army under Chiang Kai-shek, while Li Tsung-jen and Pai Chung-hsi were in return given important positions. Li Tsung-jen later became Chiang Kai-shek's deputy and in January 1949 briefly became head of state, following Chiang Kai-shek's resignation.

In September 1931, my father describes another tour he made of the Yungchow district.

Letter of September 1931:
A Country Journey in Yungchow District

Wednesday September 2nd
Leave Yungchow with one coolie at 9.30 am. Dinner at an inn five miles out. Talk with young man walking to Tung-an. One

of his legs was very bad, about twice the size of the other, bleeding and festering in parts. He seems unconcerned, and not keen on the suggestion that he pays our hospital a visit – says he has had the trouble for three years. Also talk with a Mr Li... He asks me what connection missionaries have with the British government, and when I reply that we hadn't any, he asked, 'Well who pays your expenses out to China?' In the afternoon arrive at Shih Chi Chan, fifteen miles from Yungchow. Find Church members awaiting my arrival. Change, and conduct service without delay. Talk with members...

Thursday September 3rd
Up early. Breakfast of bread, cheese and tea. Family prayers with the preacher's family. Walk ten miles to Lu Pu Tou, where we have what we call a prayer room – no proper church. Have a refreshing bathe in the river. Mr Ho, our Tung-an preacher...meets me. We visit together in the afternoon, and in the evening hold a service. Quite a good crowd of people listen. The village is situated on the bend of a river and the view all round is wonderful, but the place itself is filthy. There was a good deal of opium smoking going on.

Friday September 4th
Walk five miles to Tung-an with Ho. The fields are very interesting at this time of the year. The rice harvest is being gathered in everywhere, and, as at home, the whole family turns out to lend a hand. In the afternoon, lead a service in the house of a member... As Chinese houses usually open on to the street, such services serve the purpose of an open air meeting.

Saturday September 5th
Visit members and adherents all morning and afternoon. Take pm prayer meeting.

Sunday September 6th

Ho takes morning service. I take evening one. Together we go to the prison and harangue a bit. The Tung-an prison is a little less foul than the Yungchow one. Ho sometimes goes quite alone to the prison and preaches and chats with the prisoners. Whilst walking through the dirty, narrow streets I saw hanging on a small vendor's stall a child's hat with a ribbon round it, bearing the lettering 'HMS Nautilus'. Where it came from I do not know. It looked very odd amidst all the Chinese things on a small stall, in such an out-of-the-way place. Ho seemed very surprised when I explained what the lettering meant.

Monday September 7th

Walk six and a half miles to Pai Ya Shih. Visit with the preacher, Mr Mo, and later hold a service. Quite a large crowd gathers. I've been greatly struck on this tour by the willingness of people to listen and by the greatness of the opportunity that is ours. About 6 pm a servant arrives from Yungchow with a letter from Baker. Kwangsi troops are shortly expected in Yungchow and the Bakers are thinking of leaving almost immediately, lest it should be impossible to travel at a later date. This is the beginning of the southern advance that we have been hearing about for so long. I decide not to complete my country tour, but to return to Yungchow tomorrow. I must see Baker before he leaves for furlough.

Tuesday September 8th

Walk back to Yungchow in the day. Thirty miles. My coolie is wonderful. He does over six miles without a rest before breakfast, and my load is not light. Start before 6 am arrive at 6.30 pm. Bathed en route. Sun shines all day, but heat not trying. On arrival find Harrison got back from Kuling yesterday. He has tragic stories to tell of Hankow floods. Floods in second storey rooms of foreign houses. Most of the Chinese houses of poorer class are one storey high. Fear of cholera. In Yangtze valley thousands have been drowned and millions left homeless – without exaggeration[4]. The Bakers have not left and do not know whether to try to get away now, or wait a bit. They really need not leave for about a month. Kwangsi troops have already arrived – much quicker than expected. Probably they will have pinched all the available boats.

Wednesday September 9th

No boats – so Bakers can do nothing other than hang on. Perhaps it will be easier to travel in a few weeks time. More troops arrive from the south and some leave for the north. Walls plastered with anti-Chiang Kai-shek posters, and bills distributed in streets.

One poster announces that the Southern Army[5] does not: 1. Covet money, 2. Fear death, 3. Force coolies into service, 4. Demand money, but the Army loves: 1. The country, 2. The people, 3. The opportunity, 4. Its reputation.

Another depicts a poor man being strangled by a rope, the ends of which are respectively held by Chiang Kai-shek and a Communist, and a member of the Southern Army is dashing up with a pair of scissors to cut the rope. This is typical revolutionary propaganda.

We hold our usual weekly service. Not many come.

Thursday September 10th

Troops arrive…and leave. Wilson came over for tennis.

In 1932 my father, accompanied by Robert Harrison, took advantage of the annual holiday break to pay a visit to Peking. After spending a few days there, including visiting the Great Wall, they returned by train to

Nanking, which is downstream from Kiukiang, and from there took the river steamer to Kiukiang, before spending a somewhat shorter period than usual in Kuling.

The following letter describes part of the return journey to Yungchow.

Letter of 12th August 1932 from Nanking

We are just starting another stage of our trip. We arrived here by train from Peiping this morning and are now aboard a luxurious British river steamer about to leave for Kiukiang en route for Kuling.

We left Peiping[6] on Wednesday afternoon and had one night on the train before reaching T'ai An Fu. Here we alighted and climbed the famous T'ai mountain, China's most ancient religious mountain. Four thousand years ago people climbed its heights to worship the spirit of the mountain, and ever since pilgrims have been making the ascent to worship. But now, rather than worshipping the spirit of the mountain, they worship Taoist deities and the memory of Confucius, with whom the mountain is closely associated. The climb is hard indeed. It is over 4000 feet and includes 6000 steps — and high ones at that. Is it any wonder that today my legs are a little stiff? Amongst the pilgrims we saw making the climb were a number of Chinese women with small feet — feet bound in childhood — for whom the task is horrific, and yet they crawl up and down the steps.

We climbed up in pouring rain and a thick mist. We could only see a few steps in front of us. We spent the night at the top, the guest of a priest-like man. Harrison slept on two tables put together and I shared a hard Chinese bed with an American.

Fortunately by the next morning the weather had cleared and we were able to see all around. We saw the sun rise. The panorama from the top was fine indeed and the mountain scenes all the way down were wonderful. One interesting thing we saw was a natural bridge of boulders spanning a deep chasm from which many hundreds of Chinese have thrown themselves — a vicarious sacrifice. There is now a notice prohibiting people 'to give up their lives'!

We got down from the hill about ten-thirty on Friday morning, had a meal at quite a nice newly-built railway hotel and then caught the P'u K'ou express...

And now we're bound for Kuling. We're very lucky people and having a great time — but I shall be quite 'broke' at the end of it all!...

Lunch is ready — the British guard have had theirs and now passengers must eat.

About two years after arriving in China my father went to live in Kiyang, in the south of Hunan province, on the banks of the longest river in the province, the River Hsiang. Unlike Yungchow there were no other foreigners there, so he had to speak Chinese all the time. He shared three rooms with the Chinese minister, Rev Ma Chi Yun, above a shop on the main street of the town. The rooms were very sparsely furnished, with packing cases serving as a wash stand and dressing table. But rudimentary comforts would not have worried him.

Kiyang and the surrounding rural area formed a circuit, with the main church being situated in the city in addition to three or four small chapels scattered across the neighbouring countryside. The main church was small and in very poor condition. Soon after his arrival my father drew up plans to build a better building, which could more effectively serve the community. Even though construction in China is relatively cheap, it still required a significant sum of money, and he soon set his mother and his sister Nell working to raise money for this purpose in England.

The new church buildings were opened in 1933. In addition to the church there was accommodation for the Chinese preacher and Bible Woman, a small library and reading room, a club room and another room that could be used for a school. Chinese newspapers and English magazines were provided in the reading room, which soon became a popular place for local students. My father spent as much time as he could mingling with them and soon had a band of enthusiastic young men working with him, helping with teaching and evangelistic work, both in the city and the country.

It was a hard and lonely life, but suited him. He was out on his own, completely dependent on his ability to make himself understood and to understand. It was there that he gained his fluency in the Chinese language.

The following circular letter was written by him summarising his first full year's work in Kiyang.

Circular Letter of December 1933 from Kiyang
… the Kiyang circuit 1933 has been an eventful year… And I want in this letter… to give a brief account of its chief features.

Completion of new church premises
The most notable event has been the opening of the new church premises. What this has meant to us only those who knew our old, dilapidated, dingy and totally unsuitable premises can fully realise. Our old premises were a Chinese dwelling house, slightly and very poorly adapted to serve the purposes of a church, preacher's and Bible Woman's houses and guest rooms…our place of worship was also a right of way and a place

for gossiping with friends and receiving guests. The water carrier could not avoid it, children played in it and fowl strutted about in search of food...

We now have a fine three-storied building at the front, with three light and airy rooms on the two upper storeys and an imposing main entrance, with guest rooms on either side. Behind this there is an attractive and worshipful church, bright and clean, with coloured glass in the main doors and large side windows, and a gilt cross on a black background... At the back there is the preacher's new two-storied house with three large rooms on each floor...

Experiments in social service

We have opened on our new premises a small public library and reading room. So far the number of books in the library is very small...but the reading room, which contains a good selection of Chinese magazines and daily newspapers from Changsha, Nanking, Hangchow, Shanghai and Tientsin, attracts a large number of readers. The library and reading room are run by a committee, more than half of whose members are non-Christians. And so far this committee has provided, either by personal subscriptions from its members, or by subscriptions solicited from friends, all the necessary funds.

Another innovation is the English night school... When the scheme was first proposed some of us were not enthusiastic. We had seen English classes before and had seen the numbers dwindle as students realised that to learn a foreign language means hard work. But...we decided to give the school a trial. At first some forty students, including about a dozen children, mostly children of prominent businessmen, enrolled and paid their fee... The teachers are...one of our local preachers, a graduate of Wesley College, the manager of the Kiyang telegraph office and myself. The school has now been in progress for over two months. As expected some have dropped out, but we still have a regular attendance of about twenty-five... To say the least, the school is of value as a means of contact with educated non-Christians, and for making new friendships.

Another experiment is a weekly recreation meeting. Each Friday evening our young Church members and some of the English students meet for games and Chinese music...

These are experiments and only the future can tell whether they will be successful or not. And we are well aware that they are not our main job.

Three-circuit, short-term school for Church leaders

In November the Paoking, Yungchow and Kiyang circuits held a united short-term school for Church leaders. It lasted for nine days. Some fifty persons attended. There were lectures on theology, the teachings of St Paul, the New Testament... Two periods were given to the life of John Wesley and several meetings were held to discuss the problems confronting the Christian Church in China... Those present studied with diligence and entered into every part of the day's work with enthusiasm, and throughout the nine days there was a fine spirit of fellowship and devotion...

Looking back over the past year, we realised that everywhere around us there is very great opportunity. In the city and in the country the opportunity is the same. There is much friendliness wherever we go and there seems to be a general willingness to hear the Christian message. Realising this we look forward to 1934 with great hope. We have some difficult problems to tackle... Our greatest need is a vital personal experience of God: and our main task is to help our members, and all associated with us, to find such an experience. We are very thankful that, no longer having to worry about bricks and mortar, we can give the greater part of our thought and energy to this supreme task. But it is...infinitely more difficult than *putting up a new building, organising a library, or running a recreation club. Yet we know that only in as far as we succeed here can we claim to be taking a vital part in the working out of God's purpose in the world.*

...I am expecting John Foster to arrive on Friday, and I am greatly looking forward to...having a colleague. Though I don't particularly mind being alone, I feel I now have had enough of it. We shall have rather a squash in these three rooms, but I am sure we will manage...

Elsie is coming here for a few days next week to help the Bible Woman run a women's school... It will greatly buck up our Bible Woman to have a foreign lady to help her for a few days...

The following two letters were written on and just after a country tour which my father made with John Foster, a newly arrived missionary colleague.

Letter of 12th May 1935 from Kiyang

I am writing this...on a very hot and sticky day. I have just been taking Foster on his first trip round the circuit...

There is no big trouble here at the moment... What difficulties there are, are due to the economic difficulties of the people... It is to be hoped that this year's harvest will be better than the last. Several of our young men have gone into the army for a while. Going into the army is appropriately dubbed 'going to eat food'.

Last Sunday was celebrated throughout this district as a special Sunday for dealing with social customs which are condemned by the Church – customs such as smoking opium, concubinage, gambling, arranging early engagements for their children etc. To emphasise the Church's position regarding these things is very necessary, as a good many of our members do not keep to our rules. It was a great shock to me a few weeks ago when I discovered that our Circuit Steward had had a concubine for several years! All my Chinese colleagues and friends knew, but none, until Mr Hu told me a few weeks ago, mentioned it to me...

Letter of 18th May 1935 from Kiyang

I came back last Monday, after a week in the country. I always enjoy the pretty country and our school children there. The countryside and the children are two bright spots in a country full of dirt, distress and sorrow.

At present, with rice being very expensive and the heat coming on, things are more sordid than usual. Whenever Foster and I return from visiting the people on the street we always feel a bit depressed...there is so much that needs to be done and we are so helpless to do it...

We are all very full of admiration for Chiang Kai-shek and his wife these days. Wherever they go they dismiss corrupt and selfish officials (even the governor of a province) and set on foot movements to raise the standard of life of the people. And it does seem that they are inspired by Christian convictions...

I hear that the Hupeh District is to reduce the number of her missionaries by three... Personally I do not think the reduction of staff and grant is a bad thing for China. After all, surely the aim of missions should be to establish a few real Christian communities in a few places and leave them to evangelise the whole country, rather than...with the push of foreigners and foreign money.

Chiang Kai-shek

My father says above that, 'we are all very full of admiration for Chiang Kai-shek and his wife...' That was indeed the feeling of the foreign community and perhaps in particular the missionary community. One might add 'even more so the Methodist missionary community', who were startled by the announcement in August 1930 that Chiang Kai-shek had been baptised in the Methodist church in Shanghai. It was Madame Chiang's family church and there is no doubt that it was her influence that brought this about. Madame Chiang, who he had married two years earlier, came from a wealthy Sino-American Christian family.

Although Chiang, following Chinese tradition, treated his religious views as something entirely personal, which should have no influence on his politics, his conversion inevitably improved the standing of missionaries, perhaps in particular Methodist missionaries, throughout the country. Local officials were more likely to regard them favourably and be more helpful towards them than had often been the case before. This was most welcome, especially when it is to be borne in mind that the anti-foreign and anti-Christian riots described in the previous chapter had taken place only some three years earlier.

The great hope that the missionaries had was that Chiang's conversion would bring higher standards to public life, in particular less corruption and a more westernised approach to many problems. However, above all they saw in his conversion, which was followed by that of many senior central and provincial government officials, the possibility that China might develop, to a significant extent, into a Christian country.

Madame Chiang Kai-shek

In many ways even greater admiration was felt for Madame Chiang Kai-shek, who was undoubtedly a remarkable woman in many ways. She was an excellent public speaker, a woman of great poise and personality.

She had been educated at the best school in Shanghai – a Christian school – and followed it by studying at university in the United States. It was her mission to help bring China into the modern world and to improve the role of women in society. She was very well disposed to the missionaries and it was as a result of her influence that much relief was channelled through them in the immediate post-war period.

Her attitude to missionaries was summed up in an interview she gave to an American journalist, which appeared in the *Liberty* in August 1937. Speaking of missionaries she said:

> Back in the United States it is the fashion to condemn them. China knows better... As the Generalissimo and I have travelled from one end of the country to the other, we have been astonished again and again at the devotion of these missionaries and the hardships they endure...

Chiang Kai-shek and his wife travelled extensively across China, talking to the ordinary people in a way that few other rulers have done. In many places Madame Chiang specifically went out of her way to talk to missionaries, because she believed that they were in a peculiar position of independence. Unlike government officials they could tell the truth without fear or ambition standing in their way and unlike most other expatriates they lived among the Chinese people and understood the problems the ordinary Chinese faced.

Madame Chiang 'adopted' numerous war orphans, establishing what came to be known as her 'warphonages'. She also agreed to be godmother to the 'Sandpiper Baby', a young girl of about four months rescued in November 1939 by sailors from the HMS Sandpiper, the British gunboat stationed in Changsha, after a bombing raid. It was decided that the Sandpiper would adopt the child and look after her. The British Ambassador agreed to be godfather and Madame Chiang Kai-shek godmother. She named the child 'Water Lily'. The Rev John Stanfield took the christening service, using the ship's bell as a font. Sadly the baby died of pneumonia not long after. But Madame Chiang Kai-shek's interest in the case was typical of her caring nature.

Somewhat ironically, many of the things the missionaries and other Westerners strove to introduce into China and hoped Chiang Kai-shek and his wife would bring about – such as better health care, improved hygiene and sanitation, better education, less corruption and less superstition, tackling the problems of opium and so forth were only effectively addressed when those they regarded as their enemies, the Communists, came to power.

Endnotes

1. A light lunch. The term is of Indian origin.
2. On the southern bank of the Yangtze, opposite Hankow, now together forming part of the metropolis of Wuhan.
3. The China Inland Mission (CIM) was founded by Rev James Hudson Taylor and William Thomas Berger in the middle of the 19th century, with the goal of the interdenominational evangelisation of China's inland provinces.
4. In fact a considerable under-estimation. The Yangtze floods of that year are reckoned to have been the worst natural disaster in recorded human history, producing a death toll of approximately 3,700,000.
5. The Southern Army consisted of the Kwangsi troops, referred

to earlier, and those of Kwantung, the neighbouring province, which joined them in opposition to Chiang Kai-shek.

6. After Chiang Kai-shek transferred the capital from Peking (which means 'northern capital') to Nanking, the name of the former was changed to Peiping – 'northern peace'. The current name Beijing is a modern version of the former name, also meaning 'northern capital'.

Chapter Three
My Mother in Paoking

娘

After almost eighteen months furlough in Australia and England my mother returned to China in February 1931. Rather than travel by sea, which was the normal route, she went by rail, travelling across Russia on the Trans-Siberian Railway. This letter describes the memorable journey.

Letter of February 1931:
The Trans-Siberian Railway

We – that is myself and fellow passengers – assembled at Liverpool Street Station (London) for the 10 am train on Monday February 16th. There was a good crowd to wish us 'bon voyage' and then we were off. We arrived at Harwich at noon and boarded the Dutch steamer for Flushing. It was not a good journey. It was very cold and the sea was choppy, but it didn't last long. By 7 am we had arrived at Flushing, passed through customs and were on the night train for Berlin. We felt we were now really on our way. For the first night I shared the carriage with a Dutch lady. She boarded the train at 11.30 am, took two hours to get into her bunk, then insisted on having the light on all night. She left at six-thirty the next morning and I bade her goodbye with pleasure. I wondered how many more such companions I might expect; but I was very fortunate. The next night a charming German girl came to the carriage and we travelled very happily together right over to China.

The morning of the second day found us in Berlin, a hungry party of six with all the day before us and not a word of German between us. Sight-seeing and obtaining food in such circumstances is always interesting but in Berlin it was made easy as we found so many people spoke English. The real fun in that direction began when we got to Russia. Berlin seemed to us a very fine city. It was well laid out with wide clean streets. There were numerous significant public buildings, many of them one-time palaces of the Kaisers, who must have had a passion for building palaces and putting up statues. Most of the statues and palaces were undoubtedly beautiful, but it seemed a terrible waste of money.

We went on a Thomas Cooks' motor tour round the city and out to Charlottenburg, which adjoins Berlin. Touring round in a motor we saw only the outsides of the buildings of course and had no time to explore them fully. One sight of special interest was the changing of Hindenburg's[1] guard. About two hundred soldiers led by a drum and fife band marched round to the palace, attended by two hundred to three hundred unemployed. Why attended by the unemployed I do not know, but we were told it was the daily practice.

Back to the train. The next day we travelled through beautiful country deep in dazzling white snow. In some places the houses were almost buried beneath it. At every station the train was met by sleighs drawn by ponies. As we travelled we could see them dashing across the snow. Some had passengers all wrapped up in furs. Some were dragging loads of wood. About 10 pm we arrived at Negorelole, the border town for Poland and Russia. Here we had to go through strict Russian customs. Our baggage was thoroughly examined and our passports looked at in great detail. All money, jewellery, cameras and so forth had to be declared. There were a lot of formalities, but everyone was quite pleasant and it didn't seem so very long before we were comfortably settled in the Russian train.

We were three hours late in arriving at Moscow. Moscow was most depressing, especially after Berlin. The reason was partly that the city was under snow at that time. The dirty snow exaggerated the dirt and neglect. An official guide met the train. Some of the passengers I was travelling with, including Mr Stanfield, Mike Crawford and Miss Gardiner, went off with her to see someone about some luggage. They fared very well; but others, such as Mrs Heady, Miss Bolton and I didn't have such an easy time. First we tried to get lunch at the station restaurant, but food was strictly rationed and they would not serve us. We then went to the station bureau and got a note from the woman in charge there to say we were to be served with the 'regulation' meal. Armed with this we returned, but still it was unpleasant. Then a Russian girl who spoke French came to our rescue. She insisted on the waiters serving us and also drove away some rough men who were bothering us. It was a wretched place. By and by the rest of the party arrived and the official guide, who took charge. Then everything went well. She took us to the Intertourist Bureau where we engaged a guide to take us round the city.

Our time was limited, so, as in Berlin, we could only gaze at the outsides of the buildings. We walked across the Red Square and under the Kremlin walls, then from the other side of the river looked into the Kremlin at the beautiful architecture of the palaces and churches there. One place we did make time to see within was Lenin's Mausoleum. It was weird, but interesting, to see Lenin lying in that glass case with brilliant lights turned on him while all the rest of the room, or tomb, was in deep shadow. The armed guard standing at the head and foot of the glass case added to the impressiveness of the scene, but I heaved a sigh of relief when we got out again into the open air. The atmosphere of the mausoleum was typical of the atmosphere of the whole city — depressing, hostile, tense. To be fair I must say that not all our party felt the same way as I did. Perhaps it was my imagination, but the tense, unsmiling faces of the people did depress me. The people were warmly clad, but did look so shabby. It is, of course, part of their policy that no one should look better dressed than his fellows. Our guide pointed out to us many schools and colleges and spoke enthusiastically of the educational work that is being done.

For the next eight days while we travelled across Russia and Siberia we noticed that the people out in the countryside appeared to be better dressed and happier. The many small towns through which we passed seemed more prosperous than the big cities. I had expected those eight days to be very monotonous and had armed myself with a good supply of books to read, but it was not so. Each day the scenery varied, but always it was beautiful. Some days great stretches of dazzling white plains with frequently occurring forests of dark pine, some days high hills with deep valleys covered with snow-tipped pines or feathery silver birches with their beautiful silver trunks shining in the sun. Some days we travelled for miles along the banks of white frozen rivers and for one memorable day along the banks of Lake Baikal. Another day the train travelled up and up round and round a tortuous track among the hills then rolled and rollicked its way down the other side. The next day found us traversing a seemingly never-ending plain and we knew we were nearing Manchuria. The people and their dwellings changed as we travelled on. In some parts the buildings were high and nearly buried in the snow. In other parts they were squat. One day we passed a lot of windmills. In some parts the villages were numerous, in others few and far between. In Manchuria we saw only occasional and fortified homesteads.

Only one day of the journey did we have some snow, the rest was glorious sunshine. An added joy to the journey were the magnificent sunsets, when the snow became as red as the sky.

It was amazing how quickly the time passed. Each day we

had one inferior meal in the restaurant car, for the rest we picnicked on the provisions we had brought with us. Preparing and clearing away our meal took quite a long time. Fairly often – three or four times a day – we stopped at a station for ten minutes or so while the engine took on fuel and water. All the passengers turned out and we stamped up and down the track with one eye on the train lest it should start up suddenly and leave us behind. The rest of the time we read or talked.

Another source of continual interest was watching people coming to meet the trains. Long before we got to the station we could see the sleighs coming across the snow. Usually they were horse-drawn, but occasionally they were pulled by dogs, or, if they were bringing provisions, they were sometimes pulled by men.

The end of the eleventh day found us at the Chinese frontier having crossed Holland, Germany, Poland, Russia and Siberia. We reached Manchiuli about twelve hours behind time and wondered what would happen next, but we were informed that a train was waiting for us. So behold at 2 am sleepily going through customs, seeing to passports and baggage and transferring ourselves to the Chinese train. We lazed most of the next day trying to make up for lost sleep. At 10 pm that night we reached Harbin and once more changed trains. This time three of us were in a carriage so small that we barely had room to turn round, but it was only until 7 am the next morning when we reached Chanchuin[2].

The next stage was on a Japanese train, which was most clean and comfortable. At noon we reached Mukden and were met by Mr and Mrs Robertson of the British and Foreign Bible Society and were welcomed back to China. After a short while we were off again to Darien, some of the party having left us. We arrived there at 8 pm the next day and put up at the Yamoto Hotel – and how we enjoyed it! It was bliss to have a hot bath after all those days on the train and to sleep in a bed *that did not sway to and fro.*

The next morning we boarded a Japanese steamer for Shanghai. It was a comfortable steamer and the journey was uneventful, except that we hit a bit of rough weather one morning and everyone became rather quiet! Tuesday morning at the mouth of the river we ran into fog, which held us up until the next morning. As a result we arrived in Shanghai nearly a day late.

Such was our journey to China via Siberia, though much more exciting and interesting than it reads. The rest must be told quickly. We travelled up the Yangtze from Shanghai to Hankow by river steamer, a journey that took us three and a half days. From Hankow to Changsha we went on a smaller steamer – a journey of two days. The last stage was a motor bus – not the English sort – from Changsha to Yiyang. I have come here for a few weeks to help with a women's school. So I am already in the thick of it – and glad to be so too.

The entire journey from London to Shanghai had cost a total of £59. 19. 2d (now equivalent to approximately £2575), which covered second class from London to the Russian border and first class across Russia.

My mother wrote the following letter to her sister Jean during the last part of her journey, on board a ship between Darien and Shanghai.

Letter of 1st March 1931 from the SS Choshun Maru, on the China Sea

Last night we spent in a lovely hotel in Darien. It was great and we just revelled in it. After about twelve days of the dirt and dust of travelling it was lovely to get in a hot bath and just lie there, then get into fresh clean clothes and into a big clean bed that didn't dance up and down. Bliss!

I am not going to try and give you a full account of the

journey in this letter as I am preparing a circular one, so many people want to know about it.

Tonight I am sitting on a Japanese steamer not very far away from Shanghai – we are due there on Tuesday – and a fortnight ago at this time I was at 34 Market Lane[3]. Isn't it wonderful?

[Maud's letter] had the great news in it that at last the Consul has given the 'all clear' signal for Hunan[4]. Now ladies too may return to up-country stations. It is quite a while since he gave permission for the men and he must now feel sure of things when he has given permission for the ladies too.

Maud is very excited and is just waiting for my arrival in Hankow, then we will go up together to Changsha. Mr Stanfield is going up to Paoking with us, to take care of us and carry on the work there until Mr Lamming returns.

Mr Stanfield has travelled from London with us, but we left him yesterday in Mukden. He is travelling via Peking to Hankow… I wanted to go that way also, but the Mission House wouldn't allow it, because they didn't think it safe enough for ladies at present. Cliff has already left for Yungchow, so I shall not see him until Synod. I am glad of that for by then I will have got my 'China feet' again and will be more sure of myself.

I shall spend a day or two in Shanghai, doing some oddments of shopping, then have a lazy up-river trip to Hankow and expect to go on almost immediately to Changsha.

I still don't realise I am in China. The journey has been so quick and so absolutely unusual I feel as though I have been living in a most interesting story, something quite apart from England, China, Australia or any other part of my life. I still feel as if I shall awaken up soon and find myself back in England…

First of all from Ilkley I went to Liverpool to Mr and Mrs Cook. It is like going home when I go there. I am Mrs Cook's missionary daughter and indeed she is like a mother to me.

I have still lots of blather in me, but I think I had better close…

On arriving back in China my mother travelled from Shanghai to Paoking, now under the new name of Shaoyang. Shortly after her return the new matron Freda Wright arrived. From the beginning they were close friends and remained so for the rest of their lives. Also eagerly waiting to greet her on her return was her faithful dog Smuto. My mother described in her book some of changes she encountered.

With more experience and better knowledge of the language I was able…to undertake more productive work. Barbara Simpson came from Yiyang and with her help and guidance I ran my first three-week school for women. The faithful Mrs Tsao had retired. In her place I had a woman of some education, Mrs Tseo. Mrs Tseo had been a school teacher but now wanted to do full-time evangelistic work. She was a treasure. Together we ran women's schools each spring and summer in the city and one or two shorter ones in the country. We taught the Christian faith in its simplest way, as well as reading, hygiene, childcare and knitting. It was wonderful to see the change in the women who came…

The knitting though was something of a joke. I could sew and do embroidery with reasonable proficiency, but had always been a mutt at knitting. But since there was no one else to teach them it had to be me! We got into frightful muddles and in the evening I would appeal to Freda to help me unravel the mess. It did not take long before the women were knitting much better than I ever could – and more quickly too! They began to knit coats and trousers to wear in the winter. True, they were straight up and down, but they were warm and that was what mattered. Chinese women, and do remember our work was among the poor and uneducated, may have had little scholastic ability, but they were shrewd housewives and clever with their fingers. I soon decided it was time I learned to knit properly myself!...

Country journeys...were an important part of my work in those days and I was out of town a great deal. Usually a journey around the circuit lasted about two weeks, but if I was running a school somewhere I might be away from home for three, or even four, weeks. I walked most of the way between villages. Even when I had a chair I walked a lot. I hated to feel isolated and cut-off up in the chair. In our part of China the only decent road was the road from Shaoyang to Changsha. For the rest it was the old style Chinese roads made up of one or perhaps two blocks of stone laid side by side and end to end with a foot or so of earth on each side. Hard-baked earth in the dry season and slushy mud in wet weather. The roads meandered through rice fields, a beautiful green in the summer, along by the side of rivers, sometimes over hills. On and on they stretched from village to village, or small town to small town. Springtime was the most beautiful time to be out on the roads. Every farmhouse had its peach tree in bloom and the fields were covered with yellow rape seed flowers. The rape was later ploughed back into fields as fertiliser. Sometimes when you came over the brow of a hill and looked down on the valley below it was like a yellow carpet dotted with peach blossom. Hunan is a very hilly province and a very beautiful one too. In spring the hills are ablaze with azaleas – white, yellow and red.

The people though could be unbearably curious, especially where a white woman was concerned. In

71

some of the places I visited I was the first white woman they had ever seen. They were, however, always kind and friendly. When I was out in the country I stayed in the homes of the preachers. Usually they were humble abodes containing only the bare necessities, but clean, and one could be sure of a warm welcome from the preacher and his family. The Bible Woman and I always shared a room, often up a ladder in the loft. I preferred to be up in the loft safe from prying eyes. At ground level I was much more vulnerable. There being no glass in the country, the windows were covered with paper. All that was needed was a wet finger applied to the paper and you had a perfect peephole.

Sometimes strange things happened in the night, such as the occasion when I protested to Mrs Tseo because she kept on getting up and lighting the lamp. 'But Hsiao Chieh,' she replied, 'every time I put the light out and lie down the rats come and steal the straw from my pillow.' After that I agreed to sleep with the light on!

There was also the morning when I woke up with a huge upper lip. I had been bitten by a spider during the night. Another night I had a nightmare and woke up the whole household. The evening before when we had been sitting and talking, Mrs Wang, the wife of one of our ministers, told us she had heard a rumour that a gang were planning to rob me. She had therefore gone to see the headman of the clan and he had assured her that he would attend to the matter and nothing untoward would happen to me. Then in the middle of the night I had a nightmare and called out loudly. Everyone was sure the bandits had arrived. Before they would settle again I had to come down the ladder so they could see with their own eyes that all was well. Another night I was awakened by the rain coming through the roof and splashing on my face. I got up, opened up my Chinese umbrella, curled up under it and went back to sleep again.

Only once was Freda, who had by then become a particularly close friend, able to go right round the circuit with me, but often when I was going out she would come with me for the first weekend at Chiu Kong Chiao. We walked out the twelve miles on the Saturday morning. In the afternoon we visited members. We would then return to the chapel and soon the crowds would start to gather. Freda would see to the sick folk while I talked to the women and children. Then with the help of Mrs Tseo, the preacher, we would hold a service. The next morning I led the morning service and again many sick folk came and Freda helped them. After the midday meal she returned on foot to Shaoyang and I went off visiting again.

In later years when I travelled I always carried with me a simple first-aid box. In that way I was able to help people suffering from minor complaints, cuts and sores, and to give quinine to people suffering from malaria. In those days there was no doctor or dispensary out in the country. The more severe cases I used to urge to go to the hospital in Shaoyang for treatment, even though it was often as much as three days' journey away.

The following letter was written by my mother while on holiday in Kuling.

Letter of September 1931 from Kuling:
The Hankow Floods

...we are all very distressed about the terrible floods in Hankow. I don't know if much news has come through to England about them. They are terrible, absolutely beyond

comprehension. There has never been a flood as bad as this and that is saying a great deal, for the people out here often experience the most dreadful extreme weather. The whole of the Yangtze Valley is flooded almost to Shanghai. Hundreds and hundreds of miles of once lived upon and cultivated land are now under water. Countless villages and small towns have been swept away and even the very big cities are deep in water and half ruined. Hankow is in a pitiful state. It is estimated that at least fifteen million people have been rendered homeless and no one knows how many hundreds of thousands, if not millions, have lost their lives. It has been so vast no one could cope with it, or can cope with it now. After three weeks the water is still rising steadily. Several of the biggest dykes have burst. Hankow is now a new Venice. People go everywhere in boats, many shops have had to close down because the water has risen so high. On Saturday it finally reached the printing presses of the two Hankow papers, so they too have had to close down.

Thousands and thousands of refugees have crowded in from the surrounding countryside. The authorities have helped many with food and places to live, but the numbers were far beyond them. Our mission at Wu Shen Miao is responsible for three hundred in their institute and a thousand in another place, in addition to all the church refugees. For a long time the only dry place was the railway embankment and it was crowded with refugees and their few poor belongings, packed so close that for many there was only standing room. And, awful to think of, hundreds have died of starvation and the dead and the alive lay side by side with the water only a foot below where they were. And now even that embankment has gone – and where are those people? It is only when you get down to details you realise the full horror of it. The water is not sweet fresh rain water, much of it is just sewage. There is no means of burying the dead, there is no sanitation and all the water smells so foul – and the mosquitoes!…

...for all it is very trying indeed and food is so scarce, but what they have to put up with is nothing compared with what the folk have had to suffer at Union Hospital. Union Hospital is in the way of the flood water which has broken through one of the dykes. They are now seventeen feet deep in water there. All patients were first removed to the second floor, but now they have had to be put on the third floor. All the foreign houses are also flooded and the doctors...have all been living up in their second storeys. In the doctors' houses the water is two feet deep in the very rooms they were sleeping in. When they stepped out of bed they went over their knees in water. On Saturday Sister Gladys, one of the nurses here, had to give up and came away. It was impossible for her to stay longer, but the doctors are still carrying on. All their furniture is lashed to verandahs and such like and Sister Gladys complains it is most trying to have your belongings floating to meet you. Several nights she could not sleep because her sideboard would keep floating around banging into everything else. One night when there was a strong wind the water rose in great waves and dashed against the houses. The doctors and nurses have worked like Trojans trying to save equipment and belongings, but even so the loss is very heavy and will become worse as it is feared this water will not go down for a long time yet. It is estimated that at the earliest it will not go down before October and then what a terrible damp state everything will be in.

Of course after such floods there cannot but be famine and everyone fears a terrible epidemic after all the foul water. Last Friday we were all inoculated against cholera.

At present Hupeh[5] folk are not being allowed to return, the danger from sickness is too great and the food shortage too acute.

Hunan has so far kept comparatively free. Yiyang had a nasty flood, over fifteen feet, but it was over in a few days. Considered alone it was serious, but it pales into insignificance *against these other floods. There are many rumours of troop movements in Hunan. The Kwangsi troops are supposed to be on the tramp, but they are well disciplined anti-Communists so we are hoping the Consul won't raise any objections to our returning at the beginning of September.*

I am enjoying it up here immensely, but I shall be quite content to return and get my nose down. I have several schemes in mind for the autumn. First of which is a women's school for the first three weeks of October... I am also hoping to get started a girls' club and a children's play hour, or some such special time for the wee ones. But it isn't easy getting helpers for the new schemes...

These were difficult days for China. The Yangtze valley in the summer of 1931 suffered from the devastation of floods, judged in terms of human loss, unequalled in recorded history. The death toll was estimated at approximately 3,700,000 and the number of homeless uncountable.

In the north of the country another disaster, this time of human making, was rapidly unfolding. The Japanese had for some years been making threats to the Chinese regarding its dubious claims of sovereignty over parts of North-East China. Then on 18th September 1931, in what became known as the 'Mukden Incident', the Japanese devised an excuse for invading Manchuria. A railway train near Mukden was blown up – almost certainly by the Japanese themselves – and being in an area which the Chinese had ceded to the Japanese rights of movement over Chinese territory, under one of the infamous unequal treaties, the Japanese used the pretext of restoring law and order to justify their invasion. Despite condemnation by the League of Nations, which led to Japan withdrawing from the body, no effective measures were taken by the great powers to restrain the Japanese aggressors. The Chinese Army was no match for the better trained and more heavily armed Japanese and put up only token resistance. Within two months the whole of Manchuria was under Japanese control. On 1st March 1932 it was declared an independent country, under the name Manchukuo, with Henry Pu-yi, the infant Emperor deposed by the revolution of 1911, as its nominal Head of State. All effective power, of course, remained with the Japanese.

While the Japanese were seizing the North-East of the country the Chinese were fighting among themselves, with the Kwangsi Group, led by Generals Li Tsung-jen and Pai Chung-hsi, raising a rebellion against Chiang Kai-shek, who they claimed had betrayed Sun Yat Sen's 'Three Principals of the People' – nationalism, democracy and livelihood – by trying to make himself a dictator. They also objected to his lack of action in the face of repeated acts of aggression from the Japanese. Rather than prepare the country to defend itself against Japan, Chiang was directing all his energy into his dispute with the Communists.

My mother refers to the Kwangsi troops in the above letter, being concerned that their activities might prevent her returning to Shaoyang from her summer retreat in Kuling. As far as we know they did not. The forces of Chiang Kai-shek and the Kwangsi Group were fairly evenly balanced and the outcome of the conflict would have been difficult to predict had the Japanese not struck. The conflict in Manchuria led to a compromise being reached between the two groups, with the Kwangsi troops being absorbed into the Kuomintang army under Chiang Kai-shek, while Li Tsung-jen and Pai Chung-hsi were in return given important positions in the government.

Letter of 21st November 1931 from Hsiao Shiu Miao (Little Water Temple)

...I am in the country fifteen miles away from Paoking at a place called Hsiao Shiu Miao – Little Water Temple. I am sitting up in the loft writing this letter by the light of a lantern. I call it a loft, because it definitely is a loft, not a pretty upstairs room. You climb to it up a straight neck-breaking ladder. It's those first two steps going down that are the worst. Once you get your balance it is all right. The ceiling is the slate of the roof, the floor is the wood planks which also make the ceiling of the room below. The window is an aperture, now covered with paper, the door is an opening without even a piece of paper to cover it. But compared with some of the funny places Freda and I have slept in this past fortnight it is a good place, for it is approaching clean, which is something I never fail to appreciate.

The great trouble with this place, a trouble that is remediable, is that either they have never had a foreign woman here before, or it is a jolly long time since they had. I am tired of being stared at today! You might think that I would get used to it and I have to a certain extent, but it isn't a joke to sit in a room while about thirty women just sit and stare at you, never taking their eyes off you, but all the time discussing you among themselves.. I am afraid I have not been a good missionary today. I sat this morning until I could not bear their staring any longer, then got up and walked outside. Of course half of them followed, but it was a slight relief. Unfortunately when I returned I discovered the other half had gone to my room and were going through all my things! I am afraid I was downright cross!

Chinese folk here have no idea of privacy. If they had their own way they would never leave you alone. All you possess is for everyone to see and they would not think twice of reading a letter you left lying about.

Three weeks ago Miss Wright and I went off into the country to go right round the circuit. We were out for a fortnight...we had a very good trip round. It was Miss Wright's first experience of country travel and she groaned about the dirt etc, but she was great fun, treating it all as a glorious game. To me it was a great joy to have a companion, some one to share all the jokes with – and there are plenty in the country...

As we went round Freda saw sick folk in each town. We spent a day and two nights in each place. Our usual programme was to hold a service the night we arrived, then next morning visit the members. In the afternoon, as long as daylight lasted, we saw sick folk, then in the evening held another service. Everywhere we went our services were crowded. Most of it was just curiosity with the crowds wanting to see and hear the foreign woman, but they remained to listen to the Chinese speakers too.

One town we visited was holding a religious festival and was full of people from the countryside around. We had very crowded meetings there... We were asked to preach in the temple itself and had a tremendous group of two or three hundred people. I believe I have never spoken to a more attentive crowd...

Miss Wright...has only been out a year so I usually had to act as her interpreter and general assistant. It was great fun. I became quite an expert at measuring out medicines and so forth. An occasional visit of a nurse or doctor is very useful and can provide relief from pain for some people, but it is terribly inadequate and leaves you with an awful heartache for those who cannot be helped by one visit, those who need a doctor and continuous treatment...

One town we visited was suffering from an epidemic of

measles, evidently a malignant form for a number of children had died. When visiting one member I heard a woman crying in the next house and asked what was the trouble. They said both her children had died from measles, one aged one year and the other five years. I went to see her...

We are now beginning to prepare for Christmas. Last Saturday the three of us – that is Maud, Freda and I – made our mincemeat, this Saturday Freda and Maud are going to get on with the pudding, then when I return we are going to make our cake together. I quite expect our cook could do it all if we instructed him, but we like doing this ourselves...

Letter of 2nd April 1932 from Hsiao Shui Miao

I have an idea I have written to you once before from this place – 'Little Water Temple'. This is the place where everyone is called 'Wang'. It is the polite thing in China when you meet a person to ask their name. Here the answer is always 'Wang'. Then they politely try to explain exactly what relationship they stand to various other Wangs, and I sit and try to look intelligent, though I have not the ghost of an idea what branch of the family tree they belong to.

Relationships were always beyond me in English; and in Chinese, where they are so much more complicated, it is hopeless. There are different names for the elder brother's children and the younger brother's, and it varies again if the elder brother has sons or not. Uncle and cousins on the father's side have different names from uncles and cousins on the mother's side, again varying as to whether they are older or younger. Those who become relations by marriage, such as an aunt's husband have again another name and so on and so on. Do you understand?... No?!! Neither do I!...

The country at present is just lovely. What a joy after the brown bareness of the winter. The blossom is over in most places, *but now the trees are putting forth green leaves, the grass is green once again and there are great stretches of beautiful green wheat and yellow 'yeo tsai'*[6]*. The 'yeo tsai' will be ploughed in by and by to enrich the ground for the rice crop. Spring in China is wonderful. As we came along yesterday I saw lots of tall, beautiful Azaleas out in bloom on the hillsides…*

Sunday afternoon

I am sitting on the door of the step to continue this letter. This way I get a back rest. I am tired of sitting on high backless forms. Also I enjoy the fresh air and I am not separating myself too much from the other folk.

I was wrong about everyone being called 'Wang'. Yesterday afternoon we went visiting in another district, also part of Hsiao Shui Miao, and there everyone is called 'Chien'.

We had a big crowd to service this morning, the great majority women, but also quite a few men. I spoke on our hope of resurrection and of seeing our loved ones again after death… When death parts them here that is the last they see of them… They have a vague belief that afterwards they wander around as spirits, but always seem to think of them as being evil spirits… What a difference from our certainty that there is life after this.

The people here live in the midst of great beauty, which I am sure few of them ever see… They work from morning to night to make enough money to exist, know nothing beyond their own little spot, don't know how to play and don't have a book to read and not even a few pretty clothes to wear. I ought to say I am speaking mostly of the country women. The men, because they mostly have a little education, have a little more in their lives. Townspeople on the whole have more interest in life, but they are not all to the good…their recreation and forgetfulness of life's cares come from opium smoking and gambling. It is so sad…

My mother describes how Christmas 1932 was spent in Paoking.

Letter of 13th January 1933 from Paoking

It is frightfully cold here and has been below freezing point all day. Up to Christmas we had very mild weather, but it has been real winter since… Chinese New Year falls within this month and all the women are busy working for it… All government offices, post offices etc observe the foreign calendar, but in the homes – and in the country especially – Chinese New Year is still the great feast of the year. All the housewives are busy preparing dry meats, dried vegetables and sweet meats…

Chinese New Year is always good fun for us. The folk come in crowds to make their New Year bows. A group of eight or ten wander around together. Last year we had all the hospital servants (about fourteen of them) in and were giving them tea and sweetmeats to eat when another batch of about eight arrived. It was a job finding chairs for them all. We usually have quite a few batches of workers in before they finish – the hospital girl nurses, the boy and men nurses, the hospital servants, the school teachers, and two or three groups of various other staff members. This year the school staff and nurses came and made their bows on 'foreign' New Year's Day, so we don't quite know what to expect later… Freda and I also visit all the members' houses and eat most wonderful things…

We began the Friday before Christmas with a hospital patients' and children's party. The nurses gave an amusing hygiene play, then Mr Stanfield showed a few lantern slides and lastly we had the tree. Every member's child and every hospital patient received a small present. We had over a hundred presents on the tree and the children just loved it. Poor wee tots, they get so little. I love to see their shining faces when they come for their presents…

On the Saturday the school children performed 'The Story of the Manger'. It was written by the headmaster. It was, I believe, well written, but so great was the crowd and so persistent the noise that we heard little of the words. The costumes and acting did not appeal to us foreigners — except to our funny boxes! I like to be reverent, but the first scene of Mary and Joseph being married in the temple in Chinese styles with bows to all and sundry and fire crackers, was too much for me, as was the vision of Mary in padded gown and woollen hat. The funniest of all was Herod dressed in a kimono and khaki sun helmet!... We did manage to persuade the wise men to wear kimonos and turbans instead of overcoats and trilby hats. The play, like the headmaster's speeches, was mighty long — it took over two hours.

Sunday was a full and happy day. As usual Freda and I had saved each others' letters and parcels for almost a fortnight before. On Christmas Eve I had my camp bed put up in Freda's room and we were going to enjoy them together on Christmas morning, but about 5 am Freda was called to a midwifery case. We thought 'bang, goes our Christmas morning', but by 8 am she was back. I had waited hopefully, so we opened our parcels together in front of the dining room fire...

I have not yet heard what sort of Christmas and New Year Cliff has had. He said he was staying at Kiyang for Christmas Day then going down to Hungchow for a week. I expect he would have had a happy time with the others there. It is difficult to be other than happy at Christmas. We are all so busy and our Chinese friends are so happy...

Circular letter of 1934:
Three months at Wu Feng Pu

For a long time I have felt there is so much in the ordinary lives of my Chinese friends which I do not understand. Sometimes talking to them of household hygiene and similar *subjects I have felt my words lacked power because I could not say I had done it in similar conditions. Also, try as one will, just because one is a foreigner and has foreign standards there is a barrier... Thanks to the goodness of my colleagues who have undertaken my work while I have been away, I have been able this summer to experiment...*

Mrs Tseo (the Bible Woman), Miss Tsao (a student in training to become a deaconess) and myself set out for the town of the 'Five Peaks', a small but busy market town, and one of our out-stations. We rented two rooms on the street there and for three months lived very much as our neighbours live, except that we tried to observe all the rules of hygiene and were somewhat busy with Church work. We were a happy family.

Whilst there we ran a two month school for women, teaching reading, scripture, hygiene and knitting. We had around twenty scholars for the two months.

Another bit of service was a daily clinic. You didn't know I was a doctor, did you? One way and another I have done a fair amount of first-aid and home nursing. Before I went into the country I went down to the hospital when I could and Freda taught me quite a lot. I therefore felt able to tackle simple diseases, wash eyes, wash and dress sores, etc. 'Dr Koh'[7] became quite famous in Wu Feng Pu! Many I have helped were quite cured, many much improved and I don't think I killed anyone!

It was the everyday life that fascinated me. The house in which we lived was made of mud brick... My room was behind our landlady's guest room, where the household idols were also kept. I performed a wonderful cure, though not in strict accordance with medical rules. One day our landlady came to me and said would I please take down the bag which I had nailed to the wall of my room. The nail was just below the shelf where she kept her idols. She declared that since I had put it there, she had had severe pains in her back. I removed the bag and the nail, but her back, though much better, was not cured. She came into my room again to see if there was anything else there and decided the trouble was a small picture of Jesus which I had pinned up there. Would I remove it? Yes, I would put it on another wall. I did and her back was cured.

Our landlady was a dear, kindly soul but very, very superstitious. Each morning she lit her three sticks of incense. One she placed on the side of the stove and made her bow to the kitchen god, the second she placed just outside the door and made her bow to the 'Great Spirit', the third she placed on the idol shelf beside the tablets of her ancestors and made her bow to them. Also, each day two bowls of rice and two or three of vegetables, with chopsticks all ready were placed on the kitchen stove so that the gods might partake and be satisfied and bless the house.

We did our own washing and cooking. We sat on low stools in the courtyard each morning and washed our clothes, usually in a very small amount of cold water. I am afraid I wasn't very good at the washing. I can wash clothes when I have plenty of hot water and lux, but a spot of cold water, even with the help of a bar of soap, seemed inadequate. I found putting my gowns under my sleeping mat and lying on them for a night or two was an excellent substitute for ironing. I learned a fair amount of Chinese cooking, enough to do my own meals when left alone and one or two fancy dishes. One day I tried to teach the others to make foreign biscuits. We didn't know if they would turn out to be biscuits or rock buns. We used an old kerosene tin as a stove, but as we had no baking powder (only strong soda), there was a shortage of sugar, the flour was very coarse and brown and the lard strong tasting, they were not a great success!

The amount of housework was small, but there were usually extras. As a rule we paid a little to have our rice husked for us, but on one occasion we did our week's supply ourselves. It was hard work but good fun working the foot mortar to husk the rice and later swinging a big basket to sift it. I could work the mortar and swing the basket but I wasn't very successful at blowing the chaff away. Often the 'blow' seemed to get in the wrong place and the rice went flying instead. I also learned to work a hand mortar for grinding wheat.

So much did we become part of the life of the street that when the Summer Festival preparations began I was asked if I would make some paper flowers, or some such thing as we would use in England. I appreciated their friendly gesture; but didn't feel able to comply. They themselves make the most beautiful floral decorations. The Summer Festival was most interesting. It lasted eight days with daylight processions, night processions and plays. At night the street was decorated with lanterns and coloured oil lamps. Everyone wore their pretty clothes and all were so happy. I enjoyed the fun of it, but oh the visitors!

All the people from the country around came into the city for the festival, and all our friends brought their friends to see the foreign woman, and those who had no friends to bring them came of their own accord, just to sit, or stand and stare. It was a most exhausting business being a side-show for the festival! Everywhere I went people followed me until in the end I just fled and shut myself up in my room for a little while. Mrs Tseo put a seat in front of the door and sat on guard. They were all quite friendly and didn't mean to be unkind.

The night processions were very pretty, but one did wish it wasn't necessary for them to be so late at night. For most of the people it didn't matter. During the hot weather they find it almost impossible to sleep in their tiny rooms and there is always a little more air on the streets so they just lie about outside on forms or chairs or mats on the ground and talk and fan themselves until they fall asleep. The processions were therefore a welcome diversion for them, but not so welcome to us, who were trying to sleep indoors. The racket was certainly sleep-destroying and there were six or seven processions every night! However, the day processions with their gorgeous banners and dainty little figures on high stilts were a joy.

Processions were the order of the day. Before the Summer Festival began there were several processions beseeching rain. One day 3000 farmers passed through the town carrying their idols. They were out on a day's pilgrimage from a neighbouring district. On another occasion the 'Five Peaks' organised a procession, which one member from each household had to attend or pay a fine. It was a blazing hot day, but no one was allowed to wear a hat or carry an umbrella and they had very little to eat. They marched to the top of a neighbouring and very high hill, carrying their idols with them to see their misery so that they might pity them and send rain. They brought back with them another idol who was reputed to be especially good at sending rain. When they returned they broke into pieces one of the city's idols because it had failed to answer their prayers. Poor misguided folk...

During this period when there was no rain and daily the crops were growing more and more dry, everyone was becoming anxious lest the whole rice crop be lost. In addition to the procession a fast was called. No pigs were killed, no hens could be bought and later no fish and no eggs were to be had and also no vegetables. It was a real fast. The people lived on a short ration of watery rice. After a fortnight of this I was considerably thinner and extremely hungry. Living on light rations was not an inspiring experience.

We had several incidents of mild excitement such as the time when Mrs Tseo found an eight-foot-long snake careering across the floor. We made it a present of the house, but soon our good neighbours came with sticks and stones and evicted our unwelcome visitor. We also had a bandit scare, but they were turned back by soldiers when just a few miles away. Huge spiders, which insisted on taking up their abode with us, also caused alarm, but our landlady was usually equal to such a situation. There were always the street rows when other excitements failed. One night a jealous husband in the house near us almost succeeded in murdering his wife. A few doors away a man committed suicide because he thought he had killed another man — but the other man recovered.

There was another bit of excitement. One night a thief broke into our rooms. I had taken my faithful dog Smuto to Wu Feng Pu with me. She slept at my bedside. One night I was awakened by her low growling and I heard a noise in the adjoining room. I guessed what was happening, so I said to Smuto, 'Off you go…' She darted off — and so did the burglar, as fast as he could! I went after them, but they were already out of the house and racing across the fields. I called Smuto back. She was reluctant to come, but being an obedient dog eventually returned. I did not want her to catch the man, just to frighten him — and she had done that. As a result of this episode her fame spread far and wide and the burglars kept clear of our house.

Mosquitoes and flies were the plague of our lives. We screened our rooms with coarse netting bought on the street, kept covers on everything and waged constant war with fly swatters. Each evening at dusk, when the mosquitoes were liveliest, I went round with my 'Flit' gun, a very effective weapon!

We had one month of hot but bearable weather and one week of rain and cold. All the rest of the time we had extreme heat, seldom below 88° day or night, and the last week steadily at 100°, that was of course in the shade. Yes, it was hot! So continuously that in the end I became unwell. I was also half starved. So I decided I had better leave, being under a solemn promise that I would leave if I was unwell. I therefore came in a fortnight ahead of the other two and went up our Shaoyang neighbouring *mountain – 'The Copper Mine'. There I had a fortnight's glorious rest and am now ready to start the autumn's work.*

This letter is the story of my experiment, but I cannot leave without asking for your prayers on two matters. We have just had a Communist scare. Communist troops entered South Hunan en route for Sian. Their march[8] through Hunan has been stopped by government troops. Our southernmost circuit, Yungchow, had been evacuated; but it looks as if the government troops have the situation well in hand. The only danger is that with the Communists now not able to break through to Sian and not able to get back to Kiangsi, are they to become bandits and a menace to the South?

The other matter is that of food for the winter. At Wu Feng Pu, where I was, the farmers were fortunate in having rain just in time to save their crops, but Paoking and many other places did not have this good fortune and a great proportion of the crops have been lost. It means we will have to face a very hard winter. Some parts of the province have had good crops and some have lost all. A wise distribution of rice would save much suffering, but will it be done? Such a large proportion of the people live so near the poverty and starvation line that the least extra setback means dire distress. We are anxious to help and very willing to give our money, but we don't want 'rice Christians'[9].

I am well and busy and happy. I trust it is true of all my good friends.

A Health Week, 1934

Another project my mother was involved in was organising a Health Week, which she did with Freda Wright, with the help of Dr Pearson and some of his hospital staff, who gave lectures.

...We have just had our first Health Week in Paoking and we are thrilled about it. At first we were a bit afraid of the idea, as none of us had ever helped in a health campaign before... The ordinary Chinese citizen's knowledge of hygiene and the simplest health rules is absolutely nil. For many centuries no one has troubled about it, but now people are beginning to realise that many diseases are not the work of devils, but are preventable. It makes one especially sad and angry to see how little children suffer...

Last year we had a very serious outbreak of cholera. What happened? The town formed an anti-cholera committee, which gave away anti-cholera injections freely, but was afraid to attack the dirt and unsanitary conditions of the town, which was the real cause. The magistrate forbade the killing of pigs, the only meat source, in order to try to pacify the gods. Processions were organised and every kind of crude superstition was revived. The temples thronged with men and women offering gifts to placate the gods and save their families, but still the cholera swept on...

Some of the men took charge of the production of posters, slogans and advertising work, others undertook the writing of letters to schools, departments etc informing them that we were holding this campaign and inviting them to attend; the women members made hygienic garments etc. There was plenty of work for everybody.

Our general scheme was as follows:

(a) A general exhibition of pictures, charts and slogan posters

(b) An exhibition of various hygienic models such as fly swatters, dish covers, meat safes, babies' cradles, babies' chairs and pens, two model rooms, hygienic clothes and washable toys...

(c) Free examination of sick children, also free vaccinations and cholera injections.

(d) Daily lectures and demonstrations on hygiene in the

home, personal hygiene, children's health habits, prevention of the spread of infectious diseases, and one day for women only on the care and feeding of babies and childbirth.

Of the demonstrations the most popular was when nurse Tsao sat on the platform before a crowded church of people and gave a wee baby a bath in proper style. The baby yelled and kicked all the time, but that was the only sound to be heard. The people were intensely interested. Bathing babies is quite a novelty in China. No wonder the poor wee mites are so often covered with sores…

Each day our programme was open from 10 am to 12.30 pm for people to come and inspect the exhibits and ask questions. Several members were always available to explain anything and give out health tracts. Between 2 pm and 3 pm Miss Wright and either Dr Li or Dr Chang attended to sick children and carried out vaccinations and injections. 3 pm to 4 pm was lecture and demonstration time, followed on three days by hygiene plays. Each evening from 7 pm to 8 pm there were further talks and explanations of exhibits.

We had atrocious weather. The whole week it just poured and poured and poured with rain. Nevertheless everyday for the afternoon lectures we had the building crowded with heaps of people attending the whole time and always most attentive audiences…the most cheering thing was the way in which everyone worked. Long before the week was over people were saying, 'Yes, but next year it would be better if we did…' or 'Next year we must have more of…' etc. Next year! Blessings on them and three cheers for next year. I shall tell you about it when it comes!

The serious drought and resulting food shortages that my mother described in the section on her three month stay in Wu Feng Pu continued into the next year and widespread famine resulted. The people in the countryside were starving and large numbers were flocking into the towns and cities begging for food. My mother and her colleagues organised a beggars' shelter in an attempt to help at least a few of the most unfortunate people. Being limited in what they could do they decided to concentrate on women and children. She describes this work in the following letter she wrote to my father's parents.

Letter of 27th May 1935 from Paoking

...It has been a difficult year for us in Paoking. It has been difficult in most places in Hunan, but in Paoking we have been especially hard hit. Our streets are full of beggars. Walking back from the dispensary one morning...we counted over two hundred beggars. Every day one listens to harrowing stories of poverty, and in the midst of it all one feels so helpless. However this last month we have been able to do something. All along we have cared for our own Church folk, by private and special grants from Changsha, but now we are able to do a little for the beggars. Our grant from famine relief funds is limited, but we have opened a shelter for four months and are caring for between fifty and sixty beggar women and children — many of them just nice country women driven onto the streets by the famine.

Mrs Li[10], Mrs Tseo, Freda and I searched the streets at midnight for two nights collecting up the women and taking them to the shelter. Poor dears, some of them were so scared. After we opened we had a bad time for a while. All sorts of wild rumours went round the city — that we were putting medicine in the rice and they would all die soon, thus ridding the streets of beggars. Also the old stories that we were going to cut out their eyes and hearts for medicine; but starvation gives one courage and some stuck it out. Seeing that nothing but nice things happened to them others have forgotten their fears and the rumours have now died down.

At the shelter, which is in a Buddhist temple, we provide straw for bedding, watery rice and vegetables twice a day and a few clothes and medical care. After a fortnight there the folk look absolutely different, fatter and clean and alive again… Very soon I hope to start a school there for the children and younger women, just two or three hours per day, so they can learn to read…

I expect Cliff has already told you of my visit to Kiyang. I went down to Yungchow first to help with a women's school… From Yungchow I went over to Kiyang and stayed there a week… Cliff…really has done, and is doing, most worthwhile work there. More and more I feel that preaching is not of such great value here. What counts is the small group and individual teaching, and the influence and personal example of the teacher, and it is along those lines that Cliff shines…

I have just remembered I have said nothing about the wedding[11]… Everything went off beautifully. It was a most joyous time, because Jerry and Ha were obviously so happy and everyone else was pleased at their union… The dresses were rather novel. It is not usual for an English bride to wear red, but it was very correct in Chinese eyes… You would have laughed if you had seen us on Saturday night – Jerry, Freda, Dicky (Alice Dickinson) and I all taking it in turns to cut, wash and set each other's hair… Cliff was a most efficient best man, and a hard-working one too. I was court photographer and took a whole reel on the Cine Kodak, but alas it is a failure. A wonderful film of Chinese umbrellas, but that is all – the weather was atrocious, pouring with rain and the light hopeless…

Freda leaves for furlough in three weeks' time, sailing from Shanghai in the middle of June. She and I have been so very happy living together and are such great friends, I shall miss her very much… I am due for furlough in March, but that is very inconvenient for the work, so Synod asked that I either be put forward two months or back three months. Seeing that Freda is away from the station the Mission House chose the latter. So now I will spend a year on my own, and Freda, when she comes back, a year on her own![12] It is undoubtedly the best for the work, though we do feel a bit fed up…

A slowly maturing relationship

As we learnt earlier my father had decided to remain celibate, believing that that China was no place for a married missionary with children. When my mother returned to Paoking, after a year's furlough, he was living some distance away in Kiyang. For the next five years they saw each other little more than once a year at Synod. They wrote to each other once a year at Christmas, but that was all, although my mother wrote to my father's parents in England from time to time.

My father's first furlough and my mother's second overlapped, my father's commencing six months earlier. Soon after my mother reached England she received a letter from my father inviting her to his home in Weston-super-Mare. The day after her arrival there they were engaged again and six weeks later, on 23rd July 1936, were married in Stanhope, County Durham, from the home of their good friends Stanley and Gladys Lamming.

Two months after their wedding my parents sailed back to China, spending two months in Australia on the way.

Endnotes

1. Paul von Hindenburgh, President of the Germany Republic 1925-34.
2. See page 293 for a list of old and new place names.

3. Her brother's home in Dunston, south of Newcastle-upon-Tyne.

4. This relates to the evacuation from Hunan mentioned in the last chapter, caused by Communist activities in the province.

5. The province immediately to the north of Hunan, of which Hankow was the capital.

6. A legume with Nitrogen-fixing properties grown in order to improve the quality of the soil as part of a crop rotation process.

7. Koh is a common Chinese family name, which my parents used because it sounds very much like 'Cook', although there is no similarity in meaning. What I am uncertain about is how she came to use the name before her marriage. Although her maiden name was Cuthbertson, she was always known to her colleagues as 'Cuth'. Presumably 'Koh' was the nearest common Chinese name to Cuth, as well as to Cook.

8. This was the famous 'Long March'. Later in the year, when the threat was considered more serious, my mother and other missionaries withdrew to Changsha until the threat subsided.

9. ie people who claim to be Christians because they hope to be able to gain from it materially.

10. Hsu Mei Li was a prominent Christian women, who was very active in various social programmes, including helping run the orphanage.

11. The wedding of the Rev Robert Harrison, one of my parents' colleagues, and Jerry Chamberlain.

12. In fact my mother didn't return to Paoking after furlough, having married my father. Together they went to Liuyang, as the next chapter relates.

Chapter 4
A Working Partnership:
Liuyang and the Start of the War

During my parents' furlough, events in China had been developing in a worrying fashion. The Japanese, not being satisfied with having taken Manchuria, were slowly gaining control of the north of China piece by piece, all the while trying to incite the Chinese into attacking them and thereby plunging the two countries into full-scale war. In one of many provocative acts the Japanese landed troops in Shanghai to suppress a boycott of Japanese goods.

Despite these aggressive and provocative acts Chiang Kai-shek did nothing. He knew that China could not defeat Japan in open war and still vainly hoped that the great powers would come to his aid by putting pressure on the Japanese. Not only did he not fight, but he forced newspaper editors to desist from writing anti-Japanese reports and crushed any signs of anti-Japanese demonstrations, lest these actions should be taken as an excuse for further Japanese aggression. The Chinese people became impatient and rumours circulated that Chiang Kai-shek was in the pay of the Japanese. The Kwangsi generals – Li Tsung-jen and Pai Chung-hsi – threatened to rise again in revolt demanding that Chiang defend the integrity of the country.

But while Chiang refused to fight the Japanese he was taking all possible measures to suppress Communist opposition within the country, even though the latter were appealing for a ceasefire and a united front against the Japanese. The Communist forces, following the Long March, were now based in Shensi province and Chiang sent his trusted general, the 'Young Marshal', Chang Hsueh-liang, to root them out and destroy them. But Chang Hsueh-liang and his officers, being more concerned about the Japanese threat than that of the Communists made contact with the Communist leader, Chou En-lai. As a consequence Chang Hsueh-liang and his officers held back from taking further military action.

When Chiang Kai-shek realised what was happening he flew to Xian to speak to Chang Hsueh-liang, who placed him under arrest, demanding that he form a united front with the Communists against the Japanese. Chiang Kai-shek, showing great bravery, refused to negotiate while in captivity, and instead berated the Young Marshal for his disloyalty. While a growing number of the conspirators advocated executing Chiang Kai-shek, the Young Marshal refused to countenance this and after three weeks of deadlock, on Christmas Day 1936, he unconditionally released Chiang and flew back to Nanking with him, surrendering himself for trial on charges of having kidnapped the Head of State.

Chang Hsueh-liang was put under house arrest, where he remained for more than thirty years. He died in 2001 aged one hundred and one, a man of great integrity, widely respected throughout China, Taiwan and further afield. Even though Chiang claimed to have made no deals when in captivity, a ceasefire with the Communists and a 'United Front' was announced soon after his release. This announcement was welcomed by the Kwangsi group and the country at last appeared to be united and ready to face the enemy.

My parents' first appointment as a married couple was

to Liuyang, which lies east and slightly north of Changsha. Liuyang is a beautifully situated town on the Liu Water, a tributary of the Hsiang River. Like many other Hunan towns it is often the victim of severe flooding.

At first my parents lived in a typical Chinese house set around a courtyard in the main part of the town. Later, when air-raids threatened, this house was considered unsafe and they moved over the river to a house built originally for expatriate Europeans, who had since left the city.

In the following letter my mother describes the first house they lived in:

Extract from a letter from Liuyang (EMC)

Now about this funny house of ours, where do I begin?… In each room…there is a small window which looks out onto an alleyway, but the alley is so narrow and our windows so very overlooked, that we keep them shuttered. So near are we to our neighbours across the alley that we can hear what they say in their houses and smell what they are cooking. One of the greatest jokes of the house is that you must walk a few feet along an open verandah to go into the bedroom – it does not seem quite such a good joke on a cold, frosty night when you have to dress up to go up the very breezy, wooden, enclosed staircase and out on the verandah in order to get into your bedroom!

Another joke of the house is that there is only one door that closes by means of turning a handle. Two other doors have handles to turn, but as they have no counterpart in the door frame they are not much use. Generally speaking doors and windows open by means of a good shove! There isn't a fireplace in the whole house – no mantelpiece to put a clock on. We have put a small stove into the corner of the dining room and one into the topmost room. Cliff prefers a ho pen[1]. *For light at night we depend on oil lamps.*

But despite the funny things – and there are many more – we are very happy here and find the house has many possibilities for being made very homelike…the clock ticks and chimes on the sideboard, Smuto sleeps peacefully on the mat and altogether we have a homely, comfortable living room…

Cliff's study, also on the ground floor, is rather Spartan. He refuses to have any curtains, or rugs, or anything fussy, so it looks businesslike and studious, with Cliff's desk, a few chairs and all our books around the walls…

The rather Spartan way of living suited my father well, even though marriage inevitably led to some compromises.

A strong characteristic of my father's approach to missionary work was to place the emphasis on personal influence, example and social works, rather than evangelism. He was happier dealing with people as individuals, or small groups, and proclaiming the Christian message through example and good works.

In the following article that my father wrote for the Methodist Minister's Missionary Quarterly Bulletin about that time this emphasis can be seen.

The Challenge of China's Rural Millions

Two noted Christian leaders…have recently said they think China today is the greatest evangelistic opportunity in the whole world. I rather fancy that when they expressed this opinion they were thinking mainly of the opportunity among those Chinese who have received a modern education…students and intellectuals seem to be in a great moral and spiritual vacuum. The old is dead and nothing new has taken its place. This is a true description of the situation which presents a challenge of the utmost urgency to the

Christian Church. But in this article I am going to say something about another challenge – the challenge of China's illiterate masses...

The illiterate masses of China, for the most part agricultural people, are estimated at not less than eighty per cent of the entire population. There may well be over three hundred million of them. Most of them are terribly poor, and many live on the borderline of starvation. Their extreme poverty is one of the things that impresses the Westerner most when he first visits China. The most characteristic qualities of these people are of a passive, rather than of an aggressive, type. Centuries of hardship and dependence on the forces of nature have made it thus. Endurance, patience, resignation, cheerfulness, industry and economy are the qualities that characterise them. These people have religion. Most of them have a religion which is a peculiar mixture of superstitions, some of which definitely belong to Buddhism, some to Taoism; some are to be found all over the country, some only in certain localities[2].

To a foreign observer it seems that most of their religious practices are a means to try to procure some material benefit. Things are done that there may be a good harvest, that a village may be spared from disease, that a drought may be brought to an end, that departed ancestors may have houses and money in their present sphere of existence, that sons may be born, or that a person, or villages, may be secure from spirits that do material harm. And this emphasis on things material we see in their life generally as well as their religion. This is, of course, perfectly intelligible when we remember that so many important material necessities are known to them mainly by their lack. It is intelligible, but, we must admit, it obstructs a vision of the Kingdom whose values are spiritual.

What is the evangelistic opportunity among these poverty-stricken, superstitious people? It would not be true to say that they are standing with outstretched arms pleading for the Gospel. Yet we may truly speak of a tremendous opportunity and a stirring challenge. In the two country circuits in which I have worked in China, the problem has never been, 'Where can we find villages that will listen to us?' It has always been, 'Upon which few of the many possible villages shall we concentrate our limited resources?' Almost everywhere the country people would gladly hear our message; the trouble was we hadn't the time, or men or money to go to more than a mere handful of them...

Further, as distinct from preaching of the Word, there is an almost unlimited need and opportunity for Christian Social Service, such as the formation of Co-operative Societies, the teaching of hygiene – how badly this is needed – mass education and the teaching of values to children. And many a Christian leader in China has found that such service has been the means of awakening, within both those who serve and those who are served, the realisation that the Kingdom is within.

I can, of course, only speak with first-hand knowledge of one small part of China – it being so vast no one can know intimately more than a very small part of it. But judging from verbal and written reports of other parts...the opportunities through the whole country are as great... This is our challenge. The opportunity is there. The lack is in resources with which to meet that opportunity...

Less than a year after arriving in Liuyang my mother was expecting their first child. It was decided that the birth should take place in Kuling, where there was a good foreign-run hospital, rather than in the heat of the Hunan summer. In the following letter to his mother my father refers to this impending event.

Letter of 24th June 1937 from Liuyang (CVC)

...I'm hoping to go to Kuling about July 10th, and expect I shall stay there about five weeks. By the time you get this letter you may have had our cable! The infant should not really come until about the 20th, but the medics seem to think it will come earlier. Elsie will have told you that Maud and the Chinese nurse hope to be at Kuling by the 10th. The names we are thinking about are John Barry Vallance (John is a Cuthbertson name; Barry we are very fond of as a name), or Janet, or Jean Margaret. But there may be a change at the end. Life is awfully thrilling!

In today's letter (we write every day) Elsie asks what are we to do about your buying so many things for the infant! It is really sweet of you... Elsie revels in all the things you send. I love the brush and comb set. But please Mum you mustn't deny yourself your little comforts for our infant!

Sadly the event did not turn out as planned and the infant died shortly after birth.

Letter of 25th July 1937 from Kuling (CVC)

Thank you so much for your cable. It was sweet of you to send it. It came about 6 am this morning – about fifteen hours after I sent off my cable. We value it greatly.

Now I must tell you about the past few days. On Thursday 22nd (our wedding anniversary) Dr Sugg, the hospital superintendant, and Maud decided that the baby was big enough, and it should be given a little 'push'… On Thursday afternoon Elsie entered the hospital – a private hospital situated in lovely grounds. She was in excellent health and very excited. I'd never seen her in better health. She had a nice room, with a wide verandah, and from her bed she had a lovely view of Kuling Central Valley. That night she was given quinine. The next morning when Maud and I came, Elsie pretended to be very fed up because she had not had a pain yet! For some ten days she has been longing to have some pains – and her desire for them has caused a lot of fun. On Friday morning she had more quinine and in the evening, about 7 pm, castor oil. She was still very well and in good spirits – but longing for pains! Maud and I left her about 9 pm By that time she had had three pangs of pain. The doctor told me he expected the baby would be born on Saturday or Sunday, and Maud said there was no point in staying the night (Friday) at the hospital; as things could not begin properly until the next day.

On Saturday morning I got up early, shaved and dressed leisurely, and walked to the hospital before breakfast to see what sort of night Elsie had had. As I approached the hospital I saw Dr Sugg on his verandah. He called that he wanted to see me. The baby had been delivered about 5.30 am. It had a short cord, and was asphyxiated in the second stage of birth. The doctor told me the cord was so tight that it was embedded in the neck. Artificial respiration and everything was tried, but to no effect. So it seems that we are just one of the unlucky ones. A short cord is something that cannot be obviated, it is not known until the head appears. Apart from this the delivery was quite normal; no instruments were needed. Elsie only had very little anaesthetic – hardly any at all – until the very end when two stitches were put in… Altogether it was a sharp but short labour. The extraordinary thing was the quickness of it.

*Everyone expected, seeing that it was a first baby, that it would
be a drawn out – or at least not very quick – labour. The staff
here, and Maud, were all taken by surprise...*

*There is no need to say what a bitter disappointment it is –
you only have to think of the months of care, in difficult
circumstances, of periodic sickness and discomfort, of the
preparations and planning (cots, clothes etc), of Elsie in great
excitement, unpacking hers and the baby's things on arrival at
the hospital – to realise what the disappointment means. But
we are not down. Elsie is wonderfully brave. She has remarked
that she will be better able to understand Chinese women's
troubles now. She seems to me to have been amazingly brave all
the way through...*

*I am writing this on my knee in Elsie's room in the hospital.
She is asleep. She will probably stay here four or five days and
will then return to our bungalow...*

*At present we do not say much about the loss. That will be
spoken of more as the days, with their healing power, go by.*

*The baby, who was to have been called John Barry Vallance
Cook, was buried in the Kuling cemetery, last evening at
twilight. A few friends and our Chinese cook gathered for a
brief, simple service conducted by Baker. The little grave and
coffin were a mass of Kuling wild flowers. The service and its
setting – the cemetery is a fairyland of beauty – were all that
could be desired.*

I won't write more...

Letter of 10th August 1937 from Kuling (CVC)

*Elsie is doing well... Today for the first time, she walked down
the steps of the bungalow and for a few tens of yards along one
of the paths... I am going down the hill on about the 20th (ten
days later than I am due) and I have booked Elsie on a through
boat to Changsha, due to leave Kuikiang on Sept 3rd. I shall*

probably go to Changsha to meet her.

Today I have been preparing a sketch of a little wooden cross for the grave. For this year we will just have a little wooden cross 'Baby Cook: 24th July 1937', but next year we will probably have a stone curbing[3]. The little grave is in a lovely spot in the beautiful Kuling Cemetery. All sorts of missionaries and other Westerners of all nationalities are buried in the cemetery.

…I've never mentioned that both Elsie and I saw the baby after it was born. He looked like photos of Dick[4] when he was very small. He had a lot of black hair and a curl behind the ear down the neck. He weighed about seven pounds. We are both glad that we saw him…we certainly hope for better luck next time.

We are all wondering how the Sino-Japanese conflict will turn out. News is very scarce just now. The silence and lack of important developments may mean that terms of a peaceful settlement are being discussed. But we do not know. Chiang Kai-shek came up to Kuling again yesterday, but why we don't know[5].

Today at a meeting of missionaries to discuss our attitude towards the present crisis a notable Chinese preacher…said he hoped to learn lessons from the mistakes of preachers in Europe and America during the Great War: 1. Not to say things that in years to come he would regret; 2. To be more Christian than Chinese. He said during the Great War German, English and American Christians were more German, English and American than they were Christian.

I must pour out 'late tea' now. Elsie is in bed.

John Barry's short life came at a critical stage in China's history. Two days after his birth on 25th July 1937 the Japanese, while holding highly provocative military manoeuvres on the border of the territory they occupied in Manchuria, took advantage of a minor incident between their troops and those of China, known as the

Marco Polo Bridge Incident, to plunge into full-scale war against China. This time Chiang Kai-shek offered no concessions, nor sought a dishonourable peace. China was at last prepared to defend herself, whatever the cost, against the aggressor.

Within the next few days the Japanese handed over the Japanese concession in Hankow to China and withdrew their diplomats and other officials throughout the country. On 13th August they bombed Shanghai, followed shortly by Nanking and other major cities near the coast. By September they had 150,000 troops on Chinese soil pouring in from Manchuria. On 13th October the first air-raids struck Changsha. On 9th November Japanese troops took Shanghai and a few days later Chiang Kai-shek moved his capital to Chungking, in the far west of the country, behind the protection of the Yangtze gorges and the mountain ranges of central China. In December, Nanking too fell to the invaders in an orgy of slaughter, rape and pillage.

Letter of 21st August 1937 from Kuling (CVC)

I am still here at Kuling. I was due to go back to Liuyang over a week ago, but in view of the tense atmosphere and general disorganisation of communications caused by the war, I decided to wait here until Elsie is able to return with me. We are now aiming at returning in about six days' time, but we do not know whether we will be able to get a boat to Hankow or not. The river steamer service on the Yangtze, owing to the river being blocked (perhaps mined) somewhere well down towards Shanghai, is badly disorganised. There are boats running between Nanking and Hankow, but it is difficult to get a passage on them. We are trying, but it won't matter very much if we have to stay up in Kuling longer. We're all agreed that husbands should not be separated from their wives and families at the present time.

The Consuls (British and American) consider Kuling is very safe as the Japanese know that the hill resort is full of Westerners. Other places in the province have been, and will be, bombed from the air, but Kuling is a little 'city of refuge'. We've already seen, and heard, Japanese planes, and we have twice heard their bombs dropping on Kuikiang, the port on the river for Kuling. It is fifteen to twenty miles from here. It is a railway terminus (railway to Nanchang, the capital of Kiangsi province) and it has a good aerodrome. The Japanese are particularly keen on Chinese aerodromes just now. If Japanese planes are coming in this direction a large bell rings up here and we have to immediately cover the lights, as the lights of Kuling would be a fine landmark for planes going to Kuikiang or Hankow. If we show a little light the police soon tell us about it.

We all feel the best place to be is in our own station. Places like Liuyang, Yungchow etc are of no military importance and would not attract Japanese planes... The government is particularly emphasising the protection of Westerners. Our difficulty is getting to our stations. With the river boats disorganised, the question is how to get to Hankow. If we can get there we can use the railway from Wuchang to Changsha.

I expect the papers at home are rather alarming (I wonder if they have said anything about the Kuikiang bombing?), but we in the interior are all right. It is the Shanghai people who are in danger. The Chinese seem to be giving the Japanese an anxious time just now – they've advanced in Shanghai, their planes are worrying the Japanese fleet, and Chiang Kai-shek has announced that over thirty Japanese planes have been brought down so far. Nanking is said to have the most modern anti-aircraft guns. But, of course, the Chinese losses have been terrific – and now that further Japanese reinforcements have *arrived, what will happen! China is certainly united and determined in her resistance.*

Elsie is making splendid progress. She goes out for a while each day now, and the medics say she can go down the hill in a week's time – so long as she goes with me!

Well don't worry about us. We're well and safe – and we like a bit of excitement!

My father wrote the following letter to his mother in Hankow on the journey back to Liuyang.

Letter of 31st August 1937 from Navy YMCA Hankow

We are now well on our way back to Liuyang. Tomorrow morning we leave for Changsha on a British river steamer. We expect to spend Friday (September 2nd) in Changsha and to go on to Liuyang on Saturday. When we get to Liuyang we should be in one of the safest places in China. Our country stations have nothing to attract Jap planes; they are of no military importance. Of course, even in the big cities of central China the danger is not very great as they are at least four hundred and fifty miles from the coast, which means that to reach them Jap planes have to carry fuel for a flight of a minimum of nine hundred miles and the risk for them is very great. And flying so far they cannot carry many bombs. No Jap planes have got as far as Hankow or Changsha yet, though they have got pretty near.

Last night here in Hankow an air-raid warning was given. We were out in a busy Chinese street when the preliminary warning was given – one long blast followed by several short ones. Everyone hurried to their homes as fast as they could, as when the second alarm – a lot of short blasts in succession – goes no one is allowed on the streets. We just got home in time.

We then went on to the roof of the Lutheran Mission Building, a six floor building, where we are staying, and watched nine Chinese planes go up. It was amazing how this large, thickly populated, noisy city was, in about twenty minutes, silent, dark and the streets deserted. The only people allowed on the streets were police and special air-raid constables. China has quickly become efficient in air-raid defence organisation. We were sent in from the roof by police who saw us from the street below. But after all the commotion the Jap planes never got very near Hankow, though they had been coming in this direction, and did get as far as the eastern borders of Hupeh province.

We left Kuling last Friday and came up here by British river boat. The boat had come from Nanking (the Yangtze is blocked between Nanking and Shanghai) and was packed. Because of Elsie's special circs I managed to get her a cabin, but Maud Millican and I, along with crowds of others, had to sleep on deck or on the floors of the saloons. We got to Hankow at 2 pm the next day and came straight to the Lutheran Mission Building — a sort of big boarding house — comfortable and convenient. The Thompsons and Leighs left for Changsha by train last night. We are taking the more comfortable method of travelling! There is an enormous amount of traffic on the Hankow-Canton railway now as this is the only modern communication with the coast from central China.

Elsie is getting on fine. She's eating ices and enjoying soda-fountain drinks as she has not been able since we were engaged!

. . . The war is a distressing business and one wonders how long it can go on, and what the result will be. China is very united in her resistance just now.

How are you? Alas and alack mail is very erratic these days and we don't get our nice weekly letters and I expect you don't get all our letters to you. But never mind, you'll know that silence means we are safe — because if we weren't you would get a cable!

We really are safe in Liuyang and we are full of beans and enjoying the excitement of things, even whilst we deplore the war and the suffering it entails.

Elsie, Maud and I are going to the pictures tonight — the last time for many months I expect…

My father wrote the following letter shortly after returning to Liuyang.

Letter of 12th September 1937 from Liuyang

I think I last wrote to you in Hankow. Now we're back in our home in Liuyang after an absence of three months for Elsie and two for me. We got back here on Tuesday by bus. Bus travel is extra unpleasant now as many of the best buses have been sent to the Front and there is a big crowd of people travelling on the old ones that remain in service.

It is good to be back here. Elsie is quickly getting curtains up, things arranged properly etc and generally making the house look snug…

We travelled from Hankow to Changsha on a small British river steamer. Elsie shared a cabin with an American lady and I shared what is usually the military guard's room with an American businessman. A good many people didn't have cabins…

We haven't had any letters from home for ages. Perhaps they are held up in the north east somewhere, or in Shanghai. But I expect they will get through eventually. Letters have a way of getting through wars in China[6]…

The Liuyang/Ping Kiang bandits have given themselves up to the government to be incorporated into the government army to fight Japan, so now we can go anywhere without fear. At the end of next week I plan to go on a few days tour to visit the remaining few places in the circuit I've not yet been to.

People are naturally very obsessed with and troubled by the war just now. With us it is always present as a big cloud of sorrow and uncertainty. The fighting around Shanghai seems terribly fierce and the loss of life and suffering on both sides must be terrific. So far the Chinese have put up a fine show. The Japs have vastly superior armaments, but the Chinese have a lot of small equipment like rifles, machine guns and mill's bombs (hand thrown bombs) and they are filled with a great and desperate determination to resist at all costs. They know that if they lose, Japan's hold on China will make the country into a kind of Japanese dependency.

There has not been any air-raiding in the interior recently, though the coastal towns have been getting it. Anyhow Liuyang is safe enough. There is nothing to attract planes here. It is said the raids to central China have been very costly to the Japanese air force. They are pretty sure to lose a lot of planes on eight hundred mile non-stop bombing raids.

We are both well and at present have a crossword puzzle craze.

Although the war was still some distance from Liuyang, Japanese bombers were getting closer.

Letter of 26th September 1937 from Liuyang (CVC)

This week, after several weeks' famine, quite a lot of letters have arrived… A big batch of European mail, which had been held up somewhere for several weeks, got through at last…

The war continues fiercely, China is still putting up a good defence. During the past few days there have been fierce air-raids on Nanking and Canton. But you will be well informed as to the war news, I expect. We are not greatly affected here in Liuyang yet, though we are very much concerned about it. Our church and school here, along with other white buildings in the town, have had to be painted black; bomb shelters are being dug;

and the people are being taught how to act in the event of an air-raid. Though, of course, the likelihood of an air-raid here is very, very remote. The cost of living is going up and the people are naturally very full of the war, in their talk and their thoughts. We get news fairly quickly through a Changsha Chinese newspaper…

I had a lovely birthday. Elsie gave me two books that I wanted very much. We spent the evening in our snug top room doing a crossword puzzle! Birthdays and coming back from the country are very, very different when you are married!

Our very, very best love to you. We're both well and full of beans, and we do hope you are.

As we mentioned at the beginning of this chapter Liuyang was in an area prone to flooding. The following letter describes one such occasion.

Letter of 14th June 1938 from Liuyang (EMC to AIC)

These last few days it has rained a lot, then last night for hours and hours it came down in torrents and this morning we have a flood. The houses along the river street are all flooded up to their first storey; the river has overflowed its banks and the plain at the other side, where all the rice, wheat and vegetables are grown is now a sea of water… It is pitiful to see the folk trying to rescue their possessions. Tables and beds and such big things they are lashing to the supports of their houses, thus hoping to save them, other things are just piled up on the higher up streets. Many who took refuge in their top storeys are now having to be rescued from them.

Cliff and about five others have formed themselves into a rescue party and are helping out where they can. I wanted to go, but they wouldn't have me. Twenty years ago they say this house was flooded. It looks as though it will be again this year. Tien Ni (the cook) has just been in. He says the water is now only a few inches from the back doors of the houses on the other side of the street from us. We are about six feet higher than they are, but the rain continues and the water from higher up the river has not reached us yet…

I have been out. The water has entered the houses opposite. I also met Cliff on his way back, and he had such a dirty face. Of course he is sorry for the folk, but he has been having a most thrilling time, rescuing people and their property, carrying people through the water on his back etc. This letter is all about the flood. We don't seem to be able to think about anything else today. But it is a change from thinking about the war!

On 30th July 1939 while in Changsha, my father was asked to take the chairman, John Stanfield's, place at a reception given by the Governor of Hunan for the British Ambassador, who was visiting Changsha. Although Britain was at the time neutral with regard to the Sino-Japanese War, with sections of the government concerned that we should try to maintain good relations with the Japanese, rather than endanger our colonies in the Far East, the British Ambassador, Sir Archibald Clark Kerr, who had a bit of a reputation for being outspoken, took the bold step of proposing a toast to a Chinese victory.

During 1938 the war with Japan intensified and began to threaten Hunan. In August 1938 Hankow, to the north, and Canton, to the south, fell to the Japanese army. Changsha was heavily bombed in several raids and the Japanese moved closer to Liuyang, advancing down the Yangtze and moving south towards Hunan.

Letter of 3rd November 1938 from Liuyang (EMC to Jean)

Much has happened since I last wrote about a fortnight ago. For one thing we have had a great and glorious house removing. Air-raid alarms are now very frequent. Liuyang hasn't yet been bombed and there isn't anything here of military importance to make it worth bombing… Nevertheless we have decided it is time we took a few precautions. Our funny old house was dangerous anyhow, quite apart from direct hits. So we have come over the river and are now living in one of the very posh foreign houses. One blessing is that after Communists, soldiers and refugees have inhabited it for more than ten years, a lot of its poshness has worn off…

The walls have been white-washed and wood work scrubbed, but we don't intend doing any painting or floor staining. It is too expensive with war-time prices. Not a door in the house has a knob on it, nor have any cupboards or windows. But it is a lovely, light, airy house and very much more peaceful. There is a big garden all round, wild but open, and only a few minutes from a beautiful hill. We have the three rooms upstairs, plus a bathroom and also another bathroom I am using as a sewing room. Downstairs we have a dining room and kitchen, Tien Ni has a room and Mr Ma, the preacher, two rooms. Our boy and his family have two rooms at the back.

When the air-raid alarm goes we put on dark gowns or coats, open all the windows, close all shutters, put out our big Union Jack in the garden and go on with various jobs until the 'approaching near' goes, then we scatter over the hillside among the bushes and wait until the 'all clear' goes. A great life this! But not conducive to settled work of any sort.

Since I last wrote both Canton and Hankow have fallen. The fall of Canton has been a very heavy blow to everyone and really knocked the heart out of us. It was so utterly unexpected. It also greatly hastened the fall of Hankow. The men have just lost heart. They will pick up again, but the blow was so unexpected, they are down for the moment. Don't imagine we are defeated. We very definitely are not, but we have not got our balance back again yet.

We have always known that Changsha might go, but hoped it might not come to that, or at least that it would not be for months yet, but now Changsha's days seem numbered. The authorities are clearing the city, ordering everyone to leave. Cliff went down on Monday and came back yesterday (Wednesday). He went to have a talk with Mr Stanfield and to get some money. He came back terribly depressed. The roads are just a continuous stream of people fleeing to the west, carrying with them all the possessions they can manage, or pushing them along on a wheel barrow. Apart from Changsha's own population there are 60,000 refugees to be evacuated. They are a most pitiful sight.

All the churches in Hunan have been having a big drive to collect old clothes and money to make new ones for the refugees. There has been a wonderful response, but the Japanese advance has come so suddenly there isn't time to get the clothes to the folk. The refugees fled in the summer time and now winter is approaching and they have no warm clothing. Yesterday Cliff went to a small camp of five hundred people with fifty-six garments, but he dare not give them out, everyone was so clamorous and desperate.

When Yochow falls, and it may go any time now, the government officials, bank officials, post office staff and such like will all leave Changsha. Then the main buildings will be blown up and very likely the city will be set on fire. Isn't it terrible to think of it? All those people's homes! Hankow has been burnt down, except for the foreign concession. The Japanese victories are very empty in the end, but extremely costly to China.

When Changsha goes communications will go too. Cliff

wired from Changsha for Mr Ma and Tien Ni to be prepared to leave, while the going was good, but Mr Ma is taking his family into the country here instead, then coming back to help Cliff until the end. Tien Ni has flatly refused to go. He says he has been with me all these years and is not going to leave me now just because it is difficult. We have urged him to go while he can and not be cut off from his family, but he says no. He says he will stay on as his own responsibility, but he will stay. When the Japs come he will go into the nearby country, where he can keep in touch and will return as soon as it is safe to do so…

If Changsha falls we will immediately find ourselves in occupied territory. When the Japs come to take over Liuyang, if ever they do, all able-bodied men and women will leave. We are getting in stocks against the evil day – flour, sugar, milk, oil, salt, coal, charcoal and Tien Ni is making bacon. We are also trying to buy two goats and a few chickens.

The thing that worries us as much as anything is that for a while after the Japs take over we won't get letters and very likely won't be able to send them. By and by they will establish a route via Shanghai, but for a while they may be disrupted, so please don't get worried if there are no letters for a while. We will be all right; but it is a sad and worrying time because of our Chinese friends.

Now do try not to worry. The Japanese haven't harmed any missionaries anywhere, and we can put up with the unpleasant mess and nuisance of it all in order to stay on the spot with the hope of being of use to our Chinese friends. Our activities will likely be restricted at first, but later we hope to have more liberty to go on with our church work.

When you reply to this letter, you had better be careful as to what you say. By that time letters will most likely be censored.

We are both ever so well and despite everything this is a very cheery, happy household. It is a worrying time for Cliff. He feels so responsible for the safety of the preachers, teachers,

servants etc. Nevertheless church work is going wonderfully
these days. Many, mostly women, have gone into the country
to live, but the rest are at their best…

A few days after they moved house Liuyang was heavily
bombed. My father describes the event in the following
letter.

Circular letter of 19th November 1938 from Liuyang

I don't know whether this letter will ever reach you, but I'll try
sending it. Two postmen yesterday told us letters could still be
sent abroad from here, but would have to get to the coast by a
circuitous route.

The Japanese are nearing Changsha, so cannot be far from
here, though they may not actually come in this direction for
some time. Changsha may fall some time before the Japanese
decide to come on here. But we really don't know. Chinese
troops are hurriedly retiring through Liuyang. The city is dead.
Practically nobody is living in it, though during the day –
especially in the afternoon when aeroplanes are unlikely to come
– a good many people return from the country to collect things
they have left behind.

The deadness of the city is due to two things, the comparative
nearness of the Japanese and a bad air-raid last week. The latter
was a dreadful affair. Some eighteen planes bombed the city and
made havoc of the main streets. Then fires started everywhere
and the city burned for hours. The raid was in the morning at
about 11 am, but throughout the night the place was still
blazing. The hills behind our houses (we are fortunately on the
opposite side of the river from the city) were bright with the
reflection. For several nights large parts of the city were still
glowing. Our former house and the church were saved as the fire

did not spread outside what was once the city wall, and our place is situated outside.

The whole thing has been appalling. I need not go into details; you will be able to guess when you remember that no adequate preparations for stopping fire or rescuing people had been made, there is no hospital in Liuyang and there was no doctor in the place at the time of the raid. Houses collapsed on people and often there was no time to get them out before the fire reached them. People were terribly injured and there was no one to care for them. A few helpers at the local health station, people with a smattering of nursing and first-aid knowledge, were soon inundated with dozens of heavily injured people, for whom they could do very little. After about two days, a rumour that the Japanese were near sent them flying into the country. A military hospital in the town took some folk, but they too left Liuyang after about two days, having received orders to move elsewhere. The casualties were very heavy. Very many folk were injured by machine-gun fire when they ran into the streets.

Our church has a small, badly organised, badly trained and badly-equipped rescue and first-aid team. This was first on the spot after the raid, but we were very limited in what we could do. There were only about six of us, and four of these were needed for stretcher carrying. In despair we brought a few folk over the river to our empty school premises and with the help of our Chinese colleague, Mr Ma, who was once a 'doctor' in the Chinese army, we've been trying to treat people. We've twelve in-patients at the moment, plus some of whom have only stopped one or two nights before being taken back to their homes. What will happen to them in their homes with no proper attention one does not like to imagine. We've been able to do little more than keep wounds clean, feed people and give them a degree of comfort in the matter of beds etc. One man had a bullet in or near his spine and was paralysed from his hips *downwards. We sent him to his home – to die. A woman with twelve bullet holes in her we had to decline to take. The doctor at the health station who returned to Liuyang a day or two after the raid spent a night here, and by the light of an oil lamp, amputated two fingers from a man's hand. This man is now in the country somewhere attending to wounded soldiers and civilians. We now have only four in-patients, a woman with six bullet wounds who has been with us for a week, three bullets having gone right through her, fortunately though not through vital parts, a man with a bullet in the lower part of the back; another woman with many surface wounds and an old man with a slight flesh wound.*

After the raid I telephoned Changsha for medical help; but as Changsha was expected to fall any day no help could be sent. Hundreds of injured people are scattered about in their various homes, or in relatives' homes in the country, receiving no proper attention. There is practically nothing to buy in Liuyang now, all shops having been destroyed or shut up. Fortunately we had prepared beforehand and had got a good stock of supplies in, so we are not short of things. We have sent families away from their compound, and at the last moment the men will have to go too – at least for a while – until we see what treatment they are likely to receive under Japanese occupation. But in order to avoid being left absolutely on our own, we are going to keep three or four very old folk here. The old folk cannot be pressed into work and are sure to be pretty safe. One can help with washing, another carrying water etc.

Mr Ma is now in the country making arrangements for his family. Our 'hospital' staff now consists of us two, Mr Li, a preacher from Changsha, a very old workman, and a man who cooks the food. Relatives of the injured also help a bit. We spend several hours morning and evening changing dressings and washing wounds. Elsie is our star. Our cook is still here and looks after us well; but he no doubt will have to remove himself for a while later on.

Mr Ma and I had a narrow escape on the morning of the raid. We'd had one raid alarm already that morning, but the 'all clear' went without planes appearing. After that Mr Ma and I went to the city to visit a military hospital. We were being ushered into the presence of the officer-in-charge, when another air-raid alarm went. I was hesitant about going since it seemed so discourteous, but encouraged by Mr Ma, agreed to do so. Half an hour later the place was bombed and several people in it injured...

What the immediate future will bring we do not know. Will the Japanese come quickly? Or will we have to live alongside a dead city indefinitely? Fortunately on this side of the river life is less deadly than it would be in the city. There are farmhouses around here, occupied by farmers and their families and the farmers carry on with their work. Every time I cross the river and see the ruins, the desolation, and the corpses, I come back here feeling that this is a little haven of peace. Planes have often passed over our houses and seen our two huge Union Jacks lying on the ground; and this property has been reported to the Japanese authorities. We were over here during the raid. The bombs sounded like they were falling just next to us, and though actually they were mostly over the river, a few were dropped on a street this side about a third of a mile from here.

We feel that the worst of things is over for the moment at least. We rather hope the Japanese will come quickly and that these days of uncertainty will be over. By the time you get this they no doubt will be so. What we have seen these days makes us feel that there is practically nothing worse than war, for happenings here are but a tiny fraction of the whole suffering of this ghastly war. Our home, with dog and newly purchased kitten, this compound with its little group of Christians and friends, and the beautiful hills behind form a very much needed refuge for us.

This is quite a frank letter, but I hope it won't cause you to worry. Our being here at this time and helping a bit is worth years of preaching.

We'll write again when there seems a good chance of our letters getting through…

In the following letter to her sister Jean my mother describes the same event

Letter of 19th November 1938 from Liuyang

We are both well and safe, but we have had a ghastly time. A week past Thursday, November 10th, Liuyang was raided and half the town has been destroyed. It was terrible beyond description. Eighteen planes came about 12 am. Some flew over the city bombing and machine-gunning as they went, some bombed the little town across the river and some flew low over our houses — people who saw from the other side said they looked as though they were touching the roofs — but we were spared. We had two big Union Jacks out and evidently they regarded them. The noise of the low flying and power-diving machines, the 'rat tat' of the machine-guns and the terrible explosions of the bombs was a nightmare. Although none fell anywhere near us we could feel the earth and the whole place shaking and some of our window panes were broken. Immediately flames shot up in the air from all over the city and the place was black with smoke.

Cliff, Mr Ma, our boy and I seized our medicine bags and immediately ran over to the city to the church where some other members of the 'Rescue Party' were already on the spot… It was terrible, the roar of the flames, the smell of dust from the fallen houses and everywhere smoke, people pouring out of the city, women crying and everyone so terrified. Our rescue party was the first on the spot, but one or two others, including some members of the military, followed. Everywhere people were calling for help. Some were just torn to pieces, many were dead, others had terrible wounds, which we bound up as quickly as we could and carried them to places of safety, for all the time the fires were spreading and we were working against the clock. Some people were buried under the ruins of houses. It would have taken an hour or two to get them out and all the time the fires were closing in. They had to be left. It was all a nightmare. Finally the fire got so near we had to leave the main street and go down to the riverside. All who could had gone down to the riverside or across the river.

We were beseeched to help here, to help there, to bandage this person, to care for that. Then in the midst of it the cry came that the planes were coming back. The terror and the panic were terrible. The police came and urged us to go. They were very brave. They stood their posts everywhere. The fire was travelling along the riverside street as well, so finally we took with us one or two people who could walk with a bit of help and crossed back over the river and continued our work among the folk on the other side. There were wounded people everywhere. One of the military hospitals had been hit by a bomb, one closed its doors and everyone fled, the other took in patients until they could take no more. The Health Centre was absolutely full and still there were people to be cared for. We brought six bad cases to the school. Since we have added another six as well as crowds of out-patients for dressings. Later some more came from the Health Centre.

The fire raged unchecked all day and night. Almost half of the city has gone. People fled into the nearby countryside and by night hardly anyone was left in the city. Many of our members came over here until they could make arrangements to go to relations in the country. Along with the terror of the raid has come the alarm that the Japs are very near. Shops are all closed and most people have taken their stocks into the country. There is nothing to be bought. And now, more than a week after, there are still charred bodies lying about and they are still digging people out of the ruins.

Mr Ma was formerly an army doctor – that does not mean very much – but he knew how to tackle some of the wounds and Cliff and I have learnt quickly. At first we were very short of medicines, but we have got some since. At first someone had to be on duty day and night. We were working from early morning until ten or eleven at night, then Cliff went on duty until someone could relieve him. But gradually, as it has been possible to send people to their homes we have done so, and now we have only four cases left. The poor folk have had such a shock they want to go into the country where it is safer. When they hear the sound of aeroplanes they are just terrified.

Mr Ma left for the country to make arrangements for his family about five days ago, so Cliff and I are the entire hospital staff. I won't harrow you with details of the terrible wounds we have seen and dealt with. We hardly dare think of all the suffering that is going on around us. The military hospital, which received a lot of the wounded, two days afterwards got orders to leave for Kiangsi. So they sent their cases back to their homes and departed. The Health Centre about three days afterwards got a rumour that the Japs were almost here and the staff fled and left their patients unattended. Some of them have now returned and the Centre is functioning again. The Health Centre doctor, Dr Hu, was away when the raid happened. He came back two days afterwards.

It has all been terrible, but in the midst of it we are deeply thankful that we have all been spared… We had all grown so used to the air alarms and aeroplanes that we had grown careless, but last Wednesday night Cliff was very uneasy and the next morning we decided we must really be more careful. After breakfast we went round the various families and urged them all to take shelter in the cellar if the 'approaching near' signal went. No one was keen, but we expressed our concerns with such urgency that they agreed and that was the morning of the raid. If they had been walking about as usual they might have been shot down by the machine-guns.

I hardly need to say that now when we hear the sound of aeroplanes we take cover! It seems contrary to reason that we should again be bombed, but we take no risks. Our cellar is at the end of the house under the verandah. We are having it strengthened with sand bags, which are incidentally an excellent precaution against incendiary bombs.

This week we have sent all the women and children away into the country and have only two old women here, one of whom does the washing. Otherwise there is Tien Ni and one other man, and an ancient of about seventy. Tien Ni has been a treasure. He does not help down at the hospital, but helps keep us supplied with boiling water etc, and makes us especially nice meals. 'Keeps our strength up,' he says and tells us off when we don't come for them. He is always cheerful and ready for anything.

For nearly a fortnight we have had no news of the outside world. Changsha was burnt about a week ago, but we hear it has not yet fallen. All the bridges are being blown up along the motor road. But we feel that nothing can be worse than what we have experienced, and I think we will be rather glad when the Japanese do come and life becomes a bit more normal again. It is depressing to live by the side of a dead city.

I would not worry about us being bombed again, there is hardly anything left to bomb, just a few empty streets...

Be comforted we are both safe and well and in the Lord's hands. We are longing for letters and news.

Typhoid

As the work in the emergency hospital was coming to an end my mother fell ill with typhoid. She was four months pregnant at the time and proceeded to have a miscarriage. In the following letter, written from the hospital in Changsha, my father tells of my mother's illness.

Letter of 12th December 1938 from Hudson Taylor Memorial Hospital, Hunan Bible Institute, Changsha

I fear it is several weeks since I last wrote; and since then unexpected things have happened. The chief thing is that Elsie has had an attack of typhoid. Thankfully she is now well on the road to recovery. After two weeks of hard and anxious work in our 'hospital', she was tired and run down, she developed a fever and went to bed. Two days after a party from Yale Hospital in Changsha, an American doctor amongst them, passed through Liuyang, and the doctor, a friend of ours, had a look at Elsie. He thought she had contracted a kind of influenza that was prevalent then, and said it would probably be over in a few days. But it wasn't. Her fever increased, her strength decreased. I kept her in bed in a warm room, gave her an occasional aspirin to bring her temperature down, and fed her mainly on milk and fish. She got worse so there was nothing to do but wire (the telegraph service had fortunately been resumed by that time) for Dr Eitel, the German doctor in Changsha, who is really our doctor. He and his wife came out at once in their car. Typhoid was diagnosed. Eitel gave Elsie injections for her heart, kept her resting until the next day, and then brought her here. Our air-raid rescue party stretcher conveyed her from our house to the motor road. She was very bad at that time and naturally the journey was a strain.

For a few days after her arrival her fever was high, but

gradually, thanks to expert treatment, it began to abate, and now after some seventeen days of illness and ten days here, she is well on the road to recovery... Her temperature no longer rises, and the next stage is the gradual and careful building up of her strength. She will probably be convalescing here for another two to three weeks, and then she will be brought to Liuyang to continue convalescing there. We are deeply thankful that she has got on so well...but she has had some very bad days and we have been very worried. The worst days were in Liuyang, with no doctor or nurse, when her temperature rose to 104°F...

By the time you get this we shall probably both be back in Liuyang. I shall return for visits before Elsie. She is in excellent hands and there is a very affectionate atmosphere here. Everyone — the German hospital staff, the American Bible Institute staff and our folk — is exceedingly kind. Elsie says the people here pray so hard poor typhoid doesn't have a chance.

In spite of living next to a city of ruins, and lots of people having lost nearly everything, we are all cheerful and not a bit down in the mouth. Our cook is here helping, while our boy and Chinese colleagues are looking after things in Liuyang.

We are thankful too that the Japs abandoned their drive on Changsha, so that it was possible for us to get to Changsha. If they had come a few weeks ago, when they were expected, it would have been impossible. Now we hope they will keep off long enough for us both to get back to Liuyang first. If they came suddenly now I would have to hurry back to Liuyang. I've promised the folk here to be there when the Japs come. The presence of a foreigner will mean a tremendous amount when the changeover comes. But there are no signs of the Japs coming on here at the moment.

The 'Scorched Earth' policy

The Chinese knew their army was no match for the

Japanese forces in open battle and if they were to defeat the invaders it would have to be through strategy and cunning rather than a direct clash of the two armies. Following the example of the Russian army facing Napoleon they decided to employ a 'Scorched Earth' policy. As one Chinese general put it, 'When we retreat we will leave the enemy with nothing but a desert. Our houses will be empty shells, our fields will be devoid of crops, our streets and cities will be ruins. We'll defeat the Japanese as the Russians did Napoleon.'

This meant that before the Chinese army retreated and abandoned a town to the Japanese they burnt everything – buildings, supplies, crops and anything else that might be of use to the enemy. After the early fall of the great cities of Shanghai, Nanking, Hankow and Canton this policy was generally followed throughout the remainder of the war. The policy was first implemented in a number of small and medium sized towns; but the real test came as the Japanese approached Changsha, the great capital city of Hunan. Not only was Changsha of strategic value, but it was full of priceless loot. None of this could be allowed to fall into Japanese hands. The soldiers placed tins of petrol and barrels of oil in selected places across the city, so that when the time came there would be a complete and utter conflagration. Plenty of warning was promised to enable people to escape through the narrow streets and to give time for the wounded soldiers who filled the hospitals to be rescued.

But for some reason the expected warnings were not given and to make matters worse the fires were lit very early in the morning when most people were still asleep in bed. People only became aware of what was happening when they were wakened by the roar of flames or started coughing from the smoke thick in the air.

My mother's illness occurred just after the burning of Changsha, so she was brought into a city that was a ruin. This is how she described this tragic and dramatic event.

Our mission had two missionaries in Changsha at the time – Mr Stanfield and Barbara Simpson. On the fateful night Barbara woke about 4 am and saw a strange glow in the room. She went quickly to the window and from there saw fires blazing all over the city. She went quickly to Mr Stanfield's house and woke him and then to our Chinese minister and all the rest of the staff and woke them in turn. They tried to get out of the front door, but the fire was coming along the street. They then ran to the back door and fled down to the river and hurried along the riverside until they were out of the city.

The story of the China Inland Mission Hospital was much the same. Miss Fischer, one of the nurses, was tending to a very sick German nurse when she saw the glow. She roused Dr and Mrs Eitel and the other hospital staff. Dr Eitel had a car, one of the very few in Hunan. Quickly he got the sick nurse into the car, seized a handful of instruments and fled to safety outside the city. When they had got the nurse to safety he tried to return to rescue more of the hospital equipment, but the fires were everywhere and he could not get through. They lost everything. As Miss Fischer said, 'I had not even got a clean handkerchief.'

It was a terrible affair. Thousands of people were burnt to death… So great was the fire that we in Liuyang, sixty miles away, were able to go up and down a very rough path from the temporary hospital to our house, for two nights, without using a storm lantern. The glow in the sky lit up the path.

Barbara Simpson in her book *China Post*[7] describes the event so graphically and beautifully:

> I got out of bed, and saw flames in the sky, from various parts of the city…we could see about eight huge fires, we could hear the roar and buildings crashing… We decided we must make a dash for it…a fire was just starting opposite, to the right there was smoke, so we made for the river bank. What a sight! All who were left in the city, halt and lame, old and young crowding onto the riverbank. It was wildly beautiful. Everything and everybody was lit with fire, the little boats on the river, the big junks; and across the river the cotton factory was blazing fiercely. Soldiers were marching…women and children crying and on we walked… We walked along the river front, me wheeling my bike, carrying bits of luggage… We made for the hospital…but had to sit on the roadside as buildings were blazing all around them. The North Gate Street was just a sheet of flame… Dawn was breaking, so we continued our trek…this time on the railway line. Oh the sights we saw, sick and wounded and homeless everywhere…the city was blazing all round us. The sun was shining, but through thick black clouds of smoke; and the noise of the fire, roar and crackle continued…

The cost of the burning of the city in human lives and suffering will never be known, but it undoubtedly achieved the objective of leaving nothing in the city worth taking. Although there were three or four raids on the city over the next few years, and a brief period of occupation, the Japanese never took Changsha to hold until 1944, when they advanced to take the whole of the province of Hunan. It could be said that a victory of a sort was achieved, but at what a cost!

Chiang Kai-shek was deeply concerned about the failure to alert the inhabitants of the city and on 18th November, six days after the start of the fire, while rubble was still burning in many places, he arrived in Changsha and called a meeting of all foreigners. He apologised to them for what had happened and appealed for their help in rebuilding the city. He then ordered the execution of the garrison commander and his deputy, who were shot a few days later.

Christmas amid the ruins

Christmas must have been a strange affair that year, surrounded by smouldering ruins and thousands of refugees. My mother, slowly beginning her recovery from typhoid, was allowed out of hospital for the first time to join in the celebrations. Barbara Simpson described the occasion as follows:

> …having no letters and parcels to open, it was simpler than usual. We had a communion service at 7 am in our own little chapel… At 9.30 am we had a united service in the Hunan Bible Institute, which was gaily decorated with streamers, a Christmas tree, a large star etc. We were all there: refugees, blind girls, nurses, doctors, patients. Some of us had been burnt, some of us had been shot, all of us had been sad, and all of us had been saved. So there we were, with full hearts, singing 'Glory to God in the Highest!'…we had dinner together, not turkey and crackers, but rice and chopsticks…

In early January my parents returned to Liuyang, even though my mother was still far from well and needed a long period of convalescence. She had to return a few months later to Changsha for a minor operation resulting from the miscarriage.

After the dramatic events of the bombing of Liuyang, the temporary hospital, my mother's typhoid and the burning of Changsha life slowly started to return to something approaching normal.

Letter of 14th March 1939 from Liuyang (CVC)

... By today's post a very kind letter from Rattenbury has come – sympathetic and almost embarrassingly complimentary[8]. I think our little work after the raid was perhaps the most satisfying thing we have ever done. I think without doubt we were able to save several lives. It was more easy to be noble then than when up against all the daily irritations of life out here...

...on our compound here we have three dear old folk – two old women and one man – who are among the finest Christians I have ever met. They are poor and the old man dirty, but wonderful in spirit. If the Japs come and everyone goes they will stay with us.

I don't think I have written since Elsie came back... She returned a week last Friday – ten days ago. I went to Changsha to fetch her and we came back here in the District car...[she] is fine now and gets stronger and stronger...

We are planting a lot of trees in the garden – willows, bamboos and fruit trees. We hope later missionaries will bless us! If they don't we shall at least have the pleasure of watching them grow ourselves.

We're hoping to have a wireless set very soon. A friend returning to Changsha from Shanghai is bringing one for us. Among other stations we should be able to get Hong Kong, which transmits from London every night. We will hear Big Ben in Liuyang!… A wireless set will be an unspeakable boost at such a time as this – especially if all communications go again, as they did last November. That's why we have indulged in one.

We are both very happy and loving our home and work – and we do so hope you are peaceful and happy

The day after this letter was written, on 15th March 1939, one of my parents' colleagues Albert Leigh, who had been a fellow student of my father at Handsworth Collage, was killed in an air-raid in Pingkiang. He had only arrived in Pingkiang two months earlier on 14th January.

Letter of 26th March 1939 from Liuyang (CVC)

What days we live in! Since last writing thoughts of Dick[9] have been pushed aside by the Pingkiang air-raid of the 15th, when Leigh was killed. I was taking an appointment five miles out when the news came. Elsie sent a message out to me with a few clothes…so that I could go straight to Pingkiang without having to come back. This I did, but via Changsha. I cycled to Changsha that day, got there about 7 pm and found that Cyril Baker had just returned (having hurried back when he heard the news) from a visit to Hsiangyin. I was very glad to see him, and he to see me. The next morning, at dawn, we went by private car to Pingkiang. We found Pingkiang had had a terrible raid. Eleven bombs had been dropped on our compound, three hitting Henry Clarke's house, bringing the house down and killing Leigh, his cook, three of his cook's children, another servant and a boy scholar, all of whom were in a kind of raised cellar, above ground level, beneath the house. Clarke and a number of other Chinese were also in the cellar, but the part they were in did not fall in. Clarke jumped forward a few feet when he heard the whistle of the bomb rushing through the air, and that jump saved his life.

Many bombs fell in various parts of the city, killing and wounding many civilians. I saw some bomb craters twenty feet deep. The Japs claimed on the wireless from Shanghai that a military conference was being held in Pingkiang at the time and the bombs killed two thousand soldiers. In fact only two or three soldiers were killed, the rest being civilians. There were practically no soldiers in the town at the time. The whole business has been a terrible shock to us. Leigh was at Handsworth with Harrison and me. The Hunan missionary fellowship is small, and a tragedy like this is a big blow to us and touches us deeply. But, of course, there is a glorious side to it. Leigh died at his post serving the people he had chosen to serve. He and Clarke went to that cellar, on Leigh's suggestion, simply to cheer up the school children who had already gone there.

I stayed on in Pingkiang, helped Clarke clear things up, made hasty arrangements for the work to carry on without a missionary on the spot, took the funeral and then returned (on cycle for eight hours, then caught a military lorry) to Changsha with Clarke. He is being moved to Yiyang. He has only been in China about sixteen months. Barbara Simpson was still here whilst I was away, so Elsie had company. I fear this business will make parents and friends at home very anxious, but we do hope you won't worry unduly.

My mother described the same events in a letter to her sister in Australia:

Letter of 26th March 1939 from Liuyang

What a life it is! Our adjective for it is 'grim'. We are both rather depressed these days, anxiously waiting for news, and wondering what the outcome of the present European crisis will be. Out here we have seen something of what war means. In

Europe it would be even worse. It is a nightmare to think of it. Where national wars are concerned, I am now a pacifist. Surely nothing can justify such terrible sorrow and suffering as modern warfare brings to everybody, even to little children. Formerly we greatly blamed Chamberlain for what he did at Munich. We don't now. Perhaps war will be averted. We find it hard not having news immediately. Our wireless has not yet come and we have to depend on the Chinese newspapers and letters from Changsha – all at least three days old…

I expect you have read in the newspapers of the bombing of our mission in Pingkiang and the death of our minister there, Albert Leigh. It seemed such deliberate bombing of British property that it has had much publicity here and I expect it has in all the home newspapers. It is thought the bombing of British property was a retort to the English loan to China. It has been a great shock to us all. Cliff was at Handsworth with Albert, a year senior to him.

Formerly we felt fairly safe in our compound with our flags out, but now we are not so sure and when the air-raid alarm goes we all go off to the hills. The hills are very near so we can get there quickly… Cyril has asked us to make preparations so we can leave if necessary, but we don't feel that time has come yet. We are much better off here than in Pingkiang. We are further from the city, nearer the hills, and what is more important, further from the fighting line. If the front line changes and it becomes too dangerous here we will go into Changsha.

It is almost decided now that we won't stay to welcome the Japs! We are afraid lest war breaks out and if we are in Japanese territory we will be interned. We would then be of no use to China, England or anyone else. We must now wait and see what Japan's next move will be. If she pushes on to Changsha we will be almost sure to leave… Cliff is calling in all the preachers this week to plan with them what to do if we have to leave, also how best to carry on the work if we stay. It is a funny situation. We have just had three rooms painted; are having the dining-room and kitchen screened; are making a flower garden and orchard, as if we were staying indefinitely. At the same time we are packing up all things not in use in case we have to leave hurriedly. It's just like China. We always hope for the best and prepare for the worst...

Meanwhile we are taking strict precautions and...are carrying on as usual. I am doing crosswords to keep myself sane and calm...please send me some more Herald crosswords! I am not doing very well on the getting fat business, but I am very much stronger. I rest every afternoon still, but for the rest of the day hop round on household jobs almost as of old... I may be a bit mad, but you know Cliff is very sane and careful and we won't take any unnecessary risks...

We are rather depressed these days, as I fear this letter shows, but usually, despite everything, we are cheerful and happy in our home...

My parents' first evacuation from Liuyang took place at the beginning of April 1939, when the Japanese were expected to take the town. Acting on the advice of the British Consul the chairman, Cyril Baker, asked them to come into the relative safety of Changsha. They were loathe to do so because they felt they were letting their Chinese members down. But with much reluctance they left, leaving their house, friends and dog Smuto behind them, hoping they would soon be able to return.

My mother arrived in Changsha on 3rd April, but my father stayed on a few extra days to sort out a few questions with members, whose safety, in the event of Japanese occupation, greatly troubled him.

My father made at least one brief return visit to

Liuyang during their two months' exile in Changsha. He found that soldiers had broken into and occupied their house, but had only been there for one night. They were very apologetic and immediately moved out. He remarked on the beautiful countryside amid the terrible human suffering and the general reassurance he felt from seeing the farmers busy planting out the young rice. On the journey back to Changsha, at a small town called Yung An Shih, he held a service at the chapel there at which fifty people received communion.

At the beginning of June, since the Japanese had still not taken Liuyang and appeared to have shifted their attention elsewhere, it was agreed that my parents could return to Liuyang. This they did with much relief.

Letter of 5th June 1939 from Liuyang (EMC)

We're both very happy today. At last after two months we have been allowed to return to Liuyang. We arrived yesterday afternoon. It is good to be home again. The folk here have all given us a great welcome, not only the Church members, but the people on the street also. For a while now we have been pressing to return, but the Chairman wouldn't give us permission. It worried us very much that both Pingkiang and Liuyang should be without a minister – our Mr Ma is only in his first year of probation. We offered to go to Pingkiang, as there is more property there to lose, and Cliff would have run Liuyang from there. But it is nearer the front line and Cyril wouldn't hear of the idea. So for peace's sake he has allowed us to return here!

We had to do two days' road journey by the old road. I had a chair, but Cliff and Tien Ni tried to cycle. Their cycling ended in their having to hire a coolie to carry their bicycles, while they walked. Cliff walked about twenty-four miles the first day and about ten the second, eight miles he rode in a chair and the remaining eight miles he rode on his bicycle. The roads have to be seen to be imagined. Every hundred yards or so there is a great deep cut in it, some of them twenty feet across and usually flooded with water. When you come to one of these cuts you have to make a big detour by the narrow paths between the rice fields.

Between Pingkiang and Changsha every road, broad or narrow, old or new, has been cut and dug up. It looks a very effective way of fighting. If the Japs have to rebuild the road at every cut and make a bridge every time they meet a river or stream, with guerrillas popping at them from the hillsides all the time, they won't have an easy task. At present they seem to be held up. There is practically no fighting on the Pingkiang front.

Now that we are back we are hoping not to have to leave again for a while, or be bullied into going anywhere for the summer. The garden is all lovely with flowers. The boy has taken great care while we have been away. Faithful Smuto gave us a great welcome, but she is still a bit worried lest we should go off again. I think when the furniture arrives she will be much happier. For a few days we are camping out. All we possess is a Chinese bed, an old desk and five chairs, a bath, a wash bowl, a kettle, one pan and a frying pan in the kitchen. The rest of our possessions are now coming up from Changsha on Thursday.

Cliff joins me in sending much love and best wishes to you both.

Letter of 24th July 1939 from Liuyang (EMC)

Cliff is in the country today, and it is a brilliant roasting, boiling day. He left about 6 am while it was cool. He will do about two and a half miles on a narrow road on his bicycle: leave his bicycle there and take a service; then go on walking about half a mile to another country house to visit some members; then on about another mile to another group of houses; then on again another mile to another big country house and take a service there. Then home again. Too much really in this hot weather....

137

I am afraid my head is really full of housekeeping problems today, so I will let off steam. I have just been taking accounts with Tien Ni and having a talk with him. I have told him we like fish pie and we like tongue, but really we don't want them alternate nights... Poor Tien Ni is almost in despair about the food – and so am I. We have heaps to eat, there is no shortage, but it is all so monotonous. It is now the hot weather and there is nothing but pork, very occasionally a bit of tough goat, or fish. Fish is always the same sort and so tasteless.

Puddings are even more difficult. We have no well and no ice so jellied things won't set in this heat. We have given up using white sugar, because it is so expensive and difficult to get. We use sugar cane which tastes very strong, so whether it be custard, blancmange, ground rice, or rice, all you can taste is sugar cane. The lard is always in liquid form, so pastry in this weather is like leather. We have no jam, no treacle, nor ginger left. The fruit has played us a dirty trick this year. Usually we have peaches for another month, but they have failed and failed suddenly, before we could get any bottled. We were still waiting for the good ones to come in. We are now reduced to hard, gritty pears, which have come in and will stay until about October. We can't get any other fruit. I have about a dozen bottles of plums – sour ones – and pi paws[10] to draw on later. Being in Changsha so long spoiled the chance of some of the fruit bottling. I want to make a list of all the possible ways of cooking what we have and give it to Tien Ni, so we can have food that is interesting and not merely filling...

Yet despite all the things we cannot have, we are both well. Cliff is much better than he was and I am fatter than I have been for the last five or six years... At present all I do is supervise the household, plus a few of my own special jobs, do lots of sewing and mending, odd typing for Cliff, visit a little and entertain our numerous visitors. Also, of course, keep an eye on the goats, the gold fish, the dog, the cat and the garden. There is always something, but none of these things seem very important when there is a war on.

Financially we are all right, but we have to be a bit careful. Our salary is paid at the old rate of exchange, which reduces it to about half its value…but, of course, opportunities to spend are reduced to a minimum. We can't save but we aren't short. When we will feel the pinch will be when furlough comes. We are saving nothing ahead and are not replacing any household goods or clothes. Usually at Kuling we buy a few things each year, especially summer clothes, but now when we go home we will both need complete summer and winter outfits…and…I suppose we must face it, I am afraid there will be no Australia this furlough. What are the hopes of your coming to England?…

During August 1939 the Japanese army once again started to advance on Liuyang. Refugees were flooding through the town, moving westwards towards Sechuan, where the government was based, and the mountainous western province of Yunnan. My parents prepared for life behind enemy lines, consoling themselves with the thought that it would at least bring an end to bombing raids.

In September the Japanese moved even closer, then on 25th September my parents received a wire from Cyril Baker insisting they leave Liuyang immediately for Changsha. Baker was once again acting on the advice of the British Consul. My parents were very unhappy about leaving Liuyang again, but Baker and the Consul were adamant.

The following letter, written two weeks later described what occurred:

Letter of 12th October 1939 from Paoking (EMC)

A fortnight ago everything was going on much as it has done for the last few months, except that we knew there was a bit of fighting on the various fronts, but still nothing to alarm us. On Sunday September 24th (Cliff's birthday) we heard that the Japs were advancing on Changsha, but still no one was alarmed and we had services and carried on as usual. On Monday morning a wire came from Cyril telling us to prepare to go to Changsha, adding that he would be at home that evening if we wished to phone him. We very much did wish to phone him. We wanted to know why we should leave, what was the trouble etc. We had understood when we returned the last time, we were not to be called out again. We thought it must mean the Japs had come in on the side of Germany and all the British were leaving. We went to see Mr Hsu[11] to talk things over with him, and hoped with his help to be able to get through to Changsha on the phone. Mr Hsu did not want us to go. He said to stay in Liuyang and when they evacuated we could go with them. He had a house for us and soon we had everything arranged. The advantage of this plan was that we would still be able to keep in touch with most of our country stations, and if and when the Japs left the city we would be able to return immediately. Of course there was the danger we might be cut off for months and months, but we were not worried about that.

For over five hours we tried to get through to Cyril, but things were tense in Changsha and the military were monopolising all the lines. About 10.30 pm we gave up and came home, and went to bed disgusted with life. I forgot to say in the midst of the phoning another wire came saying 'Come at once'. All day Tuesday we packed until 1.30 am. At 3 am we were up again and off by 4 am. We knew if we were to get to Changsha ahead of the Japs we were going to have to dash for it. We had to leave the members without saying goodbye to them, our home, our Smuto. It was terrible. Tien Ni came out with us and Hu Kai Wen stayed to take care of the house and our possessions. We could only bring out what was necessary to face a winter. Hu will also take care of our dog Smuto.

Then came the journey to Changsha. We started off at 4 am in heavy rain and carried on until 3 am the next morning, only resting once for an hour, apart from meal times. All day long we heard heavy firing in the distance. It was a moonlit night so we pushed straight on. We passed a retreating army, we passed refugees, everyone was going in the opposite direction. At night the firing eased up, but there were terrific explosions and ahead of us a great red glow in the sky. We thought it was Changsha burning, but no one knew for sure. At about 1 am we were so exhausted we couldn't go on. Cliff was walking in his sleep. He walked about forty miles. I had a chair all the way, but the men were so exhausted I had to walk to help and did about twenty miles. The roads were terrible and even as we went men were breaking up even the small roads.

At 3 am we arrived at the river side just over three miles from Changsha. The two wooden bridges which crossed the river there were both ablaze, there were hundreds and hundreds of refugees on the far bank struggling to get across in small boats. They were all fleeing from Changsha, a heart-breaking crowd, some struggling with great bundles, all the family possessions, some helping the old people or sick, mothers hugging babies and dragging other little ones along, hanging onto their skirts, some crying, all frightened and with such tragic faces. They said the Japs were only a few miles away. No one was allowed to cross the river towards Changsha, the city was closed and no one could get in without a permit. We had a letter from Mr Hsu which would have got us through most likely, but we were unwilling to take our coolies into further danger. One man said he was sure he could get a letter through for us and so we sent a letter to Cyril telling him that we were stuck there, and asking *if he could get a permit and bring coolies out to us. We also asked whether he really wanted us, if not we wished to return to Liuyang.*

If we had done so we would have run straight into the Japs. We didn't know about it, but they were only a day's march behind us all the way. About 10 am Cyril himself arrived with two men from the compound, two wheelbarrows and a permit. Meanwhile we had been lying in hedges, by the side of ponds ducking aeroplanes. Finally we got to the Mission about 12 am, just in time for a much needed tiffin.

We were in Changsha three days and utterly miserable. We found we had been called in by consular advice to Cyril, because I was a woman, but Henry and John Foster had been allowed to stay on at Pingkiang! Oh, we were sick about it. To live in a neutral safety zone is not our idea of being a missionary! For Cyril and Barbara it was different. Their work was there; ours was in Liuyang. Despite all this it did not feel very 'safe'. The Japs were a bit careless at times, to say the least, and we quite expected to get bombed or shelled 'by mistake'. But most of all we were concerned about our Chinese minister in Changsha and our servants and others who had volunteered to stay on with us, but who we knew would have a terrible time when the Japs came.

Endnotes

1. *'Ho pen'* literally means 'fire pan'. It is made of cast iron, with hot charcoal on a layer of sand in a shallow iron dish and makes an effective room heater.

2. The Chinese religion is often referred to as *San Chiao* – literally three religions, or three-fold religion – which refers to the almost seamless intermingling of Buddhism, Taoism and Confucianism.

3. Sadly, because of the war, they never returned to Kuling.

4. My father's brother.

5. At one time he had a bungalow there.

6. China had a remarkably efficient postal service, which had been reorganised with some help from the French. Even at the height of the war they managed to operate across the war front.

7. Published by Edinburgh House Press in 1939.

8. From the Mission House in London, referring to the work my parents carried out in Liuyang following the air-raid. The Rev Harold Rattenbury was the General Secretary of the Methodist Missionary Society.

9. My father's eldest brother committed suicide on New Year's Day in 1939. Dick had suffered repeated bouts of depression and alcoholism since his days as a fighter pilot in the First World War.

10. A tropical fruit tree with oblong edible fruit.

11. Mr Hsu Ching-yu was chief magistrate of Liuyang. He had been educated at Oxford University and became a close friend of my parents, whom he often invited to civic functions that took place in Liuyang.

Chapter Five
The War Continues

戎

Living in Shaoyang (Paoking)

After a short while in Changsha my parents were asked to go to Paoking, where my mother had lived before her marriage, to help out while Dr Pearson was on furlough. The town was now known as Shaoyang. Dorothy Dymond, the hospital matron, and Kathie Warren, the evangelist, were on their own. My father, despite his lack of medical training, was made acting hospital superintendent.

Letter of 12th October 1939 from Paoking (EMC to her sister Jean)

As you will see from the address we are in Paoking…a wire came from Paoking asking if we could go there and help. An American doctor, who was supplying for Dr Pearson's furlough, has had to leave to take up another appointment. We do not know, because of the European war, if and when Dr Pearson is returning. The hospital is thus without a foreign doctor and at present there is no senior Chinese doctor there either. Also Dorothy Dymond, the matron, and Kathie Warren (evangelist) are alone there, which is not desirable in these uncertain days. Another point is the Church is greatly needing help. It seemed a direct call… It has meant turning our backs on Liuyang, which we have done with very heavy hearts, but we know Liuyang can carry on for a few months without us. For the past year we have lived there in a state of emergency and… If we went back it would only be a case of hanging on and standing by waiting for better days, but in Paoking there is work waiting to be done. On Monday afternoon we left for Paoking, along

Polyfoto

Map of China

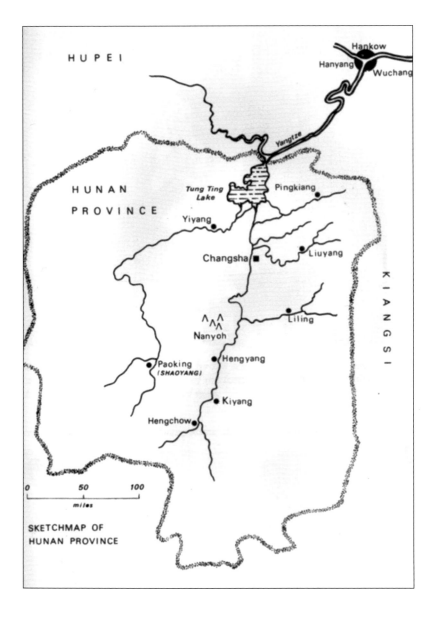

Map of Hunan

Kuling: bungalows on the hillside
Hankow: the water front

Hankow: The Bund during the 1931 floods
Shaoyang Hospital Compound, 1929

Boats on the River Shao

Methodist Boys' School, Pingkiang

Wu Feng Pu
EMC, Smuto and Maud Millican

CVC on the verandah at his Kiyang House

Sailing to Australia 1936
Raising water

Coolies on the road
Ploughing rice

A Chinese river boat

CVC on the way to the Synod 1932
CVC and Charlie Roberts bringing home pork

Coolie carrying CVC's luggage
The Great Fire of Changsha

Synod 1939
A street scene in Hong Kong

The family on holiday in Nanyoh
Squatters' huts in Hong Kong

A street scene in Changsha.

with several others who were glad to avail themselves of our protection.

The journey to Paoking was another nightmare. The road is all broken up to within sixty miles of Paoking, so it took us three and half days by bus. Travelling was terrible over the broken roads. One day it took from 2 am to 8 pm to do just thirty-four miles. The roads were crowded with refugees fleeing from Changsha. There were many thousands of them, sleeping at night in the fields, or by the road side. How they got enough food to keep them going, I do not know. Always there was the danger of aeroplanes. Whenever one was seen or heard the bus stopped and all the passengers scrambled out. We hid on hillsides, in hedges, we lay in ditches until the planes passed over, but fortunately for us they never fired. On two stretches of the road there had been bombing the day before. We saw some of the ruined buildings. The Jap planes had also machine-gunned the column of refugees and thrown hand grenades among them. Oh the wickedness of war that can transform men into fiends! And it is all so unnecessary and stupid.

England and Germany are at war, yet on the third day we called at a German mission and never doubted our welcome. They fed us, gave us a bath, helped us to get coolies and begged us to stay with them. The fourth night we spent with another group of Germans and no one could have made us more welcome, or been kinder. It is the same with the Germans in Changsha and those here in Paoking. We are fellow Christians and that is what matters most.

We have now been here nearly a week. Since we arrived Cliff has conducted a funeral and a wedding, we have had two air-raids, two feasts, two welcome meetings and hosts of visitors. The folk have made us feel very welcome. It has been good to see old friends again. The first raid was rather nerve racking. We were in an open trench and the wretched planes flew round and *round dropping bombs for half an hour. They went low over our heads about five times. There were no bombs dropped near to our compound, but lying in that trench they sounded mighty near. Wherever you are when the planes get over head, you are always sure it is the worst place on earth. It seemed such a good deep trench the day before; but when the planes came it seemed so shallow and gaping wide. It is the same with trees. A tree with good thick foliage one day seems as though it has not a leaf on it when the bombers arrive. We now go into a thirty feet deep dug-out which is well built and with three entrances, and are as safe as one can be these days. What a life it is!*

We have had news that poor Liuyang has had two terrible raids since we left, one either the very day we left or the day after. Dr Li passed through on the 30th (we left on the 27th). He said the place was absolutely deserted, not a shop open anywhere to buy food and no one about on the streets. The streets in the city were terribly smashed up. He said it was worse than the first raid; but we find that hard to believe, for there would not be anything left of Liuyang at all... We wish we could get more detailed news. We expect most of our people are safe, as they used to flee the city every fine day, but some always left it to the last minute, and you can never be sure how long a warning you will have.

For the time being at least the Japs have been driven back, following the biggest Chinese victory since the war began. Pingkiang was captured, but recaptured again by the Chinese army a few days afterwards. We have no news of John Foster and Henry Clarke, which we take as good news.

And that seems to be all there is to say on the subject of the war. We are both well, but there is a permanent ache in our hearts these days. There is so much sorrow, fear and misery all around... My next letter will give you more news of Paoking and our plans here. It seems as though Cliff is going to have to take charge of the hospital — as director or something, which seems rather a joke to us.

Did I tell you your parcel had arrived? The chocolate tin was flat and in five pieces, but I sent it to the street, got it straightened out, soldered and we are enjoying a lovely new biscuit tin!... The chocolates were just as welcome as you would expect... Alas the rats had enjoyed the garments — the top of one and the bottom of the other, but I think we will be able to make one out of the two. Thank you very much for them all.

... Let Hunan have a few special prayers these days. The war is on our doorstep, folk are suffering terribly and the winter is coming.

Letter of 12th October 1939 from Shaoyang (CVC to AIC)

Shaoyang is the new name for Paoking, which is now our station. When I last wrote we were in Changsha expecting to be occupied at any time. After a day or two, as the occupation did not come, we began to hope that we might be able to persuade Cyril to let us return to Liuyang. Then there suddenly came a telegram from Paoking urging the chairman to send us here.

There are some special difficulties at Paoking. Dr and Mrs Tucker (both doctors), who have been supplying during Dr Pearson's furlough are leaving in a few weeks' time to return to work with the Red Cross Society. Dr Pearson's return will probably be delayed. There is no one suitable to take over the superintendence of the hospital as a whole, to settle rows, to engage and dismiss staff and steer things through all sorts of difficulties. A German Jew (Dr Rynarzewski) has just been taken on the staff for a few months, but he is not a Christian and cannot speak Chinese. He is a refugee from Germany. The two young Chinese doctors are not suitable for the superintendency. There are special difficulties in carrying on the hospital in the present crisis. Due to arguments amongst the Chinese ministers, for the time being we must give up the idea of returning to Liuyang. When the Tuckers go, the hospital will probably be managed by a committee of three (Miss Dymond, a Chinese doctor and myself) and I shall probably act as superintendent. Miss Dymond can look after everything connected with the nurses – a very big task – the doctor can look after the medical side, and I will take care of the finances and general administration. Things will not be easy, but we shall muddle on...

At present we are the guests of Miss Warren and Miss Dymond, in the house that Elsie lived in for several years; but when the Tuckers leave we will probably move into the Pearsons' house next door. Dr Rynarzewski, the refugee doctor, may live with us. At present there is a Swedish doctor here helping for a few weeks. He will probably leave when the Tuckers go. He worked with the Red Cross in Abyssinia. Two days ago an Austrian doctor was here. He was sent to China by the 'China Aid Society' in England to work with the Chinese Red Cross. He has just returned from the China Front. Previously he was working in Spain among the government troops. The Tuckers are Americans. In the evenings all of us sit round the wireless listening to Manila, or London, relayed from Hong Kong.

Paoking, like so many places in China today, is deserted during the day time, with practically no business going on at all. This is because of frequent air-raid alarms and some air-raids. There have been two raids since we came, but apparently only two or three people were wounded. Most of the bombs were dropped on the aerodrome, which is no longer used. We have an excellent dug-out on this compound...

The advance on Changsha stopped about twenty miles from the city and the Japanese have retired as quickly as they advanced. It may have been because the Chinese got in behind them. Pingkiang was occupied for a few days, but has since been recaptured. Foster and Clarke are still there.

I don't know when we shall get letters from England again. All our letters are, of course, continuing to go to Liuyang, but I've wired the PO to direct them on here. However, the roads are more broken up than ever, so mail in Hunan is travelling very slowly. Also, from what we have heard, the Liuyang PO has been bombed since we left, so we may have lost the mail that had accumulated there for us.

The journey from Changsha was, as you can imagine, particularly difficult. The roads were full of refugees leaving Changsha. They slept under trees and on the roadside. Fortunately the weather was dry and mild. Three days brought us to a place sixty miles from here, where we were able to spend the night at a CIM station run by German missionaries, who were most kind to us. The German minister played a cornet, and we heard him leading the singing in the church. The tune was our National Anthem!...

We do hope you are all well and peaceful. We think such a lot about you...

Letter of 26th October 1939 from Shaoyang (CVC)

We have had letters from friends in Liuyang since I last wrote. The place was badly bombed several times after we left, but our property and all our friends are all right. The Japanese got very close to Liuyang before they started retiring.

Pingkiang was occupied by the Japanese for a few days. Foster and Clarke had a very anxious and trying time there. Soldiers lived on the compound in the unoccupied buildings. They were rigorously questioned again and again. The Japanese wanted coffee, cigarettes and biscuits. Fortunately neither they nor their staff were molested at all. Once the Japanese said their airmen were good and did not bomb foreign property. At that moment they were passing the house where Leigh was killed, so Clarke pointed it out to them. They promptly changed the subject.

We are still longing to return to Liuyang. Pearson has written from England to say that he is trying to return to Hunan. When he gets here it may be possible for us to return. Our fear is that the Japanese will get to Liuyang before we can get back... Dr and Mrs Tucker are leaving at the beginning of November. From then on, until Pearson's arrival, I shall nominally be superintendent of the hospital. The doctors will be two Chinese and a German Jew – a refugee from Berlin.

I am also in charge of the city church here, with the help of a young Chinese preacher... Meetings have to be held early in the morning, or after 4 pm, at least on fine days. People are not allowed to enter the city after 9 am and before 4 pm. During these hours the population moves to the country. It is during these periods that the planes are feared. The hospital compound does not move, but when planes are about all who can take refuge in a splendid dug-out...

Despite the problems of the war Christmas festivities still took place, as the following letter from my father to his mother reveals:

Letter of 24th December 1939 from Shaoyang

We have begun the usual round of festivities... So far we have had the Hospital Compound Children's Party, Member's Children's Party and Sunday School Party... The church and the hospital are decorated. This afternoon we are holding a special singing and baptism service with communion, tonight there is a hospital servants' meeting and mince pies next door. In the early hours of tomorrow the nurses and school children will come singing carols and we shall have to entertain them with tea, oranges and cakes.

27th December

I've not had time to write more. Every day has been packed full. Besides all the church festivities I have had much administration, supervision and interpreting in the hospital. Now I am preparing to wind things up and go to Changsha. Cyril has to go to Shanghai to attend the China Methodist Conference called by Harold Rattenbury[1], and I have to go to Changsha to take over things from Cyril for the time being. It is an awful job getting things sorted out up here – there are many things I just can't settle. Cyril too is having an awful job getting end of year schedules done and clearing up arrears… Most of us are opposed to the Shanghai Conference at the present time – it takes Cyril and a Chinese minister away for a long time and as it is we are already severely understaffed.

Christmas has been very festive and happy, though terribly busy…There is a fine opportunity here and we'd be happy to stay and work in the church. Changsha with all its responsibilities and office work doesn't attract me. If one could stay in one place and do consecutive, constructive work much more could be accomplished. But it's war time and we are understaffed. I suppose most places are disorganised now and we should be grateful we can do so much.

We're having a long spell of fine weather, which means one or two air-raid alarms every day. Yesterday a plane landed here. When it came we all ran towards our dug-out – but it was a Chinese plane bringing a wounded Chinese airman to this hospital. He was wounded in an air fight somewhere in western Hunan. He had to escape from his plane by parachute…

Thirteen foreign doctors were in Shaoyang a few days ago – almost all Jews who couldn't return to their own country – Germans, Poles, Spaniards, a Hungarian, and an Austrian. They were on their way to the Front to serve with the Chinese Red Cross. One stayed with us all the time, the others came and went — for meals, baths etc. There are some fine men among them. One we got to know better than the others was a German neurologist, who used to have a psychotherapeutic clinic in Berlin. Most of them had been in Spain[2] on the losing side!

We now have an English doctor — Dr Lockie — staying here. He is inspecting hospitals for the International Red Cross, but he's agreed to stay here and help till Dr Pearson returns. His last practice in England was at Evesham. It is a great relief to have him here, for the hospital is full with all kinds of cases and we are short of doctors.

Moving to Changsha

My father travelled back to Changsha for Synod on 2nd January 1940 and was asked to stay on there while Cyril Baker, who was the Chairman of the district, attended an all China Methodist conference in Shanghai. A few months later Cyril Baker returned to his family in England and my father took over as Chairman. This necessitated a move to Changsha.

Letter of 17th January 1940 from Changsha (CVC to AIC)

Cyril left for Shanghai on Monday morning at one o'clock in the morning! He left with a party from HMS Sandpiper, which was being escorted to the coast by the Chinese government. Cyril has gone to attend a conference of the seven Methodist Districts of China, called by Rattenbury. Whilst he is away I am to take his place here in Changsha. It was an awful rush getting him off. On Wednesday, Thursday and Friday we had District Committee meetings, to which came Harrison, Foster and two Chinese ministers. In between times and on Friday, Saturday and Sunday we all worked hard trying to get the 1939 schedules finished. At the same time Cyril tried to hand things over to me and to explain everything. It was an awful rush to the last minute. Now I am very busy with much correspondence and other things...

I ought to have left Paoking earlier and allowed more time for the takeover from Cyril, but as there was much aerial activity at Paoking at the time I felt I ought not to leave. We had a long spell of fine weather, with two or three air-raid alarms almost every day. Then we had three air-raids in four days, one with twenty-seven planes, one with twenty planes and one with nine. The first two raids were on or around the aerodrome and there were few casualties. The last was on the hills around the city and the bombs caught civilians who were hiding there. The casualties were probably between fifty and one hundred. Afterwards at the hospital we had three operating tables going at the same time. Both Elsie and I assisted the doctors. One women was brought by relatives, who carried her two crying children. She had to have both legs amputated and she died in the night. Several amputations were done, not all of which saved the lives of the people concerned.

When I last wrote I believe I said the Japs didn't seem to be interested in Paoking! They'd not come for three months, though we'd had lots of air-raid alarms and a few scouting planes. No Chinese planes had visited our aerodrome either. Then one morning twenty-seven Jap planes bombed the aerodrome. That afternoon, about 4.30 pm, eight Chinese bombers — manned by Russians — came to the aerodrome. We went on to the hill behind the house to watch them land. The next morning, before 7 am — before we were up — the air-raid alarms sounded. There was a thick morning mist at the time, which we thought would prevent planes from coming. A quarter of an hour later the 'urgent' alarm went, and quarter of an hour later twenty planes arrived. They flew around and overhead for over half an hour, delivering their bombs in six lots. We were all huddled in the twenty feet deep dug-out. We thought the city was being bombed — but it was the *aerodrome and the country round about. At least three of the Chinese planes were destroyed or damaged. How do the Japs get their information? Two days after, in the afternoon, was the third raid. The day the Chinese planes came, a Russian was brought to the hospital dead. He had been taken ill in the air and had been rushed to the hospital after landing. Because of all this excitement I postponed my journey to Changsha.*

Elsie is still in Paoking. We felt she should stay and help Dorothy Dymond, on whose shoulders falls most of the responsibility for running the hospital. Dr Lockie and Dr Rynarzewski can do the medical work, but as they cannot speak Chinese they cannot do the one hundred and one things connected with administration: keeping order, keeping morale up, finances and so on. Also Kathie Warren is ill with dysentery.

The long spell of fine weather has broken at last, for which we are very thankful. I expect Elsie will be leaving for here soon. Now that the motor road is broken up the journey from Paoking takes three and a half days, mainly by chair...

The war rumbled on as the following letters show. Sometimes the Japanese were close, sometimes they withdrew and on more than one occasion they took Changsha. On the first brief occasion my parents remained in Changsha, but after the Japanese attack on Pearl Harbour and the entry of Britain into the Asian War, they had to make sure they did not fall behind enemy lines, for this would mean internment, which apart from questions of personal comfort and safety, would render them of little use to anyone.

Letter of 14th April 1940 from Changsha: The invasion of Norway (CVC to AIC)

This is the first Sunday after the German invasion of

Denmark and Norway. During the past few days our thoughts have been full of the European situation, and twice each day we have listened-in to London and American stations. The news came as a great blow to the little foreign community here. Last Tuesday night the Changsha Missionaries Fellowship was meeting in Dr Witt's house, the house in which live the two German nurses of the Hudson Taylor Memorial Hospital and the German lady in charge of the Blind School... There were four nationalities represented in the Fellowship: English, American, Norwegian and German. There was a wireless receiving set in the room, but as there was not expected to be any special news, no one thought of turning it on. If we had turned it on we should have all heard together about the invasion. The next day Cyril and I went to the house of the Norwegians and listened to their wireless. They are all very upset. This afternoon a Norwegian is taking the English service. There will be Germans in the congregation. Surely that must be a unique happening.

On this compound are ten Europeans: Mr and Mrs Roberts[3] *('Mr' is British and 'Mrs' American), Dr Witt and the three ladies, and the four of us. The only wireless is in Dr Witt's house, so we all congregate there to hear the news. The Germans can understand the English broadcasts – at least Dr Witt can; but we, of course, cannot understand the German ones. We all remain friends, but there is a self-consciousness that wasn't present before. You will remember it was Dr Witt who operated on Elsie last year.*

We first got the news of the invasion from the Changsha Chinese newspaper, and that sent us to the wireless. I am sure you all must be having a tense and anxious time. We profoundly hope, as seems probable, that this move is going to add tremendously to Hitler's troubles...

Letter of 28th April 1940 from Changsha (CVC to AIC)

I am sure you must all be very worried and distressed at the latest turn the war has taken – the invasion of Norway... We are constantly thinking about you and listening to the wireless and studying the Chinese newspapers with great eagerness. It seems that the Allies have landed a large number of troops. The next few weeks or months will be critical, I expect. The Norwegian missionaries here are very distressed. The first time the Norwegian and German missionaries met each other after the invasion the womenfolk of both nationalities burst into tears. They have been colleagues and friends in missionary work in China for years.

We had an air-raid here on Tuesday. Five planes flew about for an hour, passing over our compound several times. There were about twenty to thirty casualties. This compound is marked with a huge American flag laid flat on the ground...

After we have been to Hengyang, we may go to Nanyoh – one of China's great sacred mountains, to see a house there that our mission hopes to rent for summer holidays.[4]

Elsie is very thrilled at the thought of getting the non-ladder stockings you mention.

Letter of 16th June 1940 from Changsha: A trip to Yiyang (CVC to AIC)

I have just been away for ten days on a trip to the Yiyang Circuit. It has been a very refreshing and encouraging time. The countryside was very beautiful and the country churches I visited seemed in a healthy condition. For some eight days I received no news, but when I got back yesterday I was greeted with a string of bad news – Paris lost, Italy joined the war, Norway surrendered, and here in China, Shashih and Ichang (important places on the Yangtze) lost to the Japanese. We are very anxious about Europe and listen in twice a day hoping for better news.

But I will leave the war and tell you of my trip to Yiyang. I travelled there by a Chinese river steamer, spending two nights on the boat. In Yiyang we have three churches…and a fair sized school… At present the circuit has neither a missionary, nor a Chinese minister. In fact it has not had one for nearly a year… We simply haven't anyone to send… The circuit is in the charge of a Chinese preacher, Mr Wu, the man who was our colleague when we first went to Liuyang. I was very impressed with the brave and able way in which he is tackling a difficult task… To see the missionary houses, which I have known as comfortable homes and full of life, now empty, shuttered up and cold was sad. The grass around them was several feet in height. Many panes of glass in the windows were broken as a result of air-raids… However, the church is far from dead. We had a fine service there on Sunday, with fifty-five for communion… I baptised seventeen people on the trip.

On the return journey I came into broken up roads – that is the old narrow roads broken up. This made walking terribly difficult, especially on the second day after there had been rain. When I saw the broken road I knew it meant the Japanese were advancing somewhere, and I feared it was towards Changsha, and wondered, with alarm, whether there was any danger of not being able to get back there. However, I learnt from an officer that the advance was up the Yangtze and not on Hunan. The roads were broken up lest the Japanese should suddenly decide to turn south. I walked back – a two day journey. I felt remarkably fit and came back very much refreshed. It was lovely to see Elsie again.

A doctor, Dr Loire, a German Jew, is staying with us for a few days. He is a man of over fifty, a nerve specialist and psychiatrist, very clever and a first class pianist. Yesterday we gave a tea party for missionaries in Changsha and asked Dr

173

*Loire to play the piano. He is working with the Chinese Red
Cross. Life must be very hard for him. He can't speak Chinese
and doesn't understand Chinese ways very well.*

*Now that France has collapsed we are waiting to know what
terms of peace Hitler will offer them. We may hear this on our
radio tonight. Britain is to fight on to the end. I fear there are
grim days ahead for England. I often wish I were at home to
share it all with you. But our duty seems to be here. Air mails
to England will probably cease for the time being. We must not
worry if we do not hear from each other for a few weeks
sometimes. And we must not fear those who can only kill the
body. I hope you will have peace at heart throughout all…*

Letter of 25th August 1940 from Changsha (CVC to AIC)

*Almost every night Clarke and I walk over to the Yale-in-
China[5] mission compound and listen to the news… We usually
listen to San Francisco, Manila and London. London comes
through very clearly. We get news of the latest raids, though place
names are not given, of course. We are all very bucked at the
failure of the first big German air invasion. At present attacks are
mainly by single planes or small groups. One wonders if this is
just an interlude before more large-scale attacks. It is good to hear
how normally life proceeds, though London did say some people
made an air-raid alarm an excuse for being late at the office!*

*We've had no planes over here for a few days. Hengyang has
been practically wiped out during the last fortnight. Over one
hundred planes bombed it one day, then about eighty planes a
few days later… Many incendiary bombs were dropped.
Chungking[6], of course, has been getting similar treatment for
quite a time. This 'scorched earth' policy does not seem to affect
China's resistance at all.*

The situation here is a little tense… Some precautions are

being made. This is due to the fact that during the autumn of
the last two years there has been a push towards Changsha. But
you know we are always all right...

Nanyoh

It was the usual practice for wives and children to go up
to the hills for a couple a months during the worst heat
of the Hunan summer, with the husbands joining them
for a shorter period. Traditionally, Kuling had been the
hill station to which Europeans normally went, but as
the war progressed it became difficult, if not impossible,
to get there and Europeans living in Hunan started to go
to Nanyoh, which is situated between Changsha and
Hengyang. It is one of the peaks of Mount Hengshan, a
popular site for tourists and pilgrims today. The summit
is 1225 metres above sea level.

My mother in her book describes Nanyoh thus:

Nanyoh is Hunan's most sacred mountain. People from
all over Hunan make pilgrimages to it, to pray to the
gods for success in business, or perhaps a woman has no
children – or no son – and she comes here to make her
offerings and prayers to Buddha. On the side of the road
up the mountain there are numerous shrines and small
temples, but close to the top, and on the top of the
mountain itself, are two larger temples, where the
pilgrims make their principal offerings and prayers.

We went up the mountain for health reasons. From
mid-July until the middle of September Hunan is
unbearably hot, both night and day. Before Kuling was
discovered and developed it was said the death rate
among European women and children along the Yangtze
valley was as high as on the west coast of Africa.

During the war it was impossible for us to go to Kuling, which was, of course, much further away. We knew Nanyoh was high enough to give us cool nights and Cliff at that time was acting chairman and deeply concerned for the health and well-being of missionary wives and children – and indeed all our missionaries. So in 1938 Cliff and I took a weekend holiday to Nanyoh and went exploring. We had been informed that near the top of the mountain there were some government bungalows. We made for these as our first stop. There was a large Buddhist temple nearby. We asked if we could lodge there, and our wish was granted.

About half an hour after our arrival one for the priests came to us, obviously rather agitated, and said the Chief Priest wanted to come and see us. Soon afterwards a most commanding looking man appeared. He had been a general in the army before retiring to the monastery. He appeared a little excited too, but was most cordial. He told us we were honoured guests and he knew we were good people. He then went on to explain. There were two swallows who for the past two or three weeks had been flying around, but would not nest. Immediately we arrived they began nesting. 'The swallows know,' he said. 'They will only nest where there are good people.' I should add that in China it is believed that if the swallows nest in your house it will bring you good luck. From then on the Chief Priest was our good friend. His word was all powerful in that area and it was he who helped us rent the various bungalows, and later buy two.

We were not far from Hengyang, the second largest city in the province and an important railway junction. During the war this made it an obvious target for Japanese bombers. It was also the base of the 'Flying

Tigers', a group of brave American volunteers, who came to help defend China[7]. We sometimes saw Japanese planes flying towards Hengyang. On one occasion we saw a dog fight near the city, which ended in a Japanese plane being brought down. Those were bad patches, but usually Nanyoh was a place of peace and quiet enjoyment and a blessing to us all.

This letter, written by my father to his mother, describes my mother's return after her summer holiday in 1940.

Letter of 8th September 1940 from Changsha

Elsie is now back in Changsha. I went to a place called Lu K'ou to meet her. Lu K'ou is nearly a day's journey by small river steamer from here. A few years ago it was hardly known, but now it is important to travellers because it is the terminus of the former Canton-Hankow railway. North of Lu K'ou the railway track has been pulled up. I met Elsie at the station; and then we went off in the dark to the river and took a little rowing boat to go and find the steamer on which I had booked a place to lie down. After about two hours search in the dark we gave up and booked a place on another steamer that was only supposed to be going half way to Changsha. However, this steamer, along with all others in Lu K'ou was commandeered by soldiers and had to go all the way to Changsha. We were the only civilians, except the crew, allowed on the boat. The steamer and the junks it was towing were full of khaki. We were glad no Jap planes came that way!...

Elsie has been at Nanyoh for about two months. She has come down pregnant, which is very thrilling...

The lovely autumn weather is starting here — dry, sunny days, with a clear blue sky, but for the third year in succession we have come to think of them as an invitation to Japanese planes. Yesterday some fifty or more planes passed over here in groups of nine, eighteen etc. We have not yet heard what poor place got it. The Japs are using new methods now. They send a larger number of planes and try to wipe a place out. How different from England things are out here – no defence, no defending fighters, very compact towns full of comparatively frail houses. A number of Hunan towns have had bad raids lately. We feel here in Changsha we are as well off as anywhere. The fact that the city has been so thoroughly burnt may save us from bad raids. Also we have a fine refuge on the Bible Institute compound – three floors of concrete above us. The compound has a gigantic American flag on the ground, and three huge white letters: U S A.

Letter of 12th November 1940 from Changsha (CVC to AIC)

I am writing this letter in our beautiful living room. We have a coal fire, which makes the room very snug. In the coldest weather we may use the central heating system. Dr Keller (an American missionary doctor), who built this house, did so for his aged mother, who was coming out to China. He promised her a house as good as the one she lived in in America.

Since my last letter I have been on a visit to the Hsiangyin circuit. It is north of Changsha and is quite near to the dividing line between 'occupied' and 'free' Hunan. The city is a ruin. It was almost completely burnt out after several bad air-raids a year last May. Our church premises were badly damaged and our elderly Chinese minister had a narrow escape.

I spent several days and nights in the country… I was in an area that suffered very much in the Japanese advance of just over a year ago. I was near the point on the Tungting Lake where they landed. There are still a good number of farm houses in ruins. I heard many stories of the killing of the inhabitants and other atrocities. Before the Japs took that area the farm houses and hamlets were bombed and machine-gunned again and again. The mother of one of our members was killed by machine-gun bullets while she was fleeing from her house. The son of another member was killed by the invaders. Everyone seemed to have friends and neighbours who were killed. Two of our 'Prayer Rooms' were burnt down. Yet in spite of all this…the earnestness and faith of the people is deeper than ever… One local preacher told me that when the Japs entered his house he sat at the table and read the Bible. When they knew he was a Christian, and that his house was one of our 'Prayer Rooms', they treated him with more consideration. One of them wrote on the wall, 'We are also Christians'. The whole of that immediate block of houses was burnt except this man's house.

At Hsiangyin city I called on the Catholic priest, a young Italian. He is the only non-Chinese in that area and seemed very lonely and glad to see me. We drank coffee together and spoke in Chinese. The poor man is much afraid of the air-raids – and no wonder. The Catholic mission is surrounded by ruins.

The day after tomorrow I leave for Yiyang. Whilst there I shall have the annual circuit meeting, the wedding of one of our women preachers, baptisms, communion and a little retreat! There is no minister there now. Ernest Wright is to go there when he arrives. The Wrights and Harrisons are on their way into the province from Hong Kong…

Arthur's birth

My brother Arthur was born in Changsha on 9th April 1941. My mother describes the event thus in her book.

On 9th April 1941, with the help of one of the German doctors, Dr Eitel, Arthur Vallance was born. There was an air-raid when he was on his way but as Miss Fischer, the

179

German nurse, said, 'We haven't time for them today'. So we carried on. Soon after he was born planes came over again, Arthur was put into a cupboard out of harm's way and I was buried in the bed clothes. Poor lamb, those first few months he spent most of his time in and out of cupboards and shelters. We were very near the front line and alarms and raids were a daily occurrence.

After the disappointment and anguish of the death of her first child, John Barry, two years earlier in Kuling, and a miscarriage a year later, my mother writes to her sister with much joy describing Arthur's birth.

Letter of 15th April 1941 from Changsha: Arthur's birth

When it gets round to 2.45 pm this afternoon it will be six days ago since our little son, and your very special little nephew, was born. I keep wishing you could see him. He really is a lovely babe and just like his Daddy. That is the unanimous opinion, but he has the Cuthbertson male blue eyes and black hair and Cliff says 'his mother's nose'. He refuses to own that nose! He weighed seven and a half pounds when born and has a lovely plump healthy look. At present he is a bit yellow, but that will only be for a few days. He seems perfectly healthy. We feel especially sure of his lungs! He cried the moment he was born, and I declare it was the loveliest sound I have ever heard… He does lung exercises at night. All day he lies in his basket looking like a cherub, but when night comes he makes his presence known…

I am keeping very well – wonderfully well really. There is no medicine like joy!… Were you beginning to get anxious when our cable was so late? The young man just refused to get a move on and had to be made to come, and even then would only come

*slowly, but I was in excellent hands and all went well and I didn't
have too bad a time.*

*He has had an interesting beginning. His parents are British,
he was brought into the world by a German doctor and nurses –
to whose care, on a previous occasion, during typhoid, his mother
owes her life. The doctor and nurse were assisted by Chinese
nurses, he was born on the American compound in Central China
and the morning he was born, Japanese planes were bombing
Changsha. How is that for a beginning? We think such a child
ought to work for the peace of the world and to the cause of peace
we are dedicating him.*

*We have had such a job deciding what to call him, but we
have now decided he is to be Arthur Vallance Cook. We wanted
a good solid English name[8]. 'Vallance' is, of course, a Cook
family name. I was rather keen on John, but there are so many
children in our mission called John…*

*Now it is time to feed the young man and as I don't want
this to go on so I will close. An added mercy is that I have
plenty of milk. Artificially feeding would have been a very
serious problem.*

Letter of 21st September 1941 from Changsha: the Japanese threat to the city

*We have another crisis on. The Japanese seem to be trying to
make another push. It came suddenly last Thursday. Today is
Monday and the Chinese army are still holding them, but the
situation is tense. We can hear gun fire in the distance and have
an alarm on and planes over all day long. So far there has been
very little bombing, but you always have to be on the alert. The
alarm goes any time between 6 am and 7 am and lasts until
dark. Yesterday we didn't get our 'all clear' until 8 pm; and then
had another short alarm at 9 pm… If more than one plane
comes over we get into the cellar of the main building and feel*

happier with three floors of concrete above us. We don't lack exercise or excitement. I would love a bit of monotony…

This letter has had a dozen interruptions, what with running away from planes, trying to get things packed up…interviewing people as to what they ought to do etc. Folk are scattering and they are coming for advice and help. Yesterday evening two friends came, one is a young woman who must get away, but her old mother is very ill and can't move. The other is an older woman with two children and her husband away from home. She must get her two boys away and keep in free China, so that her husband can join her later, but she has an old father of eighty, who cannot travel. Would we, could we, take care of the old man?

Today the pressing cases are our nice 'baby amah' (nanny), a most charming sweet girl of eighteen, who just must go, but to what? She doesn't want to go, and just weeps. I don't want her to go, but I am afraid for her, and so I weep! Then there is our old 'wash amah', of whom we are very fond. She must take to the road because of her son, who is too big to stay. And there is also our table boy who is big and strong, so he must go. And all day long there are folk coming begging us to take them or their old people. It just tears you to pieces. If only we were sure we could protect them, but who can say? And to let them go, knowing what being a refugee means, is terrible. The faithful Tien Ni stays. He is a real gift from the Lord, is our Tien Ni. But I must tell you a joke about Tien Ni. When we knew things were getting bad we sent him off to buy provisions – flour, lard, sugar, oil etc – and he bought seven hundred eggs! Seven hundred for three of us! How on earth he got them I don't know, because they are difficult to get nowadays. I have advised him to sell two or three hundred…

If we are still unoccupied next week I promise I will write again. If you don't hear from me for a while you will know it is because Changsha has been taken. But don't worry. It will be

mighty unpleasant, but I honestly believe not dangerous for us.
All the same, be careful how you reply to this letter. What a life!

The Japanese take Changsha

After many false alarms at the end of September the
Japanese advanced and took Changsha. For two days
previously the inhabitants of the city had listened to the
boom of cannons and watched the Japanese dive-
bombers raking the streets with machine-gun fire. Their
long delay in seizing the prize that had so long been
within their grasp, and the fact that they abandoned it so
soon afterwards, was almost certainly due to the great
fire, which had rendered the city of little use to them.

My father kept the following log of the brief Japanese
occupation of Changsha:

A Log of the Japanese Occupation of Changsha – September 1941

For some while there have been reports of Japanese activity in
North Hunan, but it was generally considered that the
Japanese were only making raids to capture the newly-
gathered rice harvest. North east Hunan is a very rich rice
growing area. Such raids have been made before. Then about
18th September we were suddenly told that the Japanese had
made a landing at Yung T'ien, a place on the edge of the
Tungting Lake about seventeen miles north of Hsiangyin.
Around Yung T'ien we have a number of country churches.
Two years ago when Changsha was threatened the Japanese
also landed at Yung T'ien. For the next few days we were
under an air-raid alarm from dawn to dusk and planes were
constantly flying over and around Changsha. Bombing of the
country round about was frequent.

23rd September

We bricked up the door of the Hsin Ming T'ang[9]. This meant that our only entry was through the compound of the Hunan Bible Institute[10]. We had decided that in the event of occupation we should join up with the large HBI compound, where preparations were being made for the running of a refugee camp. Very busy making preparations for the possible occupation and seeing people who were hurriedly leaving.

25th September

Nasty air-raid just after dawn. Power diving over the city.

27th September

A number of refugees have already come into the compound. About 5 pm we had gathered these together to give them instructions. While the meeting was in progress someone rushed in and said the Japanese had arrived. We went to the main gate immediately and saw retiring Chinese troops hurrying by. There was rifle and machine-gun fire on the street. A crowd of terrified people was clamouring at the gate. We opened the gate and let them in, but as soon as we had closed the gate another terrified crowd gathered. Some people climbed in over the walls. One of these was the messenger from the Yale Hospital, who was on his way to send off a cable. He had been shot by retiring troops. Two or three bullets had hit him, but most fortunately had not entered vital parts of the body. He just managed to get into the compound before he collapsed. At this time the Japanese troops had probably entered the north end of the town.

28th September

Japanese planes constantly flew low over the city. For the first time for several years we knew we need not shelter from them, though it was only after a struggle between our reason and our emotions *that we could stand out in the open and watch them go over. There is a feeling of some relief that this danger, which Changsha has faced for over three years, is, at least for a while, over. At 5 pm a Chinese service was held in the assembly hall of the HBI. The place was full. I had been asked to take the service. It was difficult to know on what subject to speak at such a time as this. I finally decided to talk on the resurrection of our Lord and His eternal presence. During the service two Japanese doctors called at the compound to inquire whether there were any infectious diseases in Changsha. Dr Eitel, Mr Roberts and Mr Wright interviewed them. Later two officers from the military police headquarters called and took the names and addresses etc of the foreigners on the compound. They also gave us a proclamation to place on the door, which forbade troops from occupying the compound.*

29th September

In the afternoon there was a surprise attack by Chinese planes. Bombs dropped on the outskirts of the north end of the town. In the night Chinese guerrillas penetrated right into the town. There was much firing, especially machine-gun firing, some of which was very near the HBI. The Japanese are concentrating in the north section of the town. Not very many Japanese troops near here. Some Japanese troops passed on beyond Changsha...

30th September

All foreigners were called to the office of the military police near the North Gate to report on their property in Changsha. Plans were required. The officer in charge was casual and did not seem to have his mind on the matter. When our reports had been given we were asked to wait a while and the Staff Officer in charge of the Changsha garrison would come and see us. Norwegians, Americans and British were asked to wait at the Presbyterian Mission (American), Germans and Italians at the

Catholic Mission (Italian). We waited a long time and were then told that the Staff Officer regretted he was too busy and could not come and see us. An officer had called at the Catholic Mission and asked that one Italian and one German go to the Staff Officer's headquarters. One of each went, only to be told that the Staff Officer was too busy. It turned out later that their headquarters were moved that night. On the way to the office of the military police we passed some Japanese soldiers carrying many paper Japanese flags fixed to little wooden sticks. They were going to the Catholic refugee camp. Later we saw many refugees streaming from this camp holding these flags in their hands. They were then conducted to an open space nearby, where they were addressed by a Japanese officer. The address was interspersed by cheers from the crowd and the waving of these flags. Just as this was going on a big passenger plane circled round overhead several times flying very low. It is probable that this was the plane referred to on the radio that brought foreign newspaper correspondents from Shanghai to view occupied Changsha from the air.

A pig was killed on the Yale compound. Mr Roberts and I brought back a joint for the HBI compound. We carried it through the street under the protection of a small US flag! We visited the Evangelical Mission and our premises at Hsi Ch'ang Kai. The Japanese had entered the latter several times. Three doors and a few window panes had been broken and a few things belonging to Mr Wang Ts'e-an were stolen. Almost every shop in the street has been broken into. Furniture and goods from the shops are strewn on the street. Mr Roberts and I brought back to the HBI compound a few terrified women and children. In the afternoon I helped a neighbour bring thirteen pigs on to the compound for protection. The suffering of the people has been absolutely terrible, but I will not enlarge upon that here. It is a cause for profound thankfulness that the three refugee camps – at Yale Mission, the Catholic Mission and here at the HBI – have been able to give protection to over fifteen thousand persons. At night we sleep in the basement of the HBI main building. There has been much firing during the night. The north end of the town has been subjected to artillery fire (small guns). One shell hit a servant's house on the Yale compound. Two amahs were slightly wounded.

1st October

Went with Mr Wright to the headquarters of the military police to get a proclamation for Hsi Ch'ang Kai premises. To our surprise we found that all the Japanese who were billeted around the North Gate had gone, including the military police headquarters. We saw a few Japanese stragglers roaming about the streets. So often during these days of occupation we have seen Japanese soldiers roaming about in twos and threes. One day we saw an odd soldier stalking down Yo Wang Kai[11] wearing a gas mask!

Dr Eitel brought in some women from a place near the YMCA house. After dark a good number of mounted Japanese passed through the outskirts of the town. They have come from the south and are moving towards the north-east. Terrific rifle and machine-gun fire during the night as the Chinese re-enter Changsha. We did not know who was doing the firing. At times it seemed to be in the compound, although actually it was never nearer than the outside of the front gate, but bullets probably flew over the compound.

2nd October

As the firing of last night was fading away, Mr Roberts came to our 'bedroom' in the basement with the news he had just heard Tokyo on the radio. Tokyo has announced that the Imperial Army will evacuate Changsha after having inflicted a

187

crushing defeat on Chiang Kai-shek's armies in North Hunan. It is not the policy of Japan to occupy this or that city, but to wipe out the entire armies of Chang Kai-Shek!

My mother relates these events in a letter to her sister.

Letter of 3rd October 1941 from Changsha

We are free again! Free and we feel we have just come out of an awful nightmare. Was it Friday when I last wrote? We have almost lost count of the days. On Friday night and Saturday morning there was street fighting, or rather fighting on the roads just outside the city, and then the Japs came in. We had them for four days – four days of continuous anxiety and stories of horrors perpetuated. Every night the Chinese guerrillas penetrated right into the city. Small cannons, machine-guns and rifles were going off all night and bullets whizzed around the compound. We all slept down in the cellars. When the Japs arrived folk swarmed onto the compound. Soon we had a thousand refugees. Of course we expected it and preparations had already been made by the International Relief Committee. There were three big camps in the city – Yale, the Roman Catholics' and ours. Many people, believing the Japs' promises, stayed in their homes. The first day and a half was all right, but after that they looted everywhere, killed and wounded anyone who dared say 'No', and no woman or child was safe. Folk just poured into the camps. Men swarmed the walls and got down on their faces and begged us to take their womenfolk, if we could not take them. The one thousand went up to two thousand before we knew where we were.

Thursday morning after a night of heavy fighting the Japs melted away and the Chinese troops marched in. The joy and relief was so great folk hardly dared believe their eyes and ears. I believe Chungking has set off millions of crackers, but there have been no wild demonstrations here. Folk are too stunned and there is still too much to face, hardly a house or shop in the whole city has not been looted, but oh the difference in the atmosphere – from winter to summer, from night to day, from a silence of dread to a joy of singing. Unconsciously people go about singing and laughing, whereas before they spoke in whispers and were so still.

Cliff, the babe and I are fine – a bit tired from loss of sleep and the strain, but in good form. We hadn't a fatted calf, but we killed two chickens last night and had a victory dinner.

No more now. This is just to let you know all is splendid with us. Yesterday afternoon the post office and police force came back – quick work!

One unfortunate result of the Japanese occupation was that on regaining control the Chinese ordered all the German and Italian missionaries to leave the country immediately, because they suspected them of having collaborated with the Japanese. The episode of flag waving at the Italian Catholic Mission could hardly have helped their cause. The case of Dr Eitel was particularly sad. He had done so much to help the Chinese people in the hospital he had built up. He clearly had no sympathy with the German government, having come to China after having been imprisoned by the Nazis for political reasons. Attempts to persuade the authorities to change their mind proved to no avail.

Another interesting follow up was a Japanese wireless broadcast which said that the Japanese would punish the missionaries when they returned to Changsha, for having spread lies and told horror stories about their occupation. This came about because a Chinese radio broadcast had reported some adverse comments made by a number of missionaries.

Continuous air-raids

Although the Japanese withdrew from Changsha, the air-raids continued, at night-time as well as during the day, so my parents and Arthur frequently spent the night in the basement of the HBI, barricaded in with packing cases as a protection against shrapnel or stray bullets. On one such occasion, on 7th December 1941, while my father was away visiting Pingkiang, my mother was awakened early in the morning by Charlie Roberts calling out 'The Japanese have bombed Pearl Harbour. We are at war'.

My father was on the road from Pingkiang to Changsha with Cyril Clarke when the attack on Pearl Harbour took place. It was only on his arrival back in Changsha that he heard the news. In the following letter to his mother he describes this event and the ensuing flight from Changsha, once again threatened by the Japanese.

The flight from Changsha (continued)

Clarke returned to Changsha with me. On our return we heard that Britain and America were at war with Japan. Japan's treacherous attack on Pearl Harbour, Manila, Malay etc had taken place three days before. This meant that our position in China was now entirely different, and our place so near to the front line was not a happy one. We decided that the missionary families should move from Changsha, the Changsha station being left in the hands of bachelors who could move easily and quickly if necessary. No dependent Chinese, who might hinder the movements of those remaining, were to stay either. We began to make preparations for moving, but we thought we should probably be able to stay until after Christmas. Then suddenly the Japanese began another push into Hunan. This was just what we hoped wouldn't happen. For two days things were very tense and people were evacuating the city in great numbers. Boats were very difficult to get. Then came a lull and I urged that this lull be seized as an opportunity for removing the families. Packing was intensified and on Christmas Eve we and the Wrights and numerous Chinese left Changsha.

We were afraid that we would have to spend Christmas on the road, but we actually spent it with some American Presbyterians at Hengyang – some very kind people. It was really quite a jolly time. Five nationalities were represented at the Christmas dinner – French, Russian, German, American and British. The German CIM missionaries at Hengyang were confined to their compound with a guard at their gate day and night, but the American missionaries got permission for them to go to the American compound for the whole of Christmas Day. That added greatly to the enjoyment of the day. The Germans were deeply pleased about it. The day after Christmas I saw Elsie and Arthur off on the bus to Paoking (Shaoyang) and I returned to Changsha. We left Changsha so hurriedly that I had left many things unattended to. Both we and the Wrights had had to leave a lot of our possessions behind, and a lot of the District stuff was left too. I hoped to be able to return to Changsha and bring out some more stuff, but as my boat approached the city I found everyone was leaving the place. Boats in great numbers were sailing up the river, and on either bank of the river was a stream of people hurrying away, carrying with them every kind of bundle and load. The military were forcibly evacuating the populace. At first the passengers on our boat weren't allowed to go ashore. Then after a lot of talking we were permitted, but with the warning that we must get our business done and leave again immediately.

At our mission I found Clarke and Fred Blundred and Mr

Roberts of the Hunan Bible Institute all packed up and debating whether to go on board a boat that they had chartered that night or the next morning. The Japanese were supposed to be less than thirty miles away and advancing. I stayed about four hours and left again. I managed to get myself a place on a launch by giving a man ten dollars to arrange it for me... I made for Hengyang, and from thence to Yungchow, to discuss a few urgent matters with the folk there. The most pressing problem was finance. I'd sent two cables to London for funds about a fortnight earlier and no reply had come. We were urgently in need of money. Another question was evacuation plans if the Yungchow folk should have to leave. My visit was very worthwhile. It was a great help to be able to discuss these things with our folk there and with Bishop Stevens of the Church Missionary Society. We sent off another urgent cable to London and also one to the chairman of the Burma District. Then I returned to Hengyang. I found Wright was still there, although his family had gone on to Shaoyang. He had not been able to get our luggage and some of the hospital supplies off to Shaoyang. The next day we left with the luggage on the truck of the Presbyterian Mission. A young English doctor, who has just come out to China with the Friends Ambulance Unit[12], travelled with us. Hengyang had a bomb or two dropped on it as we were trying to get off.

It was wonderful to arrive safely in Shaoyang and see Elsie and Arthur again. The last few days have been hard going. Out of eight successive nights I have only taken my clothes off once! Now I have been here a week. Elsie and I are living with Miss Swann, a missionary refugee, in the bungalow next to Dr Pearson, the bungalow Elsie lived in for so long when she was stationed in Paoking. Since I got here two remittances have arrived from London, so things are easier in that respect, though a lot more is needed yet. All this explains why I have not been able to write to you for so long!

Shaoyang seems very secure after Changsha – though there was an air-raid five miles from here this morning – and we are very happy to be here. Since we left Changsha the Japanese have once again reached the outskirts of the city and then pulled back. According to all accounts some terrible fighting has gone on there, quite near to the Bible Institute. The Institute is said to have been damaged and the road on which the Hsin Ming T'ang stands burnt. Yale Hospital has been burnt too. All missionaries had left. We are now longing to get reliable news about things in Changsha. I may return on a visit next week.

I know you will all have been thinking about us a lot since the Pacific War started, but I hope you don't worry. We usually seem to be in some sort of mess out here, but in the end we always seem to muddle through. We are all well and live quite comfortably and have plenty to eat... Church work here is flourishing and the hospital too. We like living in Paoking.

1942 has not started too well, but I feel sure that the year will end much better than it began. I don't see how Japan can keep going as she has during the last month. When Britain and America get properly started she will have a bad time. But we may have to lose a great deal more before the turning point comes.

Back in Shaoyang

One of my father's most pressing tasks in Shaoyang was handling the Missionary Society's finances. He was responsible for the Society's finances across the whole of southern China, which included large areas behind Japanese lines. To make matters worse inflation was rampant and it was inadvisable to hold money in Chinese currency, since it was losing its value so rapidly. So a scheme was devised to buy local products, such as bales of cotton, as soon as any cash was received. When cash was required to pay church workers, or buy food, the bales were sold.

My mother, in her book, describes some of the other problems encountered.

Cliff continued to distribute money to all the people employed by the Methodist Missionary Society throughout China – to Chinese ministers and teachers, hospital staff etc, and where possible, the occupied areas. In those days this was no easy task. Some he sent by wire to places like Ningpo and Wenchow and South China; some he gave to Chinese merchants and they paid it out to our people in occupied China. You can trust the word of a Chinese merchant. The Roman Catholic Mission helped a lot. Cliff paid money to priests in free China and they paid an equivalent amount to our Chinese ministers in the occupied areas. Some Cliff sent by courier to the various folk in Hunan.

One of the couriers we used was Liu Lao Pan. He was an elderly Christian coolie. The first time I met him he was living in a small shack with his wife and two children. The shack consisted of one small room, with a mud floor, mud brick walls and a roof made of hammered out petrol tins. It had just enough space to take a bed, a small mud brick stove and one bamboo chair. There he, his wife and their two children lived. Such was their poverty.

He worked for us for a while as our house-boy, and although he had little understanding of European habits and thought our ways very funny indeed, he was willing to try anything. Cliff had been very much struck by his honesty and reliability, so when he was looking for a courier to travel around the province taking money to the various mission stations he decided to try Liu Lao Pan. He proved just the man. He undertook these most dangerous journeys with silver dollars or sometimes gold bars tied round his waist. No one would suspect that such a rough looking coolie would be carrying such large sums of money on his person or in his small roll of belongings. For the next two or three years he travelled up and down and all over the province. It was dangerous work. Had he been suspected of carrying money he would have been robbed and probably killed. Also remember his poverty. What a temptation! Yet through all that time, though he carried large sums of money, sometimes silver bars, he never defaulted with a single dollar. There is an interesting sequel to this. Cliff had helped him by paying for his two sons to go to school. Years later, after we had left China, we heard one of Liu Lao Pan's sons had completed his education and had offered himself for the Methodist ministry.

To return to the subject of getting the money to those who needed it. Every few months one of the Hupeh ministers somehow or other got himself through the Japanese lines, over no-man's-land and came for money to take back for himself and his colleagues. Once when a minister arrived he said he had brought his wife. Could he stay and work in Hunan? Cliff's reply was yes, if he stayed in Hunan there was work for him to do, but what about his colleagues in Hupeh who needed the money? The poor man wept. It was night-time. Cliff said, 'Go and talk to your wife, and tell me your decision in the morning'. The next morning he returned very early. His decision was made. 'Give me the money,' he said. 'I am going back; but please take care of my wife'.

The chairman of our South China District, Donald

Childe, and several other missionaries had been interned by the Japanese. After consultation with the remainder of the District, the Mission House asked Cliff to take over as acting chairman for South China. As a result he was for a time acting chairman for both Hunan and South China, as well as financial secretary for the whole of free China. It also meant about every three weeks or so he had to go to Kukong in Kwangtung province. That entailed a bus journey to Hengyang and then a day's journey by train to Kukong, at a time when the railway line was being bombed almost daily. There was also always the possibility the Japanese would advance and he would be cut off. So whenever we parted we never knew when we would see each other again. The plan we agreed upon was if the Japanese advanced, I would go with the hospital folk south and west to safety somewhere, and when and if he could, Cliff would make his way to join us. It sounds simple, but it would have meant a journey of several hundreds of miles across country to join up with me wherever I might be. Arthur was just two years old and Ray was on the way. They were grim days indeed.

In the following letter to his mother my father describes some of the difficulties.

Letter of 8th February 1942 from Shaoyang

I don't seem to manage to get any letters written to you these days. It is awful, and I feel very sorry about it. But every day is so full of urgent matters that time goes by and letters to you and others get crowded out. Now in addition to Hunan, I have to give general supervision to the South China District, and am temporary treasurer for Hupeh, Hunan, Kwangtung, Wenchow and Ningpo. The chairman of the South China District is in a

Japanese-occupied part of Kwangtung. The chief job connected with the treasurership is getting enough money cabled from London to Chungking and then supplying the various Districts. The trouble at the moment is that funds from London come through so slowly. We and other Districts are as a result faced with a very acute shortage of money, although we know the Mission House was trying to send adequate funds about three weeks ago. Well, I suppose these will turn up any day now.

I've just been on a trip to Changsha and North Kwangtung that took about twelve days. The houses on the HBI compound in Changsha were not damaged very severely. The roofs of two buildings were damaged by shells, all the buildings, including our residences, were peppered with bullet marks, and several bomb craters were to be seen in the compound. Evidently there had been fierce fighting around that area. This Changsha victory seems to have been a real one, much more so than the one before, when we were in Changsha. When I got to Changsha I found the house we used to live in with Cyril had not been cleaned up. Clarke and Blundred, who returned to Changsha earlier, left it for me to see. Outside the front door was the safe, forced open (I hope the Japs spent hours trying to open it – it was quite empty!). Perhaps if we had not closed it when we left it would not have been damaged. A long wall mirror also lay outside the front door – smashed into a thousand pieces. Inside several mirrors had been smashed on the ground, just as gramophone records had been. Mattresses had been split open and the contents scattered here, there and everywhere. Crockery had been smashed on the ground. Any bedding, clothing or eatables that the Wrights hadn't taken away with them had been looted. Some vegetable oil had been spilt on the floor. Lots of other things were just smashed – but fortunately not the furniture. And the Japs had used the verandah floors as their lavatory! The strong room of the HBI had been forced and some typewriters inside smashed up.

*In the cellar of the main building there were about sixty boxes,
mainly belonging to people on furlough. Everyone of these had
been opened — usually torn open — and the contents thrown over
the floor. You can imagine the mess and the confusion. Crockery
smashed and lots of other things broken. Here, as all over the
compound, clothing, bedding and eatables had been stolen. It was
a pity we could not get more stuff out, but we were fortunate to
be able to get families, women and children and our essentials
away. There was so little time between Britain's entry into the
war and the Japanese attack on Changsha.*

*After visiting Changsha I went on to a place called
Shaokuan (or Kukong) in north Kwangtung. Now that they
are cut off from Hong Kong and Canton this place has become
the head of our South China District. We have a fine hospital
there... and three missionary families — four with the medics. I
was there four days and discussed lots of very difficult problems
with the folk there. The Chinese spoken there is Cantonese,
which I don't understand. The local people also don't
understand Hunanese — though the educated folk do. I met a
number of English military and naval men who had escaped
from Hong Kong after the surrender. They had a most thrilling
story to tell. I think it may be one of the memorable stories of
the war.*

*When I got back here there was a letter from you awaiting
me — the first letter for ages. It was quite an old letter, but it was
good to get it... We do love your letters...*

My parents remained in Shaoyang throughout 1942,
although my father spent much of the time travelling.
Financial problems continued to occupy much of his
time and proved no easier than before. Air-raids also
continued to be a regular part of their lives. Although the
Japanese army was well established in the northern part

of Hunan, as well as to the east and the south, no attempt was made to capture Shaoyang. Food supplies were short and human tragedies were all around them.

Nanyoh

It was only my mother and Arthur who went up to Nanyoh that year. My father was too busy to get away.

Cyril Baker returned to China in the summer of 1942 and my father gladly handed back many of his responsibilities – although unfortunately not the financial ones – to him.

After the serenity of Nanyoh life soon returned to the unpleasant realities of war-time. In the following letter my mother describes some of the shortages they had to put up with and how they needed to improvise.

Letter of 2nd November 1942 from Shaoyang (EMC to AIC)

Clothes are a terrific problem. Cloth is so expensive, we can't think of buying it. A plain cotton gown that formerly would have cost eight dollars now costs nearly two hundred. Of turning, patching and mending there is no end. I am thinking of bringing some of our garments home for the museum! They are so patched, there is no original cloth left. Cliff is wearing a shirt today with a collar which has the stripes running down instead of along. It was the best I could get from the shirt tail. Cliff's overcoat! It has been turned and darned and patched, the cuffs taken off and made smaller, with the frayed bits cut away, the pockets redone, the buttonholes whipped over again and again, until they are like saucers and you can almost see yourself in the shine on the tails… He looks smarter than most people, but that is because he keeps on using his trouser press and hangers and I keep them brushed clean…

I am very reduced. I now possess for winter my pale blue costume, with two woollen jerseys, and a green dress made from the coat you gave me. For the rest I depend on my heavy Chinese gowns… All Arthur's clothes are either re-knits, some for the third time, or cut downs, but he will have a new jersey made from new wool for Christmas. It is a very handsome present from Jerry Harrison. She is very generous with what they brought in. We all try to share around according to others needs. It is, of course, six years since we had any new clothes, except for a few summer dresses, which I had made three years ago. This year I am going to wear a pair of Cliff's and a pair of Dad's golf stockings, mine have gone beyond repair. But it doesn't matter, we are all shabby together, both foreigners and Chinese. In fact we would be ashamed to have new clothes nowadays. We get a lot of fun out of our makeshifts and alterations. But the servants complain. Tien Ni laughingly says we now wear our clothes for so long, there aren't any dusters in the house.

Food is also a problem. There is plenty of it, but not much variety and it's so terribly expensive. We have all been trying to economise rather too much and there are a number of people not in good health. Our household has not been too bad. Cliff has had a few ulcers and I have had two boils – one on my cheek and one on my nose – no aids to beauty!… But we are on a 'get strong campaign'. We eat soya beans every day – jolly nice too – and peanut butter. We are trying to get a little more milk and some native malt, we also eat a fair amount of honey and try not to get alarmed about the cost of fruit… But we have a goose for Christmas promised by Tien Ni's father and we have four pounds of currants and eleven pounds of raisins for the pudding and Christmas cake. I don't know what else will go into them…

Cliff keeps remarkably well and surprisingly fit. Sometimes he looks tired, but I marvel at his strength. He is working terrifically hard from early morning until 9 or 10 at night, with no break, except the time necessary to take his meals comfortably. He has a very difficult job with finances… Cyril's return has been a great joy and help to us all, but especially to Cliff. He has relieved Cliff of much travelling, but even so, Cliff has more than he can really manage. With others coming perhaps it will be possible to share out some more work. We are all so pleased about John Foster's return. He is a great soul and a splendid missionary. We will be thankful when we hear he has arrived safely in India.

Christmas 1942

Despite these shortages the missionaries living in Shaoyang, many of whom were refugees from elsewhere in Hunan, had an enjoyable and relatively sumptuous Christmas. On Christmas Eve, although no-one could offer a traditional turkey or, being China, a duck, most were happy with the substitution – a goat! On Christmas Day the morning service was taken by the chinese minister Li Chang Hsu[13], after which the missionaries retired to the Wrights' house, where there was a Christmas tree and small present for everyone. My parents gave the lunch, which, thanks to Tien Ni's ingenuity, included a goose. In the afternoon there was a party for all Church members, which included professional dancers, shadow boxing and mock sword fighting. On Boxing Day a party was given for all the children in the compound – about eighty in all.

After all the hardships and deprivations suffered by everyone over the preceding months a couple of days of rejoicing and comparative indulgence did everybody's spirits the world of good.

Raymond's birth

In the midst of these uncertain and turbulent times I was born. My mother describes the event thus:

At the time of Ray's birth we were more or less refugees. He was due in June, but June on the plains of central China is terribly hot and diseases, especially gastric infections, are prevalent. Certainly not the place to have a baby! It was decided therefore that I should go to Nanyoh, the Holy mountain in Central Hunan, to which we women and children usually went during the extreme heat of summer. Hilda Hudson, a nurse, was going to come from Lingling to be with me, and when the baby was about due, Dr Pearson would come up from Shaoyang.

The first problem that arose was the fact that I couldn't possibly travel on one of the ordinary buses without grave risk of a miscarriage. Dr Pearson said not to worry about that, the Salt Gabelle[14] people often came through Shaoyang in a private car and invariably called at the hospital. He would easily get me a lift. But during that period no car ever came.

Hilda came in June to take care of me. The baby was overdue, by nearly a month. On the 10th July, a Saturday, Dr Pearson came to see me and announced he was going to induce labour the next day. I protested that Sunday was the only day he had for any rest. He replied it was also the only day he had the time to give to me. This is interesting because afterwards he told me the baby's head was already hardening. Had he waited until Tuesday, which was the next possible day, the head would have hardened. It was a difficult birth and the baby's head would almost certainly have been crushed, and we would have lost him. Raymond was over nine pounds at birth, and put a hand to his head just to make the going more difficult. It is also interesting to note that later Dr Pearson told me that if I had gone to Nanyoh, as we planned, when he came up the mountain he would not have been able to bring with him the instrument he ultimately used. The hospital only had one, and he could not have taken it away. That would have meant he could not deliver the baby and I would have had to set off in labour for Hengyang, down the mountain and a day's journey away. Either the baby, or both of us, would have died.

The day after Ray's birth Arthur became very ill with some intestinal infection. Dr Pearson said we must get him to the cool of the hills, but how? We were still not fit to travel on one of those buses. During the morning of the next day an American aeroplane, one of the Fighting Tigers based at Henyang, had to make a forced landing on the Shaoyang airstrip. He had run out of petrol. While making the landing he broke something, I have forgotten what. He phoned Hengyang and they sent out an American mechanic in a weapons carrier. He soon mended the plane, which took off for Henyang. The mechanic came to us for the night. He didn't know us, nor we him, but he had heard there were some foreigners in the town and got someone to bring him to our house. During the evening meal we told him of our predicament. Immediately he suggested that we travel back with him the next day. We set off the next morning, Cliff, Hilda, poor sick Arthur, the baby and I – four days after Raymond's birth. Travelling in a weapons carrier, both Arthur and I were able to lie down most of the way. The American took us almost to the foot of the mountain. The next day we hired chairs and ascended into the lovely coolness of Nanyoh, where Arthur slowly recovered.

My father announced the event to my mother's sister Jean in the following letter:

Letter of 18th July 1943 from Shaoyang

A few days ago I sent you a cable to announce the arrival of John Raymond. I don't know how long the cable would take to reach you, but I hope it will get to you eventually. I know you would be anxious to get the news.

It was a week ago today – Sunday evening, about six o'clock – that the young man arrived. Dr Pearson had to be called out of church to welcome him! Everything has gone splendidly, Elsie is doing fine and is happy and well. She is far less exhausted than we'd expected. And John Raymond is all that a baby should be. He was about nine pounds at birth. I think he will be like his elder brother. Arthur looked like Winston Churchill, and now young Raymond does too!

We have been lucky in the weather. The last few weeks have not been as hot as you expect in July. But hot days must soon be here. We hope to get up to Nanyoh mountain within the next two weeks, and I hope Elsie and the boys (the first time I have used the plural!) will be able to stay there until the end of September...

Life has been too busy for me in recent months and I have had more responsibility than I like. But I suppose one must put up with such things in war time. We are wondering if we can take furlough in six months' time. We are just getting in touch with the Missionary Society about it. If they could release us and the submarine danger was less we should like to go. I expect we should have to make straight for England to avoid more sea travel than necessary, but we could see about coming back your way. We should love to be able to come on our way back to China as we did last time. But this is all just speculation. We may not be able to have a furlough yet...

Letter of 9th August 1943 from Nanyoh (CVC)

We have had some busy days since I last wrote. After the arrival of Raymond, Elsie and the baby got on wonderfully and we began to hope that we might be able to get up to Nanyoh before the end of the month. The big problem was how to get from Shaoyang to Hengyang. The few buses are very old and rickety and often break down. They are run on charcoal gas and go very slowly. Without a breakdown the journey would take six or more hours, and all the time you would be cramped on a wooden seat and the whole bus would be terribly over-crowded.

After one of the recent air fights in central Hunan, an American pilot ran short of petrol and came down near to our place. A truck was sent to do some repairs to the plane. We entertained the airman and the mechanic – and we got a lift, servants, luggage, ourselves and all on the returning truck. It certainly was a wonderful stroke of luck. We called it 'providential', but I don't know if the airman thought so! We had to rush on with the final packing in order to get away with the truck.

We had Raymond baptised earlier than we would have done, as we wanted to have him baptised in Shaoyang. We had a special little service in the hospital chapel on the day before we left. We remembered that it was your birthday, and were glad. Li Chang Hsu, baptised the baby. It was a very nice service with just a few special friends present.

On the evening of July 23rd we had had our German friends the Kamphausens (also missionaries) and Dr Pearson in – Miss Hudson was still with us, and the American pilot was there – to celebrate Raymond's arrival. During supper I mentioned that it was our wedding anniversary and that we had a film of our wedding that we had never had the chance to see screened. Dr Pearson said that he had a projector and that, if the film fitted, we could all go and see the film after supper. The film did fit, and after various manipulations with the electric light wires, the projector was got ready, and we all saw the wedding scenes, with the little car, us coming out of the church and going away from the hotel. There was a lovely bit showing you saying goodbye to us when we were leaving in the car. It thrilled us very much. Fancy seeing the film for the first time on the seventh anniversary of our wedding...

Well we got up here on the 27th July and soon got our lovely thatched roof cottage fixed up... The cottage is in a lovely fairy-land of bamboos. A stream runs down by the side of the house and brings with it a welcome cool breeze. We have our meals on the verandah, which is covered with a thatched roof. We can look up and around to the bamboos and the rich green mountain foliage, and we can look down on the distant plain, stretched out before us. It is often concealed by a low mist or a low lying sea of curly white clouds.

We have definitely got permission to take furlough at the end of the year. We are very pleased about this, though we know it is best not to get too excited. We know we shall not be able to leave until someone else has taken over my work and we do not know yet what arrangements can be made for South China. Perhaps Rattenbury has some plan. Also travel conditions may be very difficult, and we shan't want to leave unless we can be sure of coming all the way home and not being stuck in South Africa. But it is fine, we have permission to come when it is possible. It will be wonderful to see you and everyone again.

Letter of 5th September 1943 from Nanyoh (CVC)

We are still here on this lovely mountain. The weather is cooler than it was and we get quite strong winds. We have no space for a dining room in this little cottage, so we have our meals on the verandah... I'm typing this on the verandah. The near view is of a mountain side thick with bamboos and shrubs, some of the latter being in flower. Just by the house are lovely over-hanging bamboos. The distant view is of the plain below, with the biggest river in Hunan running across it. We are certainly lucky to be able to get away to such a spot. It is not quite a holiday, as I still have a lot of correspondence to do up here – but it is a change…

From this point to the time of our return to England no letters survive. This is a great pity for the events my parents encountered were among the most remarkable of their lives. I am thus once again forced to rely on an extract from my mother's book.

Kukong

In the autumn of that year we went to live in Kukong. We sent most of our belongings into the country to a China Inland Mission station, where we thought they would be safer. However as chance would have it, that mission compound had a big fire shortly afterward and in the disturbance everything was looted. Some time later Dorothy Dymond saw her sewing machine, and we saw many of our books for sale on the street at Shaoyang. We were able to buy these items back again, but the rest was lost for ever. Because the situation was still precarious and a rapid evacuation always a possibility we only took with us the minimum of luggage.

Kukong was an interesting interlude. We occupied three rooms in a house on the hospital compound. Faithful Tien Yi, our cook, of course, went with us. All sorts of people appeared in Kukong. A number of British naval and army officers came several times on what must have been intelligence missions. The bishop of Hong Kong, Bishop Hall, was a frequent visitor. Cliff and he were kindred spirits and very good friends, so he usually stayed with us. On one of his visits he made the momentous decision to ordain a woman as a priest![15] This was the first anywhere in the Anglican Church and in so doing raised a tremendous storm in England. At the time we didn't know of his decision. All we knew was that he asked if he could stay in his room all morning undisturbed as he had an important decision to make. The woman was working all alone in a remote place near Kukong, ministering to all around, doing the work of a priest. There was no suitable man to do the job, so he decided to accept the reality of the situation and ordain her. After Hong Kong was taken by the Japanese, Bishop Hall, who had been on furlough at the time and thus escaped internment, set up his headquarters in a room on one of the college campuses in Kukong. He wasn't often there. He spent most of his time travelling round Kwangtung province caring for the scattered Christians.

'Friends Ambulance' men also often passed through and spent the night on the compound. They were a very interesting group, most of them conscientious objectors who had volunteered for relief work. They went with their trucks to Kunming, picked up a load of drugs which had been flown in over 'The Hump', and took them to hospitals scattered all over China, some several weeks' journey away. Once the truck was loaded they never left their precious cargoes. They slept on the trucks. It was up to them to repair their trucks and keep them going. As well as being capable, they were very brave men.

Leaving China

We had by then been out eight years and my health was poor. The following spring we decided we must try to get back to England. The only way to the coast was by a long and difficult journey by small boat. Arthur was not yet three, Ray was a few months old and I was in ill health. Clearly such a route was impossible. In Kukong there was an American army unit. We approached them and they said they would fly us out to Kunming[16]. It was a rough journey. The plane was a cargo plane with bucket seats around the sides. Soon most of us were airsick. When we arrived in Kunming Cliff hurried off to get coolies to take our suitcases. Just as he had gone the air-raid sirens sounded and the call 'Clear the airfield, planes are taking off'. Everybody started shouting, 'Run, run!'. Someone seized Arthur and ran off with him. I could hardly hold Ray let alone run with him. The Japanese planes were expected, all the American planes were taking off and everybody was still shouting, 'Run, run!'. Suddenly someone dashed up and took Ray from me and I managed to stagger to the edge of the runway as a plane went up just over my head. It was nasty! Then Cliff dashed breathlessly to me and helped me along.

Three days later we boarded an old Dakota to fly to Calcutta, over the notorious 'Hump'. Again bucket seats. Again almost everyone except Cliff was airsick. It was a terribly bumpy flight, then we hit an air pocket and dropped dramatically. The pilot righted the plane; but he had had enough. We were due to climb up over the Hump and there was already icing on the wings. He turned back. So there we were after four hours flying, once more back in Kunming. We tried again the next day; but I fainted as we were walking over to the plane, so that was the end of that. The pilot wouldn't take me. Still not all was lost. The pilot was so sorry for us he went straight over to the office and booked us on a proper passenger plane flying out on Easter Sunday – Arthur's third birthday.

A few days later we were on the plane flying to Dum Dum Airport, Calcutta. I behaved reasonably well this time, but it was Ray who was the star turn. When we were at our highest point, he passed out. The plane, as was normal in those days, was not pressurised. There was fortunately a doctor on board and he gave Ray artificial respiration. Soon afterwards the co-pilot came along to say we were losing height, and within minutes Ray was his usual cheerful self again. It is amazing how rapidly children recover!

The 'Hump' referred to was a notorious air route over the Himalayan foothills connecting India and China. At that time with the Japanese forces occupying north, east and south China and the mountains to the west it was the only route into non-occupied China. Six hundred aircraft were lost attempting this hazardous crossing. At the time cabins were unpressurised and many passengers passed out during the journey.

My mother continued her description of the journey back to England:

After a few days in Calcutta we boarded the train for Bombay. Though terribly hot, it was a fascinating journey right across India, that took two days and two nights. We then spent three tedious weeks in Bombay before embarking on a troop-ship for England. The war was still on, so we travelled in a convoy with two protecting frigates and a barrage of balloons. A strong wind soon blew the balloons away. After we passed through the Straits of Gibraltar we were sent off on our own because we were a fast boat and carrying troops we were too much of a target in the slow moving convoy. From there until we reached the Irish Sea we had to rely on our own speed.

Each night we were sent to bed with comforting words from the Bridge! 'All lights out. We are now travelling in dangerous waters. All passengers are advised to sleep in their clothes. Keep your life belts near you. Good-night'. Ray and I were in a big cabin with a number of women and children. Cliff and Arthur were next-door with a number of men and boys. Poor Ray was suffering from prickly heat and couldn't sleep so Cliff and I spent most of the nights walking up and down the passageway.

Finally we arrived at Liverpool, then travelled to Bristol where Cliff's sister Nell was waiting for us, then on to Weston-super-Mare where Cliff's mother was waiting to see her two grandsons for the first time.

It would have been a time of great joy for my grandmother seeing her son again after eight long and anxious years as well as meeting her grandchildren for the first time. But it would also have been a time tinged with sadness for my father knowing that neither his father nor elder brother would be there to greet him. His father had died shortly after his return to China in 1936 and his elder brother, Dick, the vicar of the lonely Cornish outpost of St Just, had committed suicide on New Years Day in 1937 in a fit of depression.

My parents spent their furlough in a house on the outskirts of Weston-super-Mare, which my grandmother had found for them.

Endnotes

1. General Secretary of the Methodist Missionary Society in London

2. In the Spanish Civil War.

3. Charlie Roberts was in charge of the American run Hunan Bible Institute, next door to the Hsin Ming T'ang.

4. With travel to Kuling for the summer break now impossible because of the war, Nanyoh proved a worthy substitute.

5. The Yale-in-China Association was founded in 1901 by Yale University as a private, non-profit organisation, financially and legally separate from University. It focused on the fields of medicine and education. Currently, under the title Yale-China Association, it promotes mutual understanding between the peoples of China and the United States, through a broad range of educational, medical, environmental and cultural programs in the United States, Hong Kong and China.

6. Chungking had become the capital of China in November 1937, just prior to the fall of Nanking.

7. Several films, including a 1942 Hollywood action movie, *The Flying Tigers*, starring John Wayne, have been made about their exploits.

8. Although interestingly enough when my mother told Dr Eitel of their choice of names his reaction was, 'Artur, a good German name'.

9. Hsin Ming T'ang – literally 'New Life Hall' – was a large, three storey, multi-purpose building within a walled compound, originally built as a theological college. After the burning of Changsha it became the main Methodist Missionary Society building in Changsha.

10. The American run Hunan Bible Institute (HBI) was situated in the next compound.

11. One of the main roads in Changsha.

12. The Friends Ambulance Unit were a Quaker organisation, staffed mainly by conscientious objectors, who throughout the war worked near the front line tending to the wounded of either side.

13. Rev Li Chang was the first Chinese chairman of the Methodist Hunan district. When the Communists came to power he was appointed by all the Christian denominations in Changsha to act as their spokesman in dealings with the new rulers. During the Cultural Revolution, when all churches were closed down, he was not allowed to work or beg and was forced to leave his wife and family. It is believed that he died of hunger.

14. Salt in China was a government monopoly, run a by state-owned organisation called the Salt Gabelle.

15. Florence Tim Oi Li became the first woman priest in the Anglican Church, when she was ordained by Bishop Hall in 1944. When the news reached Britain there was such an outcry she was forced to cease exercising her ministry. After many difficult years under the Communist government she visited Britain in 1984 and was honoured in a special service in Westminster Abbey. In the same year the General Synod of the Church of England voted in favour of women priests and Florence Tim Oi Li's historic role was at last recognised. Her autobiography *Much Loved Daughter* was published in 1985. She died in 1992.

16. The capital of Yunnan province, which lies adjacent to the Burmese and Vietnamese borders.

Chapter 6
The Post-war Years

大

My father returned to China as soon as possible after the war ended, leaving my mother, Arthur and me behind in England until the situation was more stable and we could come and join him. He sailed from Liverpool to Bombay aboard the SS Exeter. From Bombay he travelled across India by train to Calcutta, where he stayed for several weeks. From there he flew over the Hump to Kunming in Yunnan province of China and completed his journey to Changsha by road.

The first letter we have was one he sent my mother while passing through the Red Sea.

Letter of 16th November 1945 from the SS City of Exeter on the Red Sea

We got to Port Said about 3 pm on Wednesday, and soon after arrival I was given your letter. I don't know when I have been so thrilled with a letter. I'd been just longing to hear a word. The inevitable silence since we said goodbye on the doorstep has seemed so long…

We had about twenty-four hours in Port Said and went ashore several times. We shopped, visited Simon Arzt's Café¹ twice, walked to the de Lessep's statue, strolled about the streets and visited the new Catholic cathedral. The cathedral is one of the most beautiful churches I have ever seen. Not too ornate. The lighting effect from orange, yellow and blue windows high up in the building was gorgeous. The floor was a lovely, and not too elaborate, mosaic. There was a great dome over the sanctuary with lots of painted representations, including the signs of the zodiac. In big letter were the words 'Mary is the Mother of the Universe' – in French. Around the building, inside it, were marvellous statues of various saints – mainly French, I think. I was particularly struck by one of Joan of Arc.

Port Said is as full of swindlers as ever, and is I should imagine, as iniquitous as ever. We were diddled over some oranges and even the post office was going to give us an unfair rate of exchange. Simon Arzt had some useful things, but was pretty empty compared with pre-war days. They had watches and fountain pens. The watches were over twenty pounds. Some of the Chinese bought them. I bought a British made (Valentine) fountain pen for under two pounds. I don't know whether I was wise. I also bought some summer cotton socks and some stockings for shorts. We also bought a big tin of boiled sweets – lovely ones.

Coming through the Suez Canal was lovely. It was a beautiful moonlit evening. There was a gorgeous red sunset. After dark the lights of motors, trains, buoys and canal stations were very interesting. At one point we saw a plane come down onto a floodlit airfield… When we awoke this morning we were in the Red Sea. It is a gorgeous day today, sunny with a calm, blue sea and a strong cooling breeze. The barren hills of Egypt are clear – looking a brownish red…

Saturday 17th November
Another lovely day – clear and sunny. The sea is blue with white horses, created by a fresh breeze. It's warm and I am in my shorts. A swimming pool has been erected, but not many people have been in it yet. We've passed a good many ships… On this trip we have seen many more ships than on any other trip. One gets the impression of a huge amount of British shipping on this Eastern run…

Yesterday we had a boat drill… We are due at Port Sudan

tomorrow and Bombay on the 26th or 27th...

The Chinese missionaries and some of the Chinese had cholera inoculations yesterday. Apparently there are no side-effects. We have the second jab in a week's time. Before flying into China we have to have cholera inoculation certificates dated within three months...

Sunday 18th November

...I must now finish this letter and have it ready to post at Port Sudan. We get there around midday...

The purser is now receiving letters, so I must hurry. I hear we shall not be able to go ashore...

Letter of 19th November 1945 from the SS City of Exeter on the Red Sea (CVC to EMC)

We had a very short stay at Port Sudan yesterday – less then two hours. We tied up at the quayside about 11.45 am. Passengers weren't allowed ashore except to step off the ship on to the quay, where there were Africans selling things like shells, slippers, coral stones, necklaces made of coral, etc. The docks looked neat and clean, and there were several handsome buildings within sight. You'll remember the general picture of the docks and harbour buildings with a background of desert. If there had been time we could have had a ride in little boats with glass bottoms, through which you look at the beautiful coral and brightly coloured fish. Port Sudan seems a great place for fish. Some of the crew caught them. There was never long to wait before a bite. I saw several bright yellow and bright red ones caught. My dislike of catching fish was deepened as I saw these lovely little fish with their flesh torn by the hook and gasping for breath.

A good many passengers got off. Everything was very orderly. On the quay were two groups of Africans. At the back were men in blue robes who pushed luggage trucks on the quayside; in the foreground were rougher looking men with long, black, curly and rather dusty hair. The latter belonged to a tribe that inhabits the coastal region... These men filled up the gangway and carried the luggage of the disembarking passengers to the men in blue, who put them on the trucks and then pushed the trucks to the railway station. Each time one of them stepped off the gangway they were searched by the native policemen. Most of the passengers who got off were going up to Khartoum.

Sudan is a condominium, a place ruled jointly by two countries – Britain and Egypt. The Union Jack and the Egyptian flag were flying on the buildings. I'm told that Britain does all the work! We only took on two passengers – both Indians. We didn't take on any at Port Said. So now the ship is half empty. At our table there is only Fred (a fellow missionary) and myself and the Malay man. All three of us have left behind a wife and children, and this morning we were wishing the empty places could be taken by our families!...

It is very hot at the moment. Last night we had the wind catcher in our porthole and the electric fan on.

Tuesday 20th November

We are now in the Gulf of Aden, having left the Red Sea and turned East. About two hours ago we passed the island of Perim. It is a British island, of course, as it occupies a strategic position. It is in the Straits of Bab el Mandeb, the entrance to the Red Sea. For several hours this morning we saw land on both sides, Abyssinia and Arabia. Now that we have turned the corner we have land only on one side, the south Arabian coast near Aden.

It is another gorgeous day. The sun is shining, the sea is very calm and there's a refreshing breeze. On the whole we have had wonderful weather on this trip. Through the Red Sea the sun has shone by day and the moon by night... Last night it was a full moon, and we saw the moon come up from behind a solitary mountain. Later we saw a group of twelve islands – the Twelve Apostles. We could count them in the moonlight.

This morning Fred Cram and I had a long talk with Mr Bryan, a Baptist missionary, about the policies and work of our respective Missions. In Shantung the Baptists withdrew many missionaries and annually reduced their grant. The result was that their outstanding Chinese went to other Christian organisations...and things got so low that they had to alter their programme, send more missionaries and increase the grant. A very interesting example of the folly of pushing self-support and devolution too quickly. In Shansi, where Bryan is now, having had the Shantung example before them, they've gone more slowly. Most of their village churches in Shansi have no resident pastors. Their services are taken by lay leaders, who have had some training in short-term schools.

After talking together for a while Mr and Mrs Bryan played Fred and me at quoits. We won every game!

Saturday 24th November

Another lovely day with the sun shining and the sea like a mill pond... I'm told that India won't be too hot at this time of the year – it's the coolest time. Calcutta will be cooler than Bombay and there we shall probably need ordinary suits in the evening.

We may stay in Bombay only a few hours... I wrote to our Mission in Bombay (air mail from Port Said) asking them to do what they could to book us places on the train... Bombay customs are said to be 'sticky'...

I have made some notes on the Tambaran (Madras) Report that I was reading and have added some thoughts of my own. I think the result can serve as a kind of guide for my next term in China. I have put down as part of the programme such things as: 1. Get the China Assembly (Seven Districts Conference) going; 2. Push lay leadership, providing short-term schools at the slack periods of the year; 3. Make use of things of value in Chinese culture (eg. reverence for ancestors, baptising children at a time of importance in the child's life); 4. Advocate united action where two or more denominations are working in one place; 5. Church leaders to take an active part in China's reconstruction, through various forms of social service eg. better health, better homes, better recreation, better education etc; 6. Advance self-support.

I think it will be a help to have this programme in mind. I am very glad I have had this leisure to think things out. When I get to China the trees will loom so large I shan't be able to see the wood!

Sunday November 25th
We are getting near the end of the journey now. When we awake tomorrow morning we shall probably be at Bombay.

Well, my dearest, I think I'll bring this letter to a close… All my love to you, very dear wife…

On arriving at Bombay my father took the train across India to Calcutta. The journey took two nights and a day.

Calcutta

My father stayed in Calcutta for several weeks. With many missionaries returning to Yunnan, Hupeh and Hunan provinces of China via that route, Calcutta, where they changed from surface travel to air, was seen as a serious bottleneck. The Mission House asked my father to stay for a while to help with the necessary arrangements to get people back into China. He had to arrange air flights to Kunming and get heavy baggage off by sea. Although there were Methodist missionaries in Calcutta it was considered unreasonable to ask them to take on this extra burden.

Letter of 5th December 1945 from 14/2 Sudder Street, Calcutta (CVC to EMC)

I've been wanting to write to you for the last few days; but I've been so rushed that I haven't managed it...

I've written a long letter to Harold Rattenbury reporting on the situation here and making suggestions... Rev Culshaw, the minister here, is too busy to take on the extra work of the China agency... I've said, after consultation here, that I think the best solution is for Hector Chick[2] to have full responsibility for China affairs... I've gone to lots of places and made lots of enquires about getting the stored baggage transported to China. Thomas Cooks suggested it may not be so long before they can send it. The freight departments of their offices in Hong Kong and Shanghai have been re-opened...

The services here on Sunday were very impressive. The morning service was splendidly attended... For the evening service the church was quite full before the time to begin had come. Extra chairs had to be brought in. The great majority were service men, including some Americans. There were sixty-eight to the Communion Service...

I never told you of the train journey. Fred and I shared a four berth compartment with a man, his wife and a little girl aged three. They were Indian Jews on their way to Calcutta from Palestine. He was strong in his views on British policy in Palestine. We ought to 'keep our promise' and make Palestine a Jewish home! The little girl spoke Hebrew. She called her Daddy 'Abba'. It made the New Testament words 'Abba, Father' live as never before.

Well...it won't be so long before you'll be coming out. I miss you all so much...

Letter of 11th December 1945 from Calcutta (CVC to EMC)

A very Happy Christmas! I've got reservations for myself and Miss Scott to fly to Chungking on the 28th. Ted Outerbridge, a Bermudan missionary doctor, advises Chungking rather than Kunming. By the 28th all the other China folk will have passed on, and I hope I shall have been able to list all the stored baggage – there will be about 120 pieces – so that, when the way to China is properly open, Cooks can deal with it.

Rattenbury's latest cable and letter tell me to push on the others as soon as possible, to relieve Calcutta staff, make arrangements for the future managing of China affairs in Calcutta and get to China myself as quickly as possible.

I'm very busy these days mainly helping the ladies to get off. It means long waits at the CNAC (China National Aviation Corporation), customs etc and filling in forms, helping to undo and do up boxes. The five ladies have forty-one heavy pieces to be stored here. Imagine my dismay when I met them at Calcutta station!

Reverend Conibear wires from Shanghai that the route from Shanghai to Hankow is now fully open. Things are looking up. I hear Moody has been left lots of things by the Americans, including a jeep, cases of soap, shaving cream, stores etc, many sleeping bags and some sheets. If I go that way I hope to collect a bit. There are many razor blades – huge numbers apparently.

Mrs Redhead is wearing eight dresses, three pairs of underwear, jumper, costume, scarves and an overcoat to go on the plane. She looks square with it all on!...

I have received another lovely letter from you... I felt so sad to think of Arthur being subdued and sad for his Daddy. I long to see them both again. They are so little and can not really understand why their Daddy has gone from them...

Back in China again

At last on 27th December 1945, after most of the other returning China missionaries had passed through Calcutta, my father flew to Kunming. Arriving there he was delighted to discover his old colleague Rev Ma Chi Yun and his wife, with their three children, anxious to get back to Hunan, but unable to find transport.

Letter of 28th December 1945 from Kunming (CVC to EMC)

I got here a few hours ago. Last night about 11:30 pm I went to the Great Eastern Hotel and sat to await going through customs at 2 am... I dozed for about an hour. No difficulty with customs. At four the bus left for Dum Dum (Calcutta airport). Just before five the plane started. It was a passenger plane like the one we went in before. For about an hour we were flying in the dark. Then the horizon grew red and gradually, very gradually, the sun rose. It was a very red sun.

For the first part of the journey the plane was very smooth and I felt more at ease than on any other occasion when flying. We got to Bhamo in north Burma about 8 am. But the airfield was covered in a thick ground fog and the pilot – an American – could not find it. He tried for fifty minutes, circling round and round at sharp angles and diving down into the mist and up again. I think all the passengers were thoroughly scared when he flew very low in the fog. We feared he'd hit a tree. We all wished he'd leave the fog alone. After fifty minutes he moved away to another landing strip, which was near a big river, in which we could see destroyed launches and other boats. He was just going to land when he received a message that the Bhamo fog had lifted. So back we went and landed there – at 9.45 am. It had taken four hours and three quarters to get there. The pilot told us he had only taken 'reasonable safe risks'. The passengers weren't so sure about the 'safe'!

At Bhamo we were supplied with a coffee and a good lunch box – much more than I could manage – on the plane. Bhamo to Kunming took about one hour and three quarters. It was a little bumpy going over the Hump, but I never felt at all sick. This trip made me realise how bad some of her journeys were last year. This is a good time of the year for weather, though they say April is a bad time. My flying hours are now twenty-three and a half! At Kunming I had to wait about an hour for the CNAC bus. From the CNAC office I got rickshaws – $400 each! The waiting room at the aerodrome is just the same. It brought back so many memories.

I am staying at the Moodys' and have the top room that we had... The Moodys are just the same. I brought a little doll for Beryl and she seems very pleased with it... This house looks dreadfully shabby after England and the Methodist Church in Calcutta. In fact China looks dirty and shabby and very inefficient after England! But the Chinese people look cheerful.

Tomorrow I'm going to the Friends Ambulance Unit and the BMM to see about convoys. I hear the FAU have trucks going through to Hsiangtan. I hope I can get to bed early. I had no real sleep last night and a very short one the night before...

Letter of 8th January 1946 from Kunming (CVC to EMC)

There are now good hopes of getting a truck to take all the Hunan folk back to Hunan. Also to take some of the American stores. If the plan works it will be worth my arriving in Changsha two weeks later than I might have done. If the Chinese were left to get back by themselves, it would be a very long time before we saw some of them. The Ma family might have to wait a very long time.

The plan now is to take a truck to Changsha – a big US one – which is supposed to belong to the Hankow YMCA. A young American YMCA man called Charlie Jorgensen ('Call me Charlie', he says) will drive. He has had a lot of experience driving trucks. Actually the ownership of the truck is in question. It was given by the US army to the YMCA Emergency Service Unit. An American called Paul Sung was in the unit. Now he claims the truck is his, or ostensibly, the Hankow YMCA's!

The truck was recently damaged…and I have to get it repaired (at South West China District expense) before we go… Tomorrow Jorgensen and I dine with the Chinese general of a transport unit. We hope to arrange for our truck to travel with a Chinese convoy en route to Nanking. We shall then have protection from bandits and company in case of engine trouble.

If I'd not considered our Chinese here I could probably have got off about two days ago on a FAU truck – but I couldn't have taken any stores. It is disappointing to be held up again, but the advantages outweigh the disadvantages of an extra two week delay. In the meantime I am doing some finance for the South West China District, while Moody is at Synod…

The pound is changing at about $4,400. Today I have wired Chungking for £10,000, which should bring $44 million! Actually the financial situation is better than it has been for a long time. The cost of living is down and the dollar has been steady for a while. Goods are beginning to reach Shanghai from America, and it is thought that as more goods appear on the market things will get cheaper…

Since I last wrote I've had several talks with Ma. The first time we met he had a weep before he could talk. They walked with the six children, carrying some of them, about twenty li a day. The Japs got nearer, they could hear the gunfire. They gave the three youngest children to three different people, two to *country women who said they would take them to the hills, or out-of-the-way villages and the third to a military man in a good position. They have been in correspondence with the latter, but have not heard about the others. They'd like us to look for them on the way back, but I don't know if we can manage it. It's out of our way – we shan't take the long road via Kweilin, and it would not be a good thing to leave the truck stationary for a day, when there is a risk of bandits. It would mean leaving the convoy, but we will see. I've offered Ma leave from Hunan to go and look for them later when the weather is better. His idea is if the children are well cared for to leave them, if they are not, to try to negotiate for their return. I think Mrs Ma wants them badly.*

The Moodys were awfully good to them when they arrived. Their sitting room had to be de-loused after the Mas sat in it. They were all given a bath in the Moodys' bathroom, their clothes burnt and various odd new garments found for them. Moody has now given me $70,000 relief money for the Mas to get 'mien i'[3] for the truck journey and the colder Hunan weather. Ma's religious experience seems as strong as before. Our Hunan folk are outstanding in this district...

I do long to hear that you have news of sailing, and yet I feel I ought to see the housing situation in Changsha first... Also I ought to know what the milk situation is. Hollman says there is a dairy in Changsha, but very expensive. I must find out what it is like and explore the possibilities of keeping a cow or goats! Conditions will improve rapidly, I think, and American goods will soon be generally available...

Circular Letter of 13th January 1946 from Kunming
The reports I have heard of the flight have been ghastly. Of the handful of persons known to me there have been the following losses. Ma – three children, Lung Si Fu – two children, Bible Woman Ch'eng Yu – one daughter, Mrs Cheng Chi-kwei –

one child. I dread to think what the complete toll of death and suffering must have been! There were corpses all along the road and many children lost contact with their parents. Bandits played havoc with the folk. Lung Si Fu left two girls in the charge of a person known to him, a person whom they considered quite reliable — left them for just a few minutes. They've never seen that person or the two girls again…

Prices are still ridiculous — a box of matches costs $80, a short rickshaw ride $400, average Sunday collection at Zion $35,000. The pound gets about $4,400. Prices have been higher. They have now been stable for a little while, but they have gone up by leaps and bounds in what was occupied China. It is said that American goods are pouring into Shanghai…

Kunming is an amazing place. Jeeps and US trucks everywhere. You see jeeps with markings like 'Chinese Commandos', 'Chinese Army X Division' etc… Every mission seems to have a jeep. Moody has both a jeep and a truck and petrol — all free. Also our folk and some other missions in Kunming have had a staggering windfall of US supplies — stationary by the case, two cases of razor blades (tens of thousands!), two cases of good tooth brushes, two cases of tooth powder, cases of coffee (12lb tins), butter (10lb tins), chocolate, tinned vegetables, meat, puddings, cheese, lemonade powder, milk etc. Also sleeping bags, army clothing, big rubber over-boots, anti-bug powder, footballs, cases of matches, cases of chewing tobacco etc etc. In Kunming shops there are plenty of watches and clocks, fountain pens etc. Chinese military police go about in US white jeeps…

The 'flight' referred to in the previous letter occurred shortly after we left China in 1944. In the summer of that year, after several years when the Japanese front line had changed very little, they suddenly advanced with great rapidity to take the whole of Hunan and parts of Kweichow. This offensive, named '*itche go*', had the twin aims of linking up Japanese forces in the north with those in the south, which was of strategic importance now that the Americans had control of much of the coastal seas, and secondly to take the airfields in south Hunan and Kweichow, from which the American and Chinese planes were bombing their forces. Hundreds of thousands of refugees fled to escape from the advancing Japanese army.

Letter of 17th January 1946 from Kunming (CVC to EMC)

I am very busy getting ready to go. We hope to leave on the 20th. The Chinese military have repaired the truck and we think we can get a pass for it... Jorgensen is making various calls to try to get some petrol... We shall need at least five drums to get to Changsha. All our Hunan folk are here now waiting... I've got a lot of US stuff packed up, but I do not know if there will be room on the truck to take much...

The journey will be tough and cold, but being all together will make it quite fun. Moody has given the Ma family some relief money to supplement their clothing and I have given them some US army winter underclothing! I shall wear US army uniform, minus badges, for the journey. Most foreigners in Kunming look like US soldiers! I am taking four US mosquito nets with me to give to needy colleagues, also a little clothing, rubber overboots, lots of air mail paper, razor blades, tooth powder, tooth brushes, lots of soap, 24lbs of coffee, 18lbs of peanut butter, chocolate, about twelve tins of baking powder, a very big tin of tomato juice and one of tomato puree, a very big tin of bacon, some tins of lemonade, three big (about 10lbs each) tins of cheese, tinned chocolate pudding, lots of anti-insect

powder and lotion, some face towels, two or three old towels...
I do hope I can get it all on the truck. We hope to get to
Changsha in about nine days.

I have achieved one of my ambitions. I've driven a jeep! I drove
one back from the lake — about eight miles — a few nights ago. It
was in the dark, and I did not know the road, I was driving on
the right-hand side of the road for the first time — so I was very
cautious, but I loved it. A jeep is wonderful to manoeuvre...

It will be thrilling to get to Changsha. I expect my next
letter will be from there, though I may be able to send one from
Kweiyang. Jorgensen and I will probably sleep on the truck en
route. I'll use a US army sleeping bag as they are tough and
heavy and have a khaki blanket.

All my love to you dearest and to the lovely imps. When I get
to Changsha I'll begin planning accommodation.

Letter of 24th January 1946 from Kweiyang: The journey back to Changsha (CVC to EMC)

I'm in my room at the China Inland Mission, Kweiyang. It's
after 10 pm, but I want to scribble a few lines before I go to bed
in case I can't manage it tomorrow.

We left Kunming about 10 am on the twenty-first. Mrs
Moody, Dr Galbraith, the Sellars and a group of Chinese were
at the gate of Zion Church to see us off. The truck is a big US
army one, with ten wheels. It was packed with luggage, perched
upon which at the back were CVC, Ma, and two of the Ma
children... We have had many jerks and bumps at the back and
at times it has not been too comfortable, but we've all been in
good spirits — enjoying travelling together and glad to be on the
way back to Changsha. The children have sung a lot.

The first day we did 170 kilometres and stopped at a place
called Chan Y, where the US formerly had an airfield and base.
Before we left, Jorgensen had succeeded in getting a paper from

the Chinese SOS[4], giving us the right to get petrol, oil etc and have any necessary repairs done at CSOS stations en route to Changsha – and all free! Jorgensen wangled this through an introduction to the CSOS from an American officer.

On arrival at Chan Y, after leaving the Chinese at a hotel, we took the truck on to the Chinese SOS. It was dark then. We were received with honours – given coffee, and a room which used to be occupied by US officers, with spring beds and a 'huo p'en'. A sentry was put to guard the truck all night. In the morning we had a posh breakfast with the Chinese officers and interviewed a general. We had coffee with him and wrote in his Visitors' Book. Then we were taken to the officer in charge of the repair shop, where we had a new spring put in the truck and some other repairs done, and filled up with petrol and oil then departed without paying one cent. There were no Americans in the place then, but we received such honours as an American officer would have received. We were quite frank about who we were, though we were both wearing US khaki – without badges of course. The next day we had a very late start – we only did about 140 kilometres, staying the night at P'an Hsien. Jorgensen and I spent the night with Bosshardt of the CIM.

Bosshardt talked about his eighteen months captivity in the hands of the Reds. He is a great man and lives in a modest rented Chinese house in P'an Hsien, a small place, tucked in among the mountains. When we arrived he was teaching English to four people, one of whom was his own servant. From Chan Y to P'an Hsien we climbed and descended many hills. But the next day made the day before seem like a level run. We only did a hundred kilometres between 10 am and 4 pm.

We got a late start because of going to the Chinese SOS to fill up with petrol and oil. The truck was guarded by a sentry again that night! The road is just amazing – mountain after mountain was crossed by long steep, zig-zag roads. The curves *were terrifically sharp sometimes, and the roads sometimes ran along precipices. The roads would reach summits higher (I should think) than Kuling. I'd heard much about the Burma Road – the Kunming-Kweiyang section of it – but it is much more wonderful than I'd ever imagined. It goes over mountain after mountain – mountains that would be famous in England – for about 200 miles. There can be no other stretch of road like it in the world. One sharp climb was done in twenty-three curves. On the top was a board in which were written the following words in Chinese 'It is the strength of the War of Resistance that has built the S.W. road'.*

We stayed last night at a China Travel Service hotel. Today we have done about 240 kilometres, part of it over mountains. I used to wonder why cars took so long to do the journey from Kunming to Kweiyang – about 450 miles. Now I know! We've also had a spot of engine trouble and two punctures… We had US flags on the trucks and to all the folk on the way we looked just like GIs. Everywhere people shouted 'ting hao' ('very good') or 'lao mei' ('foreigners'), sticking up their thumbs and grinning. Even the mountain villages could say 'OK'. There are no Americans stationed on the road now, only in Kunming, but when the convoys were passing regularly, the bigger places on the road all had convoy service stations with a group of Americans stationed there. We've had nothing but friendliness everywhere…

We intend to stop in Kweiyang for one day – some repairs are necessary – and then push on into Hunan. We will take the truck to the CSOS in the morning. Tomorrow night I may sleep on the truck. Someone will have to, unless we get another Chinese sentry!…

Letter of 2nd February 1946 from Chih Kiang, Hunan (CVC to EMC)

We've been thirteen days on the way from Kunming to

Changsha and here I am writing this letter in Chih Kiang, western Hunan. Since leaving Kweiyang a week ago today we've had mishaps and adventures. The first day out from Kweiyang we got to the fork where the roads to Hunan and Kiangsi separate. We purposely took the Kiangsi road for a few miles to try to find one of the Ma's twins – the little girl and the child they were most concerned about. The other two are boys, given to people for whom they will be only sons and who therefore are likely to care for them well. We got to the village and Ma got down from the truck to enquire. The first person he asked knew at once where his daughter was. The Ma family and some of the others walked into the countryside for a few li. After about two hours they returned greatly rejoicing with the little girl. She'd been well cared for and the foster parents wept when they let her go. Ma only paid $30,000, which at present rates is a small amount. The Ma family were most excited and happy. The other three Ma children almost quarrelled as to who should nurse the returned child. We could not go a long distance out of the way – we had thirteen people on the truck and petrol limited – searching for the other two children, and the Mas seemed content just to have the girl back. They are sure the two boys are well cared for.

The next day was spent mainly stationary on the road repairing the engine of the truck. But everyone seemed cheerful enough. For the third night in a row Jorgensen and I slept on our truck. The next night was spent here in Chih Kiang with the Germans at the CIM… The next day got us past Ankiang. Then our big troubles began. Late in the afternoon as we got near to the top of a mountain the engine of the truck broke down – the piston broke, part of the crank shaft etc. It was impossible to repair the damage. A brief 'pow-wow' followed, and the outcome was that we decided to get our folk down the mountain before nightfall and get them to Changsha by other means if possible. I would return to Chih Kiang to get the help of the Chinese SOS, Jorgensen and T'an would stay on the mountain with the truck. Passing motors were hailed, and the rest of us went back to Ankiang for the night. I, at least, felt wretched, not knowing how we were going to get out of the mess.

There was a lot to do in Ankiang. We bought food (eggs, mien, peanut toffee, biscuits etc) and gave them to Chinese soldiers who were leaving for Changsha by jeep the next day to give to Jorgensen when they got to the top of the mountain. I interviewed the drivers of various trucks that were spending the night in Ankiang, and being a foreigner, I managed to arrange for our Chinese to proceed on their journey in various trucks — mainly military — the next day. Then I had to supply people with travel money etc. I got to bed about midnight. In the night the prospects seemed grim. I was awake soon after 3 am longing for dawn to come. I got up before dawn, went out and found a charcoal-burning commercial van about to leave for Yu Shu Wan en route for Chih Kiang and managed to get a lift on it. At Yu Shu Wan I got a lift on a similar vehicle to Chih Kiang, paying $6,000 for this and nothing for the first. At Chih Kiang I went to the Chinese SOS who were very helpful. They agreed to send out another truck engine, but a good deal of arranging had to be done. They could not get going until the next day. So I spent most of that day and night at the SOS Headquarters, had supper with some of the officers and spent hours that night chatting with various soldiers. We set off the next day about 10 am and got to Ankiang about one o'clock.

We got to the top of the mountain about 3 pm. Ma had remained with T'an and Jorgensen, his family going on with some of the others. Great rejoicing to see me back so soon and with another engine and mechanics and a car with a crane on it. The mechanics got to work at once. Alas one was careless with a cigarette and the engine — the broken one — caught fire. Huge

*flames arose. The truck was by a mountain house made of wood.
It looked as though both the truck and the house might be
destroyed. The occupants of the house shrieked and wanted to
pour water on the burning petrol, but we managed to stop them.
The rescue car pushed the burning truck away from the house,
then foolishly pushed it back still nearer to the house. More
shrieks followed before it was pushed away again. Then
Jorgensen remembered his fire extinguisher – got it out – and
put out the fire.*

*The result of the fire was that all the rubber and wiring
connected with the engine was quite destroyed. There was
nothing to be done but for the car, plus me, to go back to Chih
Kiang – 75 miles away – to get new parts. It was New Year's
night and we'd brought up food and 'tien hsin'[5] for everyone
on the mountain to have that night. But the driver, the
mechanic and I returned to Ankiang and spent 'kuo nien'[6] in
an inn. I was up early this morning, had mien at Yu Shu Wan,
then went to Chih Kiang aerodrome. The Chinese are in
command – all the Americans having left. They gave us most of
what we needed from an old truck. Then we went on to the
CSOS for more petrol for the rescue car for this extra round
trip. It was very difficult to get it. The CO wanted to help, but
regulations were very strict and petrol short. Also there were
many people off duty because of kuo nien.*

*I urged the CO not to punish the careless mechanic, as he'd
given up his New Year in coming up the mountain, and they
agreed. However, various wrangling had to be done to enable the
CO to give the extra petrol. Everything was fixed about 3 pm.
Hoped to get well on the way back to Ankiang, but the driver
and mechanic said the rescue car needed minor repairs. This I
took to mean, 'We want to have New Year festivities with our
friends'. I protested a little, but not too much. Left them to go
to their friends and came on to the CIM.*

233

The rescue car is to call for me about 5.30 am. We should get to the mountain about midday. I hope we shall be able to get the engine fixed up. My next letter should give the answer!...

In Kweiyang all movement in the streets stops from 7 am to 7.20 am, when loud speakers give directions for physical exercises...and people are supposed to do them!

Back again in Changsha

Letter of 9th February 1946 from Changsha (CVC to EMC)

Here I am at last — actually in the Hsin Ming T'ang!

When I got back to the top of the mountain with the coils and wires to replace those that were burnt out, about a day and a half's work was needed to get the new engine fixed and working. When at last we got away we all held our breaths for the first few miles, especially since we were still travelling uphill. Would the engine keep going? It did, although once some oil caught fire and we had to use the fire extinguisher again.

On the second morning we reached Shaoyang and stopped there for several hours... It was a joy to be there and to see so many old friends, but the destruction made me sad. The Wrights', the Pearsons' and our house are all in ruins. The church has little else than its walls... I walked over the ruins of the missionaries residences. The fireplace in our sitting room was there, but only part of its wall. I picked a violet from the garden for you... The Chinese minister's house is in surprisingly good condition, also some of the hospital buildings, especially the hospital chapel. I felt nostalgic as I walked the familiar paths of the hospital compound and saw the paths outside where we used to take Arthur...

The headmaster, Mr Ts'ai, and his wife both have

tuberculosis badly. Mr Ts'ai was very pathetic and has nearly lost his voice. He wept when he spoke to me. I don't think he will live very long...

I was very pleased with the way Dr Tang has got the hospital restarted – on a small scale. He has got very little equipment, but has recovered a few iron beds from somewhere...

Our truck got to the Hsin Ming T'ang about 3.30 pm... Nobody I knew, apart from Miss Hsieh, was there. The gatekeeper has changed... Li, who was out, returned when we were unloading the truck and...Mrs Li and the other children, as well as the Paoking orphans, are now on their way here. John Foster did not return until quite late. I think he is very relieved to see me...

I have sent a cable to Rattenbury to say that I have arrived and there is accommodation for the family here... I can't make up my mind whether or not it would be right for you to come out before the summer. I long for you all to come, and I know how you long to come, and I should just hate to disappoint you by suggesting a postponement, but there are some snags... John has got the Hsin Ming T'ang free for the use of missionaries, but there is very little furniture in it – just a few odd pieces. The walls and the ceilings are very dirty and the plaster is down in places... There are no stoves. The third storey is full of post office people, including wives and children – all seem very noisy. In the big room outside the flat are some Chinese relief workers... The servants' rooms outside are full of refugee workers, as is the storeroom... The compound seems crowded – too crowded I think. It is almost impossible to keep the place clean. It's dirty now. The drainage was always bad here. It is now very bad...

I cannot free the compound of our tenants yet, though I shall try to reduce their numbers. There is great economic stress in Hunan and a great shortage of houses in Changsha. Since Synod rice has risen from 5,000 a tan to 25,000 a tan. In

Hengyang it is 40,000 a tan. There is a shortage of rice and famine is expected in parts. Our workers have not enough to live on and many are in debt. The Mission House has not agreed to Synod's request for increased salaries and for an advancement of money to buy rice... Everyone is living very simply. Only absolutely essential repairs – repairs to preserve property – have been done. Only a few pieces of furniture have been bought... John has a semi-foreign breakfast, but has Chinese food with the Chinese for the rest of the day. No money is expended unless absolutely necessary. You feel you have to be super-economical when your Chinese workers are so hard put to...

I hear that locomotives have reached Shanghai from America. I believe the bridges are being repaired. The few trains that there are are very crowded. In view of all this I can't help wondering whether I ought to send a cable advising you not to arrive until after the summer. Another difficulty would be finding the time to meet you. The district is alive with problems, and the rice shortage, which will be at its most acute as the summer approaches, presents urgent questions. When John goes, and until Harry returns, Jefferies and I will be the only missionaries here. For me to go away for a month or so during the next three or four months would be very difficult.

Once back in Changsha my father was able to start reorganising the Church's activities throughout the province and repairing damage to Church property after the turmoil and chaos of the war.

Letter of 17th March 1946 from Lingling:
Relief work (CVC to EMC)

I am writing this in Bishop Stevens's house...having come here with UNRRA (United Nations Relief and Rehabilitation

Agency) and CNRRA (China National Relief and Rehabilitation Agency) people. Lingling hospital had written me urging me to come and see the difficulties. So I decided to take the opportunity to come. I've brought with me five million dollars for hospital rebuilding. CNRRA had promised this, but have been slow in fulfilling the promise. We left in two weapons carriers — US army cars a bit bigger than a jeep — and a Ford car, on Wednesday. Horatio Hawkins, the UNRRA director, three of the UNRRA ladies and various CNRRA officials came. The first day we got to Hengyang. We rested at the bus station at Nanyoh. The China Travel Service place was in ruins and some other buildings in the area seemed to be damaged, but for the most part things looked much the same as they ever did. The mountains were enshrouded in clouds. Hengyang is just ruins.

The Presbyterians have got the hospital building repaired and the work is going on there in full swing… I stayed with Hawkins at the CNRRA headquarters. The next day we got to Kiyang for lunch. I went to the church at once… The church premises are in remarkably good condition. It is the only city church in the district still intact. The rest of Kiyang is badly knocked about…

The road from Changsha had been very bad — slippery, wet and muddy. At some places the Ford had to be pushed through the mud. We skidded most dangerously and once were two or three feet from a deep cut in the side of the road. Another CNRRA motor that left Changsha just before we did turned over near Kiyang and one man was killed.

We got to Lingling in the late afternoon. Near Hsiangtan we had to cross a river in a slow ferry. There was a line of cars waiting, but we were given priority… At Lingling I came over to the Bishop's and the other foreigners went to the Catholic Mission.

Lingling is as complete a ruin as I have seen anywhere. It really is a mess… Our Church compound on the street is just a pile of bricks and debris. The buildings on the hospital compound are burnt out. The walls stand, but that is all… The hospital carries on heroically in the school building. It has about fifty beds. Dr Huang is terribly over-worked. Things are not going well in the hospital. Dr Huang's superintendency is not acceptable to the staff… There's a lot of dissatisfaction and nasty insinuations about him are being made… There are probably faults on both sides. Huang does not have the qualities of leadership…he needs to share the financial responsibilities with others. If others have it they will realise how difficult things really are…

The famine is worse than I had expected. In some parts of the country people are dying of starvation. Herbs and roots and the husks (milled to a powder) of rice are being eaten. Beggars abound. And a big proportion of the fields are not being ploughed. The men have gone to more fortunate areas to find food. There are very few beasts to do the ploughing. CNRRA is building roads and paying people in flour, but it seems there is the usual squeeze and corruption… I have attended various relief t'an hua hui[7], one at the Yamen. It is all rather overwhelming for these foreigners who know nothing about China and have never been to the country before. They sometimes make the most impracticable suggestions!

I've seen Lung Si Fu. His story is one of the saddest I've heard. After days of walking the two older girls – there was a baby girl as well – could hardly struggle on any further. A truck came by belonging to a military establishment in Lingling. Lung knew one of the t'ai t'ai[8], who offered to give the girls a lift to the next town. One cried to go, the other cried not to go. They both went. After that the Lungs never saw them again. It appears that the truck broke down and the little girls, aged about eight, were left. One of them said to the other 'You wait here and I'll run on and tell the soldiers (from the truck) to wait and take us *with them'. She couldn't find the soldiers and when she got back, she could not find her sister. That sister has never been found… The other was eventually cared for by some country people. Lung got her back about a year later by extensive advertising in that neighbourhood, and by offering $200,000, which he had earned with the US army in Kweiyang. He found people who said that they had cared for the other girl, that she was with them several months, that she consistently went down to the motor road to look for her parents, but that she got ill and died. But the people who buried the child were no longer there and so the grave couldn't be found. The Lungs think she may have been sold to another family and may still be living. They are very distressed. I want to find out if they would have a chance of getting the other child if they offered a huge reward…*

We shall probably go back tomorrow or the day after. I have to wait for the UNRRA people…

Well, my dear, all my love to you and the imps. I wonder if there is any news of passages?

My mother describes our eventual passage to China to join my father. We arrived in Hong Kong in September 1946, where my father met us, and travelled by train from there to Changsha, the railway line by then having been repaired.

After a non-eventful passage to Hong Kong, we travelled to Canton and then spent four days on the train to Changsha. We were to live once more at the Hsin Ming T'ang. The Hsin Ming T'ang had been designed as the main building of the old Union Theological College. It had three storeys. On the ground floor was the chapel, where Arthur was christened, and the rooms of the Chinese Minister and Deaconess. On the first floor there was the Library – now a big bare room – our flat and several guest rooms. On the second floor was Cliff's study, the Chinese guest rooms and our servants' quarters. It was not as segregated as it sounds. Those Chinese guests often came to meals with us.

She goes on to describe the conditions we found:

At the time of the surrender, Japanese soldiers were living in the Hsin Ming T'ang, but after they left the place was so badly looted that virtually nothing remained. Cliff had the walls, which were black with smoke, white-washed. Then we brought furniture of the same type as our Chinese colleagues had. Each person was allowed a bed, a desk, a bookshelf, a table and a few backless benches, and that was all there was when I arrived. Under normal circumstances the Chinese make quite acceptable furniture, but this was rough, crude stuff. I confess I was a bit stumped when I first saw the conditions. Trying hard to find something cheerful to say, I said 'Those two chairs in the corner are nice'. 'Yes', said Cliff, 'They are Paul's. They are going to Pingkiang tomorrow.'

I think it was the table that gave me the horrors. The Japanese had cut it down to about eight inches so they could sit cross-legged around it on the floor. But we returned it to its normal height by nailing four pieces of rough white wood! We couldn't go to bed until the coolies had brought my luggage from the railway station. The boys were already tucked up in the only bedding Cliff had, so we sat and waited and talked until 4 am when the luggage eventually arrived. We unpacked the bedding and rolled into, or rather I should say 'onto' the bed – a rope frame supported on two trestles.

The next day I unpacked what I had brought. Soon there were curtains in the windows, one or two pictures on the walls, vases, photos, a few knick-knacks around the place and a cloth over that hideous table. I sent the boy out to buy a couple of rush mats and two or three cane chairs. It was amazing how different the place soon looked. It was home, our new home.

Letter of 18th November 1946 from Changsha (EMC to her sister Jean)

It is absolutely disgraceful, only my second letter to you since we arrived two months ago… It isn't that I have nothing to write about, I have, but never seem to have time to write letters. This evening is the first for weeks that I have had clear, but really I ought to take accounts with the cook – he may come along yet. Also I am expecting a guest on the Yiyang launch. She may arrive this evening, or during the night, or may not get in until tomorrow morning.

Since we arrived in the middle of September, ie two months ago, we have had two days on our own. For the rest of the time we have had one or two visitors staying with us. This is the district house and it is always like that. It is in the centre and must always be open for people passing through. At present we have two guests. One is Barbara Simpson, who arrived a fortnight ago from England. She is stationed in Changsha, but will live in a flat over the main church, on the other side of the city. She is with us for a few weeks until her rooms are ready. The other is Stella Griffiths, a newly appointed worker. She is very gay and cheery and we are greatly enjoying her company. She is with us until after Synod, when most likely she will go out to some country station. Tonight we are expecting Kathie Warren… When Synod begins we will have four more guests, making seven in all. We always enjoy these meetings together, but with such a shortage of accommodation and furniture, placing everyone comfortably isn't easy...

I am sitting writing in the diner/sitting room. It is a big room with three windows in it. Until a week ago many of the panes of glass were missing and their place taken either by pieces of wood or paper, but now we have glass in them. The floor is bare boards, which used to be painted... The walls are white-washed. The furniture consists of a patched-up rusty stove...a table with a black top and unvarnished white wooden legs, something that used to be a sideboard...a rather crude bamboo settee and two arm chairs, four unvarnished white wooden chairs, a small black table with a lovely fern on it – my birthday present – ugly unpainted bookshelves and lastly my desk in the corner... Most rooms are similarly furnished, with bits of furniture rescued from here, there and everywhere. Everyone is sleeping on rope mattresses and most people have no bedstead, only the rope mattress frame resting on two trestles. But we are all so thankful to have a building to live in, so many people haven't... For us the great thing is to be together again...

The children are settling down well. They are still the only British children in the town... I am teaching Arthur every morning for two and a half to three hours. It is difficult with so many guests and so much housekeeping, but I enjoy it. He is a bit of a dreamer and needs a lot of prodding to keep him to the point... While Arthur does lessons Dee Dee[9] plays quietly and is no trouble at all...

Food worried me a lot before we came out, but the situation is much better than I dared to hope. We are able to buy fresh milk; also plenty of powdered milk and army butter... This army butter isn't real butter, but a sort of mixture of butter and cheese – some people say India-rubber!... Of course everything is terribly expensive and variety is lacking...

We have been having an adventure with our cook. Before we

arrived Cliff was eating Chinese food, as were most of our workers. The cook is very good at Chinese food, but knew very little about Western cooking, but he was keen to learn… He has done well, though his cooking still leaves much to be desired, but other things about him and his wife aren't so good. In two months he has resigned or been sacked about four times! One day Cliff and I had to separate him and his wife who were having a fight. Another night he came home dead drunk. Then there was a row over a plate of tarts he ate. Last night Miss Simpson had a robbery – a room was entered, a case forced open and eight or nine pounds was taken. This is the fourth robbery in the house within a year and all of them obviously inside work. Suspicion rests heavily on the cook's wife. And now the last episode is the use of 500lbs of charcoal in the kitchen in two weeks, when we usually use only 300lb in a month. At the end of the month the cook will be sacked once again, and this time I am afraid we won't be moved to pity by his pathetic looks…

The next day

Our guest did arrive last night at 11.30 pm, just as we were going to sleep. I then had supper to get for her etc. We went to bed again about 12.45 am. Later the dog barked a good bit. There must have been someone prowling around. I am afraid tonight all I desire is to go to bed… I am just dead sleepy and must give up.

Numerous visitors

As the above letter reveals this was a period of many visitors. Ours was the main British residence in Changsha and with no hotels of any acceptable standard, passing British, Australians and other nationalities frequently descended upon us, even though they had little, if any, connection with the Methodist Church. My mother at times felt as though she was running a boarding house.

243

In her book she talks of these visitors thus:

All sorts of people were returning to China. Our visitors were many, very many. There were people returning to China from England. There were people who had been inland and unable to leave earlier now trying to get home. We were the only British family living in Changsha, so they all stayed with us. To complicate matters trains from Canton always arrived in the middle of the night and launches to inland places always left at dawn. I think our worst night was when we received eight visitors at 1 am, fed them and then put them all to sleep in the children's playroom and then after about an hour's sleep got up and saw off five other folk at 4.30 am. It was impossible. In the end we resorted to thermos flasks and a note. 'Help yourself, bed down in the living room. Will see you in the morning.' And we never knew who we would see in the morning! Some were expected, some got there before their letters, some just turned up!

Letter of 19th January 1947 from Changsha (EMC to AIC)

Best wishes for 1947... I know I don't need to apologise to you, Mums, if this letter is mainly about the children. Cliff writes to you of Church affairs and general happenings. My letters must be about family details... [The children] long for freedom, for hills and fields, for places where they can play without people crowding round and watching them. That we hope we can give them for a while in the summer... Here in Changsha it is a dirty town and rather dull, flat countryside around and there are always curious – in the sense of inquisitive – people crowding around them...but they like the Chinese people. They seem to have no fear at all of them. People on the streets touching them, catching hold of their hands etc sometimes annoys them, but doesn't frighten them in the least and usually they are most friendly and willing to talk, especially Dee Dee. Arthur is always a little more shy and slower to make friends, but people are fond of him and appreciate him when they know him. Dee Dee, of course, makes easy conquests wherever he goes. It's that funny face of his…

As I expect you know Cliff is now in Hankow at the Seven Districts Conference[10]. He has been gone for more than a week, though the children say it is years and years!… For various reasons the delegates from other districts have been late in arriving and the conference has been delayed. I will be glad when he returns. I am as bad as the children. I hate him to be away.

I have just remembered I have not mentioned Christmas. I am afraid my chief memory of Christmas 1946 will be one of toothache! I began with toothache two days before Christmas and continued with an abscess and infected antrums, which was just like severe toothache, until a week afterwards… Nevertheless we did have a happy time. The children loved the fun of their stockings… Cliff had found quite a few stocking things on the street – ping pong balls, marbles, a rubber mouse each, crayons etc. The main present was a wheel barrow each, made (badly) by the local carpenter. They looked splendid, but turned out to be faulty. To encourage them to make yet more noise, we gave them a drum each!… Everyone was out at Christmas service in the Hsi Ch'ang Kai church except the children and I. The servants were there too, so I made Christmas dinner – only a simple meal. Cliff came back to have it with us, then went back to join the others for the afternoon Church party. Then all returned to a proper Christmas tea – Christmas cakes, mince pies, fancy cakes with icing made by Dorothy, jelly, sandwiches and home made sweets and fudge.

After tea we lit lanterns and went round the building singing Christmas carols... Just as we were finishing two UNRRA folk came in. They had to have Christmas tea and stayed with us for the evening. They had brought little motors and mouth-organs for the children, so off to bed they went very happily, Dee Dee asking whether there would be another stocking again the next day!

Boxing Day was our 'foreign' Christmas. Barbara came over for the day and spent the night here. We had a proper Christmas dinner − Christmas pudding, mince pies and tinned turkey. Then again a Christmas tea. In the evening after the children had gone off to bed, tired out with excitement, we five adults − I forgot to say Dorothy spent Christmas with us − sat round the stove and played games.

And now I think I must bring this letter to a close, except our best wishes...

Letter of 18th August 1947 from Nanyoh (EMC to AIC)

Raymond celebrated his fourth birthday on 11th July, with proper excitement. He had a number of presents, including a hobby horse...also a birthday party with six little friends present and altogether had a lovely day...

A perfect finish to a happy day came when just as they were going to bed Paul Jefferies arrived in from Pingkiang with a little pup for them − just what they wanted more than anything else. The pup has been christened 'Judy'. and is a constant source of joy and interest.

The children are having a lovely time up here on the mountain... They are such a lovely sun-burnt brown and look so healthy and full of energy... They are thrilled with the freedom of life up here. They are always exploring somewhere or other, and now is added the joy of the bathing pool and learning to swim. They are neither of them actually swimming yet, but are both quite near it. I hope they will be off before we go down…

This letter is being written at various times and it is now the 25th. Even up here on the mountain I find my days very full, but in a lazier, more amusing way. You see Mummy promised her boys to play with them when they went on holiday, and not for a day am I allowed to forget that promise. Mummy has to go for walks, go to the pool, scramble up hills and always be on call to look at this, examine that, help with something else… It is part of the holiday having Mummy on call…

Since I began this letter Cliff has come up the hill. He is looking tired and lean after so much work and the terrific heat, but three weeks up here will do wonders for him. He loves Nanyoh and is going to be absolutely lazy… It is wonderful to have time just to talk and wander about together, and not always be thinking of all that needs doing and other people…

The messenger wants the letters to go down the hill very early in the morning so I must close…

The following is a letter my father wrote to his former colleague and friend Robert Harrison, who, after many years in China, was now living back in England.

Letter of 26th August 1947 from Nanyoh (CVC to Rev Robert Harrison)

I promised you a letter from Nanyoh; and you deserve it. You've been so good at writing – and writing such really interesting letters. I, on the other hand, don't even answer your letters. I've felt bad about that, but I really could not help it. One man in Changsha just cannot manage everything. Relief affairs are numerous and in the Hsin Ming T'ang flat we run the usual Changsha boarding house and are never alone. Much building work is going on all over the District and so on. Finances were never so complicated. The accounts alone are almost a full-time job – at least for an amateur...

Lai[11] is doing quite well as chairman, but he is finding it hard going and is supposed to be thinner... One of his problems is the stream of visitors at the Hsin Ming T'ang, who impose on him, eating his food, calling him up in the middle of the night etc. He has so many acquaintances from various circuits and there seem to be so many of his former P'ei Yuan students. This is something that must be faced next Synod. You refer to Confucius's 朋朋[12]. I'm inclined to think that the general application of it is one of the curses of China. We've got to see that 'obligations' to friends, relations and fellow students doesn't seriously impair the efficiency of the Church, as it does the efficiency of government and other organisations.

We try to give Lai all the authority due to his position, but the present inflationary situation inevitably puts a lot of responsibility on the Committee's representative. Estimates expressed in Chinese currency are useless so the MMS has to give the MCR a sterling ceiling for almost everything. This means that things are concealed from the Chairman and that his decisions are so often dependent on my saying whether there's enough money or not. I pressed for Cyril to become MCR, but Rattenbury was unmoveable. He said Cyril was only out for two years and continuity of responsibility was important. Synod had not helped my case by asking Cyril to do special evangelistic work throughout the District. Cyril did some fine work in Pingkiang and Hsiangyin in April and May, but on his return he was taken ill with typhus. He was very ill and we were concerned. Dorothy Dymond nursed him in the Hsin Ming T'ang. He is now recuperating in Kuling. I fear it will be some time before he is restored to full strength.

Moral standards have suffered here, as in other parts of the world. CNRRA/UNRRA have done some good work in

China, but they've also, with the best intentions, provided temptations stronger than most people can bear. The distribution of masses of foodstuffs — flour, some rice and lots of US army surplus canned goods — has provided the opportunity for much graft and corruption — high officials, magistrates, pao chang, chia chang and CNRRA employers all have been caught up in it. The spirit of 'What can I get?' is never weak in this land of economic insecurity, and has been fed by the influx of these huge quantities of relief goods. In Changsha today you can buy plenty of tinned butter, powdered milk, salmon, meat, Vienna sausages — and lots of other things. We missionaries have had one or two windfalls, such as a big gift of UNRRA foreign personnel commissariat supplies. We are better off than you in many ways.

Still we often feel homesick for England. England is such a fine country for children. It is hard for children in Hunan — though, of course, there are compensations. Nanyoh is one of them. This year we and the Clarks are sharing the Mission bungalow. It is now coloured outside with a pale yellow wash and is better than ever before...

There is more criticism of the government and the Kuomintang than I have ever heard before... There is really little freedom of speech in China today — though I saw in a Chinese paper recently that if all the wealth of H.H.Kung and T.V.Soong[13] were taken over it would be enough to stabilise China's currency! Justly, or unjustly, these two people are attacked from many quarters. With so many critics of the Kuomintang — secret critics — it is surprising the other parties — Democratic League, Youth Party etc — don't make more progress. But you know the immense difficulties in the way of Anglo-Saxon democracy in China.

Inflation goes on. Rice in Changsha is now $160,000 a 'tan', ordinary letters are $500. Our cook's wages are over

$300,000 a month. Shanghai is worse than Hunan. Kunming and Chungking are now cheaper than the east. Curious things happen. UNRRA recently shipped tons of rice to Hunan for famine prevention. Concurrently Hunan was shipping large quantities of rice out of the province! I saw a boat at the river front being loaded with Hunan rice. It was returning to Shanghai after bringing in relief rice! A crate of prophylactics was delivered to me for Pingkiang hospital – from UNRRA/CNRRA. I opened it and found thousands and thousands of contraceptives – US army surplus! I returned the crate to CNRRA and told Pingkiang nothing about it... The large quantities of US army goods – milk, butter, meat, vegetables, cereals, dehydrated fruits and potatoes – could have met a crying need in Europe. True they were of some value during last year's famine in the south. But since then, at least, the need is in Europe rather than here...

... We were so glad to get news of you all... Our two lads thrive. Arthur's lessons get sadly interrupted at the Hsin Ming T'ang, which is a great pity...

Extract from a letter of 1947 from Changsha: Celeste – our cow (EMC to AIC)

We have a cow! UNRRA has been distributing some cows sent to China by various organisations. Our cow is from a church in California. UNRRA reckons to give them to philanthropic institutions. The children wish the cow to be called Celeste, after the Queen of the Elephants in one of their stories[14]. Celeste is black and white and is a Holstein heifer. She is two years old and has only had one calf. The calf has either died, or got separated from its mother on the journey. Celeste has suffered a great deal en route, but is now gradually picking up. Her milk increases day by day. Our cook used to keep a dairy and he is helping with her, but we are trying to get a cowman. We have heaps and heaps of fresh milk and are giving away and selling some.

Fixed to the ear of the cow was a little metal disk with a cap to it. We unscrewed the cap and in the disk was curled up a message on paper. The message reads:

'Greetings of brotherhood from the Church of the Saviour, Hanford, California, USA. May the milk of human kindness gladden your heart as the milk from this heifer nourishes your body.'

…The children love Celeste. When it is fine they spend quite a lot of time in the garden.

The idea of sending these cows was to help introduce dairy farming into China. It was suggested that foreigners should look after them at first, since, with the patronising attitudes of the time, it was felt that they would be better able to take care of them and they could train the Chinese to do so.

Letter of 2nd November 1947 from Changsha: Lord Ammon's visit (CVC to AIC)

You will know that Lord Ammon[15] is the head of a British Parliamentary Mission to China. I sent him a letter from the Methodist Church in Hunan. I had the following reply:

Dear Mr Cook

Thank you very much for your letter of the 8th instant, which reached me here a few days ago. I leave, with my colleagues, tomorrow morning for Tientsin. I fear that Changsha will not be on our itinerary. As you will know, on these sort of tours one is kept at it from breakfast until bedtime. One or two of my colleagues have found the pace a little severe.

We have been overwhelmed with generosity and kindness from

*the moment we landed in China. I too am glad that in some small
measure credit is reflected on the Methodist Church by my being
the leader of the delegation.*

*Yes I well remember my visit to Birmingham in connection
with COPEC. It is pleasing to know that you are the son of
my then good host and that you follow in your distinguished
father's footsteps*[16].

Salute the brethren for me.

Yours sincerely

Ammon.

*… All goes well here. On Hallowe'en the children went to a
party in an American home at which all the children dressed up.
Dee Dee was a pirate with a patch over one eye; Arthur was
the Mad Hatter, with a very tall hat. The Americans make a lot
of Hallowe'en.*

Isn't it nice that letters are getting through so quickly?

Educating the children

Among all her other duties, including those of running
'the guest house', my mother was responsible for Arthur's
and my education, which she writes about thus:

When we first returned to China I tried to teach Arthur
to read and write myself. We were members of the
Parents' Home Education Association. They sent me all
the books I needed, also each month a set of questions
for Arthur and me. These I duly returned and the next
month came a criticism of Arthur's work and my
teaching along with a new set of questions. Some time
during the second year after our return the American
families returned to Hunan. With the returning families
there came a wife of one of the members of staff who

was to start a school for the American children in Changsha. Arthur and Ray were invited to join the school, which they did, duly saluting the American flag each morning. Unfortunately the school did not last very long. Just over a year later the Communist scare came and the American families left again. While it lasted it was a great pleasure for the children...

Letter of 28th December 1947 from Changsha: Christmas (CVC to AIC)

We do hope your Christmas has been as happy as ours. We've had a lovely time. Our big diner/sitting room has been brightly decorated with the usual paper chains, bunches of holly, a beautifully decorated Christmas tree and a large number of Christmas cards fixed to doors with drawing pins...

Presents were easier to arrange this year. Money was easier than last year and there was plenty to buy in the shops. I did most of the Chinese shopping. We got a good carpenter to make a big, painted engine for Raymond and a big painted closed-in lorry with hinged doors at the back for Arthur. They are big enough for the children to sit on. They are really lovely things – big, bright and strong...

On the 24th there were Chinese services in both our Changsha churches. I took one of them. On the morning of the 25th I played the organ at the service at the Hsi Ch'ang Kai and helped Mr Li with communion...

We've had wonderful food this Christmas – no rationing here! We've had, or are having, mince pies, turkey (US army canned boneless turkey), Christmas cake, different kinds of sweets (some made by Stella), several kinds of fruit etc. I wish you could share the good things we get...

Paul Jefferies has been with us over Christmas and we have been a happy family. In spite of sickness in the house it has been an especially nice Christmas.

The children have both got chicken pox and Arthur's worst day was the 25th! He is still covered with spots and Dee Dee is not far behind him. They are not in bed, but keep mainly to our warm living room. They are not bad in themselves, but the spots are very irritating…

Letter of 6th June 1948 from Changsha (CVC to AIC)

…This afternoon I took Arthur and Raymond out for a scramble and a bathe. First we had a rickshaw ride for about one and a half miles. We all sat in one rickshaw – a bit hot for father – and the puller! The rickshaw puller was very pleasant… We alighted at a certain spot, told the puller to wait and then walked along little paths through the paddy fields for about another mile until we came to a little river. The boys undressed and bathed, splashing in the mud and shallow water. The water was very muddy I fear, but they had a lovely time. We found a fish that had got itself on to dry land by the side of the stream. By throwing it from one pool to another we eventually got it to the river. The first announcement to Elsie on our return was 'We saved a fish!' After an outing like that the boys look red, sunburnt, hot and very bonny. Last Sunday they bathed in a pool and two leeches nipped Arthur and I had to pull them off with force. He did not care for that much!

One day last week I visited the 'school' that Arthur and Raymond go to. It was visitors' day. The teacher just carried on as usual, but two or three visitors sat at the back. There are seven children in the school – one older than Arthur, one younger than Raymond. They begin with prayers, then salute the American flag and make some sort of vow to it – which Arthur and Raymond do quite willingly…

I must stop now and go to bed. This letter seems to have been all about Arthur and Raymond, but I know you won't mind.

In the autumn of 1948 John and May Stanfield arrived back in Changsha. It was intended that Stanfield would eventually relieve my father for furlough. Their arrival approximately coincided with the appointment of Chang Mou Sheng as Chairman of the district, in succession to Lai I-Hsioh. My parents gave a reception in honour of Chang Mou Sheng's appointment and to welcome back the Stanfields. There were over one hundred guests, including Chinese, Americans, Germans, Norwegians and other nationalities.

Letter of 11th December 1948 from Changsha (CVC to AIC)

We've just had a most exhausting fortnight and I fear I've not managed to write to you for at least two weeks…

Synod committees and Synod proper lasted for just under two weeks. We were kept busy morning, afternoon and evening with one meeting after another… I had to attend almost every one. At the same time I was having to do the work of Treasurer and much money was passing through my hands. Finances are extremely difficult as I was dealing in sterling, Hong Kong dollars, Chinese silver dollars and Chinese paper money. The various exchange rates were changing each day. Then we had a packed house here, with people coming and going. For a while we had twenty people, including children, feeding here…

Then during the first days of Synod, most of our American friends were evacuating Changsha by plane at very short notice. As we were all remaining they had lots of commissions for us. They wanted to give and sell us lots of things. They even wanted us to take over their houses and furniture. They are so well furnished and well supplied with everything. And we had to make time to see people off by plane and train...

We were all rather conscious of the uncertainty of the political situation and of possible changes in the future that might alter the whole structure of society. The present government with Chiang at the head has lost the confidence of the people. Many do not want Communism, but they do not want the present set-up either. Chiang is regarded as a good man, and he is said to be more spiritually minded than ever before, but he seems to be blind to what is going on around him.

At the moment there is a battle a hundred miles north of Nanking. It may be quite a decisive one. If the central government loses, they will have to leave Nanking and then nobody knows what may happen.

The American government warned their nationals of the seriousness of the situation and told them if they wanted US help in getting out they must leave at once. Planes would be sent to Shanghai and other places to evacuate people. Thus our happy foreign community in Changsha has been broken. All Arthur and Raymond's schoolmates have gone. The American mothers and children have all left. It has been a very sad time.

The British Consul has warned us of the difficulties that there might be under a new regime – difficulties in getting supplies and of tight regulations. If people wanted to go he urged them to do so while normal communications existed. All of us in Hunan feel it is too early to decide to pull out. Also we feel a strong nucleus ought to consider staying for the moment, unless there are fresh developments that make such a prospect too forbidding. Chinese leaders of the National Christian Council have expressed the hope that some missionaries could stay and face any changes that may come. But for the present we in Hunan will just wait and watch developments. Americans are definitely persona non grata with the other side. The British are in a better position.

One interesting decision of our Missionaries Meeting was that the Cook family should go and live in the new house built at Hsi Ch'ang Kai. It has just been completed and has three rooms upstairs and three down, is one room wide, and has two verandahs. The servants' quarters are in an enclosed courtyard joining onto the house. We don't really want to move, but the plan seemed to fit with the general needs of everything. Now that the little American school is closed Elsie will have to give a lot of time teaching the boys. It is very difficult for her to do that if she has to run the 'hotel' over here. I expect we shall move just after Christmas... The Stanfields will live over here at the Hsin Ming T'ang and do the entertaining. It is good to have such experienced people as the Stanfields back...

So it was decided we should move from the Hsin Ming T'ang to the compound attached to the new church on the other side of the city.

Letter of 1949 from Changsha (EMC to Jean)

Cliff longs to get back to his work as a pastor. He is so sick of all this office work. At the moment he is just about silly trying to do last year's financial statements. Last year's accounts began in national currency. When they got to the place where he was working in billions and trillions of dollars he changed all the accounts into sterling. Then came the currency reform, and we began to work in what was called 'gold dollars' (they were paper of course), so the accounts had to go into 'gold Yen'. Now that currency has gone 'phut' and we are working in silver dollars – real silver – and so everything had to be changed to silver. It is so annoying its almost funny...

Letter of 6th February 1949 from Changsha
(CVC to Robert Harrison)

I am as busy as ever. For two or three years now I've had far more to do than I could manage. Accountancy is a full job in itself, not just something to add on to other more important duties. In the current circumstances it is a most difficult and exacting task. When the currency changed last summer my ledger total in the balance sheet was over 75, 000, 000, 000.00 – thirteen figures! Then there was all the bother of starting with a new currency. Now the new one is going the way of the old. Silver dollars are stable and are used a lot, but there aren't nearly enough to go round. As a result I now deal in the new paper currency, in silver dollars, Hong Kong cheques and in sterling. The only way to keep accounts is to establish a sterling equivalent for every individual item. It's an awful fag, especially since there's always so much else to do.

Synod was a time of great pressure. Then came Christmas with a full house at the Hsin Ming T'ang. Donald Childe (from the Methodist Mission House in London) was here for Christmas. Directly after I took him to various places – Pingkiang, Shaoyang, Kiyang and Lingling, driving the jeep. Then we moved from the Hsin Ming T'ang to the nice, new house at Hsi Ch'ang Kai – a much smaller house than the original one and facing south. It was a hopeless task with all the visitors and comings and goings at the Hsin Ming T'ang. During the first days of Synod we were all disturbed by the evacuation by air of most of the American missionaries in Hunan. We all decided to stay on and watch events elsewhere and await further developments.

The civil war is a constant worry and the future is all unknown. Apart from the possibility of fighting in one's area and some temporary local disorder, there doesn't seem to be much risk of personal harm. The Communists apparently respect foreigners and foreign property these days. We hear too of the Church carrying on under the Reds in various places… But what restrictions will the Church be subject to later on? Shall we all be squeezed out eventually? If so, and this is my chief worry, how shall we get money to carry on? I rather feel that we have too big a missionary staff (four families with children) in Hunan to face the uncertainties of the future.

Chiang having stepped aside, it looks as though Li Tsung-jen[17] is trying to arrange peace with the Communists. They have been very stubborn and have been demanding the punishment of 'war criminals', among whom they include Chiang, Li Tsung-jen himself, Sun Fo[18], T.V.Soong… and lots of other prominent members of what they call the 'Reactionary Nanking Government'. It looks as though some prominent people from Nanking and Shanghai will be able to go to Peiping as representatives of the people – not the government. Whether there is hope there I don't know. By going to Peiping I mean of course going to talk peace with the Communists.

An interesting point is that a number of non-Communist revolutionaries are in the north with the Communists and they talk about forming a coalition… The people everywhere desperately want peace. I should think this fact, along with the military reverse, was responsible for Chiang having to 'retire'. If peace talks break down there may be a rallying of the various Kuomintang groups – the Kiangsi group, the Cantonese group and others. Whether Chiang will reappear on the scene – only time will show. It is all very sad and disturbing. One would like to see a strong coalition with a Socialist, rather than a Communist, programme.

I broke off at that point to listen to the North Shansi New China Broadcasting Station (Communist) broadcast their English news bulletin. They spoke of the establishment of a Provisional Administration for the area between the Yangtze and the Yellow River. Communists were to co-operate democratically – whatever that means – with non-Communists.

'Enlightened gentry', industrialists and representatives of the professions would be represented. There was also talk about the bogus peace talks of the 'Reactionary Nanking Government'. They were very angry that a Nanking Military Tribunal had acquitted some leading Japanese 'war criminal'.

Following that I heard the Nanking news in English. They said the Nanking People's Peace Representatives were flying to Peiping today. One of them had engaged in a long distance telephone conversation from Tsingtao with a Communist representative in Peiping. The latter said that arrangements were being made to facilitate the landing of the plane taking the Nanking People's Reps to Peiping etc. Altogether it is a curious situation…

You ask when we are coming home. That is a problem. We are not due until the end of 1950. But at Synod we asked for permission to come home a year early. Now we feel we ought to come so as to get Arthur into a school this September. Donald Childe felt strongly that we should do this. We may have to go. The only alternative seems to be the CIM school which is now in Kuling. They could probably take our two boys as day boys this September, and later take them as boarders. We might be able to arrange for Elsie to live temporarily in Kuling. But will the situation permit the school to carry on? We don't feel we can risk Arthur not getting into school in September, so, unless the situation settles down, you may be seeing us at home this year… On the whole we have a fair amount to worry about these days.

Letter of 10th April 1949 from Changsha: Malaria (EMC to AIC)

It is a very long time since I wrote to you myself. Perhaps Cliff's letter this week – if he manages to get it written with Arthur and Raymond about – will tell you he is in sole charge while

Mummy is in hospital. He is making a very good job of it too, though he does look a bit harassed sometimes. I have felt very unwell for a long time and since Synod have been so tired I have hardly known how to keep on going. A fortnight ago I came into hospital for an examination and a series of injections, supposed to last three or four days, but I have had two weeks here. It looks rather as though it has been malaria that has been holding me down. Certainly since it was discovered and treated I have been a different person. There is also the nuisance of a heart murmur and low blood pressure, but I think I will be able to cope with those. I will still have to rest a lot, I am afraid, but it is good to be feeling so much better.

Yesterday was Arthur's birthday. I did so want to be home for it, but Dr Eitel[19] was unmoveable. Tomorrow (Monday) is the earliest date he will give me. However, I think Arthur had a very happy day. Daddy brought them both over in the afternoon and they were very excited and happy…

With the political situation deteriorating my father sent the following circular letter to his colleagues:

Circular Letter of 15th April 1949 from Changsha
The Situation and our Policy

Since Synod we have carefully been watching developments in the China situation. We have been particularly interested in any information from the Communist areas that concerned missionaries and the Church, for such information might serve as a guide for us. In general the news received has perhaps been a little better than we feared it might be. From time to time I have talked to some of you about our place in regard to the changes we expect to come and the uncertainties of the future. Until recently it seemed we were no more ready for any special action than we were at Synod time. If the Missionary Society has any guidance for us it is perhaps contained in the words of Mr Rattenbury – 'We do not want mothers or children, or those who cannot bear it, to suffer undue strain, but I am quite sure speaking generally our folks will continue to stand by the side of their colleagues, as they always have stood.'

However, at a time like this the Society relies upon responsible people on the spot to make any necessary decisions. Some ten days ago, when the situation was especially tense – the Communist armies were nearing Hankow; a crossing of the Yangtze at some point seemed probable; the peace talks seemed to be in danger of breaking down; the money situation was very critical; and regional disturbances were numerous – I felt we needed to consider seriously whether in view of all the uncertainties, it was right for mothers and children to stay any longer. I consulted with Mr Stanfield and we both felt it would be right for me to communicate with the Clarkes, Hollmans, Piles (and Cooks!) and advise they should be ready to move their families at short notice. I am now in correspondence with these families.

During the last few days hopes of a settlement being reached in Peiping are considerably brighter. According to the press after a period of exchange of views, the peace talks proper have now begun; most fighting has stopped; the Communists have modified some of their demands; and Nanking has sent to Peiping some more senior officials to help with the talks. This is encouraging… However, there are still many uncertainties. Will a final settlement be reached? If not what will happen in Hunan? If a coalition government is formed what then? Will there still be centres of resistance? Will our financial supplies be cut off?… We should all realise there are serious problems in the matter of financial supplies. There is no need to point out the need for a reasonable conservation of such silver as we have.

I think it may help if I make two or three statements.

1) If, for any reason anyone feels he (or she) should not face the uncertainties of the future, it would be good to raise the matter now. Anyone who leaves temporarily would have the full understanding of the whole District.

2) Families should seriously consider what Mr Rattenbury said about not wishing mothers and children to suffer undue strain. Any preparations that are now possible should be made so that families can move to Hong Kong at short notice. We in Changsha are willing to give our advice when we think families should delay no longer, but it may be difficult to get word to you quickly, and we may so easily be wrong in our judgement. Until we give strong advice, the actual decision about moving must rest with each family. You will realise the advantage of moving while the going is good.

3) If for financial, or other, reasons it seems necessary to consider further reductions in our staff, we will communicate with you again.

This letter is not intended to cause alarm, but during the tension of a few days ago, I felt some sort of statement was necessary. Your views would be appreciated...

By that time my father had been back in China nearly four years and was soon due for furlough. With my mother in poor health, still recovering from a recent attack of malaria, and John Stanfield, who was to take over from my father as Missionary Committee's Representative, already in Changsha, it was decided that we should return to England as soon a passage could be booked. My mother describes those last days in China as follows:

When the Communist advance had reached the north bank of the Yangtze and the China Inland Mission school in Kuling, to which we had intended sending the boys, had been disbanded, it seemed best for us to come home on furlough.

At the time it was still hoped that Chiang Kai-shek would be able to prevent the Communists from crossing the Yangtze and that the southern part of the country would remain under his rule. With these thoughts in mind, it was our intention when we left that after furlough Cliff would return to Hunan, but I would stay with the boys in Hong Kong, where they would attend the King George School. The school did not take boarders. At Christmas it was intended we would go to Hunan and in the summer Cliff would come to Hong Kong to join us.

What actually happened proved to be very different. While we were still in Hong Kong on our way home the Communists crossed the Yangtze and begun their push to take the whole of the country. Soon all China fell to them. There was no hope of a return.

Thus it was we left China vainly hoping some way would be found to enable us to return. Cliff went out to Hong Kong just over a year later to help the Chinese Church there; but I never went back.

Was it all worth it?

So I have come to the end of a rather factual account of our life in China. Behind these facts there were many other elements. Sometimes there was real danger, often there was stress and sometimes near exhaustion. We worked long days – that was the norm. We never lived in anything approaching luxury, in fact most of the time very simply.

Balanced against all that was the joy we had in our work and the satisfaction it brought us. Someone once said to me, 'Was it all worth it?' A quite startling question. We missionaries, certainly Cliff and I, were in China because we believed God had sent us and we believed we were doing the work he wanted us to do. We were called upon to do all sorts of things that normally we would have thought beyond our powers, and yet we were able to do them.

We did not work for rewards, but the rewards there were in abundance, in the pleasure we got working with the children and the radiant enthusiasm they showed, in the joy of seeing a peasant woman flower into a new life because she now felt she was someone who mattered, who could read and write. The joy of seeing people's lives changed when they found God and were sure of His love and care. And the great joy of seeing God's Church established in China – a Church that has since suffered thirty years of persecution and yet has emerged stronger than ever before – self-governing, self-supporting and self-developing. What greater rewards could we have had?

As a bonus we have experienced the wonderful friendship of our Chinese colleagues and fellow Christians. We have made friends who would give their lives to help, as we would have given our lives to help them.

What more can I say – except thanks be to God for allowing us to serve Him.

On 4th August 1949 Lin Piao's Fourth Field Army took Changsha and on 1st October 1949 Mao Tse-tung declared the birth of the 'People's Republic of China'.

Leaving China

I remember the long railway journey from Changsha to Canton, a journey of several days. At Canton we took a much faster train for the short journey to Kowloon, where we caught the ferry to Hong Kong.

We remained in Hong Kong for several weeks trying to get a ship to England. Large numbers of people were once again fleeing from China and as a result it was difficult to get a booking. We stayed at the 'Soldiers and Sailors Home', a Methodist hostel for members of the armed forces.

We eventually got a ship – the SS Carthage – to Singapore. It was an old and not a very comfortable boat. In Singapore we spent a few days. I remember visiting a park and watching monkeys chasing each other up coconut palms. We then caught the SS Dorsetshire back to England, where we arrived on 5th July 1949, just six days before my sixth birthday.

My parents on their return to England regarded their stay there as a mere interlude before they resumed their work in the missionary field and at the time they still hoped a return to China would prove possible. However, as it turned out no more missionaries were allowed to return to China and apart from a few – such as my parents' colleagues, Dr Pearson and Paul and Stella Jefferies, who stayed for a while after the Communist Revolution only to be expelled a few years later – missionary work effectively came to an end in China with the advent of the Communist Revolution. The new government were highly suspicious of missionaries, partly because of their perceived links with Chiang Kai-shek's administration, but also because of the Western ideas and values they promoted. The only condition under which they would allow the Christian Church to operate was as a genuinely Chinese affair without the help of, or allegiance to, any foreign power. Under such terms, and even then constantly viewed with suspicion, the Church survived in China until the Cultural Revolution, which sprung to life in 1966 rapidly gathering momentum until its impact was felt throughout the whole country and in all walks of life. For the next ten years observance of the Christian religion was not permitted, churches were closed and the clergy sent to work with the peasants in the fields.

After the Cultural Revolution had run its course, in the late 1970s, the Church was once again allowed to operate, provided it adhered to the 'doctrine of the three selfs' (self-governing, self-supporting and self-developing). To the amazement and delight of my mother, and those surviving colleagues of my parents, reports drifted back to England that the congregations attending these services far exceeded the numbers who used to go to church in the days before the Revolution. A totally unexpected outcome of thirty years of repression; but one that caused much rejoicing among those who had served the missionary cause with such dedication.

As the possibility of a return to China became more remote I remember my parents talking about offering to their service to the Church in Africa. But it wasn't to be. After spending a year in a church in Torquay my father went out to Hong Kong for two years and thereafter served in the home ministry until his death, while still in service, in 1972. Arthur's and my education was a major consideration in their decision to remain in England.

Endnotes

1. Simon Arzt was a well known stop on the way out to India, where Europeans used to stock up on pith helmets and other tropical wear.

2. Rev Hector Chick. Another China missionary, who took over responsibility from my father for organising the return of Methodist missionaries to China via India and 'the Hump' until the rail track from Hong Kong to central China had been reopened.

3. 'Mien' means noodles, or food in general.

4. A Chinese-run relief organisation, although mainly funded by the Americans.

5. Literally means 'good luck', but in the context probably some New Year decorations or lucky charm.

6. Chinese New Year

7. Roughly translates as 'meetings'.

8. Wives, or women (in the sense of a girlfriend or partner).

9. Yes, I'm afraid that's me!

10. In effect an all-China Synod, the Methodist Church in China being divided into seven districts, of which Hunan was one.

11. In accordance with the policy of handing over responsibility for church affairs to the Chinese, the chairman of the Hunan district was now a Chinese, the Rev Lai I-Hsioh, and my father was the Missionary Committee's Representative (MCR) ie the representative of the Methodist Missionary Society (MMS) in London.

12. The Chinese character 'chung' meaning 'loyalty'. It is one of the Confucian virtues; but also often a source of corruption.

13. Chiang Kai-shek's two brother-in-laws. Dr Tse-Vung Soong, or T.V.Soong, as he was always known, was Madame Chiang Kai-shek's brother and Dr H.H.Kung

married her eldest sister Eling.

14. *Babar the Elephant* by Jean de Brunhoff.

15. Lord Ammon of Camberwell (1873-1960), formerly Charles Ammon, was a prominent Labour politician and, among other things, a well known lay Methodist.

16. My father's father, the Rev Vallance Cook, was a well known evangelist.

17. General Li Tsung-jen, who some years earlier had been one of the Kwangsi warlords opposing Chiang Kai-shek, was at the time Chiang's deputy.

18. The son of Sun Yat Sen.

19. Dr Eitel had been expelled from the country as a German in 1941, despite years of selfless work among the Chinese people. He returned to China as soon as he was able after the end of the war and was once again running the CIM Hospital in Changsha.

Chapter 7
Refugee Work in Hong Kong

Two years after our return to England my father was asked by the Methodist Missionary Society (MMS) to go to Hong Kong as the Missionary Committee Representative for a period of two years. He took up this appointment, leaving my mother, my brother Arthur and me in Bristol.

The job had two main components – liaison with the Chinese Church in Hong Kong and working with refugees who had fled to Hong Kong following the seizure of power by the Communists.

Following the fall of the Kuomintang government in China more than one million refugees fled to Hong Kong, thereby almost doubling the population of the colony. Most of them were well-educated and formerly well-to-do people, who either held positions of importance under the Kuomintang in the government or the military, or else were magistrates, merchants, shop owners, landowners or landlords. And these groups fled with good reason. The Communists shot many senior and middle ranking government officials and military officers who had been closely linked with the Kuomintang, along with rapacious or corrupt merchants, landlords or shop owners; and at times the ordinary people, with little bidding from their new masters, took revenge on those regarded as having used their positions of power to exploit the poorer sections of the population. The peasants and workers and others of little standing, education or wealth generally had little to fear from the new regime and thus few of them joined the ranks of the great exodus.

These refugees arrived in Hong Kong penniless, uninvited and unwelcome. The colony had totally inadequate resources to deal with such a deluge of new arrivals, while the British government was reluctant to become actively involved, perhaps fearing that any display of generosity might encourage others to follow.

The refugees, once they crossed the border and arrived in Hong Kong, had no option but to stake out a few square feet of muddy ground on some hillside and with any materials they could reclaim from rubbish dumps – such as cardboard, bits of cloth, pieces of scrap metal – try to provide some protection against the elements and create a semblance of privacy. These shacks were huddled together in large groups, separated by narrow, muddy, unlit paths, with no running water or sanitation. And that was only the start of their problems.

The Hong Kong authorities were overwhelmed by the situation and generally treated their uninvited guests as little more than vagabonds and beggars.

Although my father thrived on the challenge of working to improve, in however small a way, the lives of these unfortunate people, it was often a very frustrating task. Frustrating because without massive backup resources – and he had virtually none – there was often so little he could do to help them. These desperate people needed housing, food and jobs, as well as help in restoring their dignity. He would always treat refugees, when they called on him, as though they were still men of importance, following the accepted Chinese etiquette – the correct bows and greetings, the cup of tea correctly served – and after the visit he would accompany the guest to the outer door, where once again he would make the traditional bows and farewell phrases. While they were with him, they were his honoured guests. This meant a great deal to them. Several of the refugees told him it helped them more than any monetary assistance he could give. It helped to restore their self-respect.

My father sailed out to Hong Kong in October 1951 on the P&O liner, the SS Carthage. As this book intends to concentrate primarily on my parents' time in China, I include only those letters that my father wrote from Hong Kong which are of particular significance and beginning with the first letter we have that he wrote to my mother from Hong Kong:

Letter of 16th December 1951 from Hong Kong

This is your Christmas letter…I've got quite a programme between now and Christmas Day.

On December 17th there will be a feast given by the biscuit man[1], then staff meeting and Hong Kong ministers fraternity. The next day is the opening of the Kowloon School by HE the Governor and the Quarterly Meeting. December 19th is Margaret and Geoffrey's wedding, then the united choir service of various churches in our new Kowloon Church. On December 20th is the party for the forces in the S. and S. Home. December 21st – Police band concert in the English Methodist Church. December 23rd there are Sunday services including children's toy service and the Messiah on gramophone records.

Then Christmas Day Services. My colleagues The Brays and I have asked me to spend Christmas Day with them. I suppose that will begin after the morning service…

I am to write up the Kowloon church opening for the Methodist Recorder *– which will give me a bit of a headache!…*

To begin with, tonight I'm going to the evening service at Kowloon. I am making a little progress in understanding Cantonese...

There has been a great deal of publicity in the press here recently about missionaries in difficulty in mainland China – in prison, public accusation meetings etc. All the Hunan missionaries are safely out; but some in Kwangtung are in difficulties.

I've had two Hunan folk asking for help. I didn't recognise either of them, but both said they knew me. They certainly knew our places and our people in Changsha. One said he owned a house in Hsin Chun Lu just below the Hsin Ming T'ang, the house that was rented by the bus company. He said he had been a general in the army in Hsieh Yo's time. He certainly knew a lot about Changsha. He's been out of Hunan a good while.

Just to let you know, I am moving to a flat in the Soldiers and Sailors Home. I shall have two rooms, an upper and a lower, both of which look out towards the harbour...

This letter brings a specially big measure of love and deep wishes for a really happy Christmas... I do miss you and the boys so badly. There is a very important job to do here, but oh for the two years to be up!

Letter of 24th February 1952

The best way to end a Sunday is to write to one's wife!...

Though I am a little reflective right now. The Brays left yesterday on the SS Chushan. What a farewell they've had. During the past two weeks there's been such a run of feasts, farewell meetings, presentations as to overwhelm anyone. Towards the end Bray was about bowled over...

On Friday there was a funeral in the English Methodist Church – one I shall never forget. It was the funeral of Miss Gertrude Cone, an American Methodist missionary from China, who'd been in China twenty-seven years. She came out less than a week ago...close to death. She died two days later.

*She'd suffered great pain. The authorities wouldn't let her out.
She had no money and…for several months she had been living
on a bowl of 'hsi fan' (rice gruel) a day… At last – no doubt
realising she was dying – the authorities finally let her cross the
border and enter the Matilda Hospital here. Bishop Ward (an
American Methodist bishop) was with her a great deal before
she died and gave a most moving address. From her deathbed,
in the hospital, Gertrude had said to him, 'I don't hate anyone.
I don't bear any resentment to anyone.' When the Bishop said
to her, 'You are now with those who love you', she replied, 'And
I've come from those who love me. They had their way of
showing it.'*

*She'd had a terrible time with accusations in Nanchang. The
Bishop said that at the beginning, before things got difficult, she
could have come out, but she chose to stay… Then the Bishop
finished his address with the words, 'And I'm glad she did.'*

*Hong Kong is a very interesting place, but the poverty and
the problem of the refugees is so distressing. And I hate the idea
of the British governing the place.*

My father had long been in favour of the rendition of
Hong Kong to the Chinese and had written a letter to
The Times on the issue some years before. Such views
were not popular among the British at the time, although
some fifty years later it did, of course, come to pass.

Letter of 16th March 1952

*…I went to see a refugee living in a hovel in the midst of a
squatters' settlement. His room, shared with another man, was
in the middle of many rooms, divided from one another by dirty
wooden boards. The room had no windows and was quite dark
in daytime as well as at night. A little oil lamp was lit for me
to see the man. He was obviously very ill. He hadn't been out*

of bed for days. His face was swollen and one of his eyes was almost hidden by the swelling. His ears were suppurating. There was an unpleasant smell. There was noise all around – people talking, children crying – in the rooms on the other sides of the boards. This man had been a magistrate in China. He had no money and said he had no one to turn to. I talked to the man and left some money. I'd already discovered that he could go to a Chinese charitable hospital, though he'd probably have to sleep on the floor as the place is so crowded. So I said I would try to get him a bed in Kowloon Hospital...

Letter of 21st July 1952: The baptism of Wu Te-chen

I've had quite an interesting weekend...Most notably, after Sunday's evening service at our English Church, a prominent Nationalist leader was baptised. The man is Wu Te-chen – for several years Mayor of Shanghai. He has been Governor of Kwangtung and for a while was Foreign Minister of the Nanking Government². I think he has been Governor of Taiwan. He wanted to be baptised in the Methodist Church, as he was at school in the Methodist School in Kuikiang. His two sons, one in America, are Methodists... At first I didn't know what to do. We knew it would be a great embarrassment if the Chinese Church was presented with the problem, however, I was one hundred per cent convinced of his utter sincerity. He said it was six months ago that he decided he must become a Christian – also asking if he was too old! There was no Methodist Church in Taiwan. I talked it over with Phillipson (the minister in charge of the English Methodist Church) and Dr Anderson, the American missionary here. Things had to be kept very quiet, as Wu's presence in Hong Kong was supposed to be a secret, but we decided the deed must be done and arranged to baptise Wu quietly in the English Methodist Church after the Sunday service. Only members of the family and a few representative leaders of the English Church were to be present...

Peter read the scriptures, then I baptised Mr Wu. He will later let it be known that he has been baptised, but he won't say where. (It will be surprising if it doesn't come out sooner or later, however.) He said to Dr Anderson and me sadly, 'I am to blame that we couldn't keep peace in China.' That, of course, wasn't really so, for when General Marshall was in Nanking, Mr Wu tried very hard to bring about peace...

We are not mentioning this to anyone in Hong Kong and please make sure you don't tell this to a soul who might mention it in public...

If news of Wu Te-chen's baptism were publicised in Communist China it could have been acutely embarrassing for the Church there, which was already perceived by the Communists as having been both an agent of Western imperialism and an ally of the Kuomintang. Chiang Kai-shek's conversion to Christianity and Madame Chiang's forthright support of missionaries, although they appeared to be a blessing at the time, proved a troublesome legacy.

Letter of 23rd November 1952

It has been an unusual Sunday. I went to the 11am service in our Church, mainly to meet the last American Methodist missionary – Rev Olin Stockwell – from China. He came out of China a few days ago after fourteen months solitary confinement and nine and a half months in a prisoners' 'Thought Reform Training School'. In prison in Chungking, he was not manhandled or tortured, but he must have suffered in other ways. Special prayers of thanksgiving were said in the English service this morning...

Mr Stockwell made a confession of being a spy before he was released. He said that was the only way of getting released. His confession was recorded in English and Chinese. He told the judges that what he was saying was lies, but they accepted the statement. Some folk here are very troubled about this...

After the service I went to the Nethersole Hospital to see our Kowloon Bible Woman, who has tuberculosis.

Letter of 8th December 1952:
The visit of the Rev Middleton Brumwell

After a few minor hitches, our expected guest — the Rev Middleton Brumwell CBE, MC — arrived Saturday morning in the end. He is a Methodist supernumerary, and for most of his ministry he has been a chaplain in the armed forces where he reached a very high position — as high a position as a non-conformist chaplain can reach. He's met all sorts of VIPs, as well as kings: George V, Edward and George VI! no less!

Yesterday morning I took Brum to our Kowloon church. The church was full and some three hundred took Communion. He was very impressed. I'm afraid he doesn't understand, or appreciate, the Chinese. I was helping administer Communion and he — very much an army type — was alone in the congregation of these three hundred Chinese. He even refers to them as Chinamen!

Letter of 14th February 1953

Yesterday evening around seven o'clock a young Chinese man came to see me. He said he was from Hunan and he seemed in very great distress. He said his wife had left him suddenly four days ago, leaving him with a baby girl, five months old. He couldn't feed the baby and look after it and it was gradually weakening and would soon die. Did I know of any babies' home that would take the infant? I said I thought there was no chance at all, as the babies' homes and orphanages here don't reckon to take any children who still have one parent about. Moreover all such homes are full. But the man seemed in such distress – he even said the only thing he could do was leave the baby in the street so that the police would take it and arrange for its care. I got in touch with a babies' home run by some Americans belonging to some independent Church. They agreed to try and help, because of the man's distress. But they said the father must hand over the baby and not come and see it. In fact he shouldn't be told where the babies' home was. The man agreed. I was to go where the baby was and have a look at it and see the actual circumstances of the case. The father agreed to my going there and then.

So I accompanied the man to the squatters' area near Kai Tak airfield. On the way I treated him to a Chinese meal in a second-rate Chinese food shop in the heart of a Chinese area. It was very interesting, as it was the last night of the old year. Firecrackers were being let off and people were playing with dragons. The squatters' area was dark. We followed narrow paths and then got to a place where there was a public lavatory, built to serve that part of the squatters' area. The man excused himself to go in. I said I would wait on the path nearby. I waited half-an-hour and the man never came out. I went in and he was not there. He'd given me the slip in the darkness. I can only guess that in the end he wasn't prepared to accept the terms of admittance into the babies' home. I wonder if I shall ever see him again.

Letter of 6th March 1953

Life is still very busy. This week I've typed the minutes of our Synod. I'm having Cantonese lessons five mornings a week from 8 to 9 am. Then I go to the Literature Office until lunch where, though there are extra things to do, I find time to get letters written.

You ask about raising funds for refugees. I think the MMS would give a good sum if we had a good plan. I think the main trouble is not so much the money as getting the people and time to dispense it.

Most afternoons I have talks with several refugees. I don't give financial help (usually) until I've got evidence of the people's genuineness — until I feel they are amongst the most desperately needy. I prefer to try and get them jobs if possible.

This kind of work is thrilling in some ways, but it can be very wearing. One gets a bit frightened of a building project.[3] Those who have experience tell us that administration after the houses are built is very difficult. If an extra two months here would be of value perhaps I ought not to be too definite about coming home exactly on time — though I shall aim to do so. What do you really think? You know I'm just longing to see you and the boys. But I can do little for these people once I leave. I haven't done anything yet about the offer of a home circuit in Manchester.[4] It is such a big thing to get committed to — perhaps for four or five years. I'm thinking much about it.

Letter of 13th March 1953

On Tuesday I went to visit a little Hunan family in a squatters' hut. The 'home' was a tiny place made of bamboo matting and oiled paper. I sat on the bed boards and the folk managed to cook three eggs for me. The man is out of work, but the woman begs a bit and does embroidery work at home at slave-labour rates. They were awfully nice, friendly dignified people. The wife is only twenty-five or so. He looks nearly twice that age. I left a parcel containing some clothing, including a bright red dress for the girl, a doll, some hankies, soap, sweets, etc — also fifty dollars for improving the roof of the house. I'll go again sometime...

Last night I got on a tram and sat downstairs (third class downstairs, first class upstairs). I sat next to four children — very

*small. They started giggling and talking about me in clear
Mandarin. I waited a little while then suddenly joined in their
conversation. The other people on the tram laughed like
anything. I left on very good terms with the children*

Letter of 30th March 1953

*I'm spending a lot of time these days dealing with refugees, but
I've been down for supper since I started this letter – and an
interesting thing has happened. I was sitting next to an
American newspaperman and I happened to mention that I
thought I saw that American launch that was captured by the
Communists on the morning of the day it was captured. I
passed it on my way back from Silver Mine Bay. He suddenly
became all ears and fired at me one question after another. And
now he has been in to see me. He's reported what I said to the
US Consul and he's cabling the story to American newspapers!
Curiously enough I had specially noticed the American craft
that day, thinking it strange to see a boat flying the US flag at
that point. Also I had noticed one of the pilots of my ferry boat
go to the side window of the pilot's cabin and look at the craft.
In this newspaperman's report I am down as 'Clifford Cook, an
English minister, from Bristol'!*

Letter of 13th April 1953

*This weekend has been rather dominated by refugees, but at
least I've succeeded in getting jobs for a few people – an almost
hopeless task in the present situation. Mr Hu Hsioh-li, brother
of our Hupeh minister, and two of his friends are all pretty well
destitute. I agreed to give three of them letters of introduction to
the British army to do coolie work. After days and days of
waiting at the Army Employment of Labour Office they were
all suddenly given jobs, two to carry stores, to load and unload
trucks etc and one to clean cars and other things (belts, shoes*

etc). They are thrilled to bits and came together on Saturday to express thanks. They get $3.50 a day. They are ex-landlords, or military officers etc!

After lunch, which I took in a Kowloon cafe, I went, by appointment, to the house of an out-of-work young man. He wanted me to see his sister, whose baby was ill. The house was one of the very worst of all the squatters' houses. Bits of wood, bamboo matting and tarred paper were thrown together to make the rough tinny shack. The floor was wet mud and the rain was dripping through the roof. Cracks and holes were plentiful. I found a woman, aged about thirty, sitting on an old bed hugging a sick child, about two years old. The woman's eyes were very red with much weeping. The child was ill and covered with raw sores. The child didn't look Chinese and in the course of conversation I discovered the father was a British soldier who had left the colony for over a year. There was another young child – fully Chinese, who I suspect is the son of the woman's real husband. The woman was obviously desperately fond of the whiter baby. She was crying most of the time she talked, and she kept hugging the baby and sometimes kissed it. The father never wrote and had deserted her completely. He wasn't in Hong Kong now. There was never a word of blame, but she several times said in broken English, 'He was always very kind to me.' They weren't married of course.

She said that people said she loved the Englishman's baby more than the Chinese baby, but, she added, that was not true; she loved them both. She was absolutely penniless. She said that if she didn't love her children – both boys – she could sell them and then she would be free. She said her father was in Kwangtung. I asked if he knew about the 'English' baby. She said, 'No, he would ma ssu *(curse to death) me if he knew.' She also said the father of the Chinese boy treated her cruelly, but the English soldier treated her kindly. She begged for work to*

281

do, saying she could sew and make clothes. At one point she wanted to hand the sick baby to me to look after. I've never seen a more disturbing sight and all the time rain was dripping onto the bed. While we were talking the baby wet the bed and the woman. The place was filthy. She's a northerner and spoke to me sometimes in Mandarin and sometimes in broken English. I felt quite helpless. I gave her twenty dollars, but she didn't want to take it. She said what she needed was a job, so that she could support the children. The brother said, 'If you can do something for her I can somehow manage to look after myself.' Not knowing what to do, I said I was terribly sorry for her, I had no plan to help her, but I would think about her difficulty and come and see her again. I'm thinking of going to the Salvation Army to see if they can help. What is needed is a real Christian family that would employ the woman and patiently help her and the children. But I don't think I can find one in Hong Kong that would do it. I may suggest that I try to get the children into a children's home of some kind – but that is no easy thing. What is the father of the white child doing now? I wonder if he's in England going out with an English girl. He may even be a married man.

Letter of 1st May 1953

Communist flags – not many – are out today – May Day. A Government education officer has asked me to keep an eye on two of our school teachers, as they are suspected of being Red. This was told to me in the strictest confidence...

Letter of 7th May 1953

I'm sitting on a deckchair on a lovely sandy beach at Silver Mine Bay. Sea breakers are rolling within a few yards of where I am sitting. Reverend Bowers is on leave for two weeks and he's brought a group of us here for the afternoon... The bay – a lovely one and quiet – is at the east end of Hong Kong island.

Life is still very full and I continue to see a lot of refugees. Yesterday afternoon I went out to a squatters' area to visit the family where the little girl has tuberculosis in the spine. The family – father, mother, girl aged nine and a little boy about five, live in one tiny room. The girl, called Li Li, now has a slightly deformed spine. It all came on very suddenly a few months ago. If I'd known earlier I might have been able to get her into a hospital and perhaps the deformity could have been prevented. When I knew I gave the family an introductory letter to a voluntary relief organisation called the Family Welfare Association and they are providing free Streptomycin (or something like that). The little girl is very sweet, very pretty and gentle, with big eyes that look straight at you. The mother was cruelly treated by the Reds before she fled to Hong Kong.

Our Literature Committee met on Tuesday and passed more books for publication, including a number of books for rural work in Malaya, Formosa and elsewhere.

Preparations are being made for the Coronation celebrations. There are going to be elaborate decorations. One feature of the celebrations is going to be a procession of huge Chinese dragons.

I've just had a spot of encouragement in relief work. A week or so ago a young man, who is very short-sighted, called with broken glasses. He'd got a job with the RAF, but couldn't work without his glasses. We talked a while, then I gave him the necessary money as a loan, asking him not to return the money to me, but to deliver it to another refugee, whom I named. I've just heard the other refugee has received the money…

Letter of 19th July 1953

…I preached in our Kowloon church this morning. Last Sunday I preached in our Chinese church. In Hunan I rarely preach as much as I do nowadays, but I still do as much refugee work as

I can. The living conditions of these people are so dreadful and they are so undernourished that one after another goes down with tuberculosis; and when they have got it their chances of recovery are almost nil. They are told to rest, to eat good food and have plenty of fresh air.

Yesterday a woman of twenty-eight called. I know her family – father, mother and little boy. She'd been ailing for several months. A few days ago she was told at Kowloon Hospital that she had TB. She was terribly upset and frightened. Several of her relatives had died of TB. She wept and wept as she told me. Her husband has no work. She labours long hours each day doing embroidery at slave labour rates. They live in a tiny upstairs room in an awful wooden house. The room is terribly hot and has no window. What chance of recovery has she? I'm hoping to be able to get powdered milk and injection serum for her...

I'm not worrying about a circuit. There's an important job to do anywhere. I wrote to Manchester a few days ago and said that if they hadn't got fixed up and were still interested in me, I was now available... I shan't be at all concerned if they aren't, though I think that kind of church would suit me very well...

...I'm planning to come home on the January boat. How lovely and cold it will be when I get home!

Letter of 11th September 1953
I've just had a visit from the family of which the mother has cancer. The whole family – father, mother and two boys – all came. I think I am pretty well supporting them these days, but they know I can't do it much longer.

At that point in my letter I was interrupted by the visit of the first of several refugees and now it is 11 pm, so this will be rather hurried. The other refugees included a couple called Mr and Mrs Wang of Changsha. Then I had a messenger from the brother of our Hupeh minister. He – the brother – has been in the Nethersole Hospital. He is now out and is living in a squatters' hut with another refugee. After that I had a messenger from a man whom I got into the Nethersole yesterday. And finally I had an absolutely destitute Hupeh woman with her arms and legs covered with sores. Her husband, who seems to have deserted her, is in Indonesia. She had written him and had given this address for the reply. She cannot read. The reply has come and I read it to her. He cannot help her. I gave her ten dollars. She has one child and a baby...

Has Hong Kong been in the news at home recently? Two Roman Catholic Chinese priests were murdered in bed a stone's throw away from here the other night. The papers haven't said so, but the general theory is that it was a political murder perpetrated by the Communists. Then six British sailors have been killed in a attack on a naval launch. The funeral of those killed was almost opposite here this afternoon. Colonel Waller of the Salvation Army told me on the phone this afternoon that his life had been threatened because he'd had to dismiss a Communist headmaster from a Salvation Army school and now the police were following him around for his protection! He was joking about it...

Letter of 25th September 1953:
Trip to Silver Mine Bay

Yes I had a lovely birthday, thank you for the cable! I went to Silver Mine Bay for one night, which was marvellously relaxing.

While I was reading after supper at the Guest House at Silver Mine someone suddenly entered the room in which I was sitting. To my surprise it was a young European police inspector, who said he'd come on a police launch from Cheung Chau on a routine visit. A little while later, when I was strolling to the village, I met him coming back to see me. In his hands he had an opium pipe. He said, 'I couldn't tell you before, but this is what I came for. We've raided an opium divan. Then I saw several handcuffed men under the guard of Chinese policemen. The young officer shouted out one of the few Chinese sentences he knew – 'Fai li, Fai li!'(k'uai li, k'uai li)[5] – and off they all went to the awaiting launch… He was obviously very pleased with himself. As I walked through the village afterwards the street was full of people talking excitedly about what had happened…

I do hope Raymond didn't feel too bad about leaving home to go to boarding school, I long to know how he has settled.

You ask me, why is it good for boys to go to boarding school? I can think of one point. These days, at nineteen or so, boys are thrown into the army (or air force) and have to live a pretty tough life. Boarding school should be a good preparation for that life. Otherwise, having never been away from home, it would be terribly hard.

In fact, a school party has just arrived here for an outing. The place is now alive with children. But how different from China! I sit and write in their midst and hardly anyone takes the slightest notice of me.

I return on the 2 pm boat. It's been a particularly happy birthday.

Lily

Although that is the last letter we have that my father wrote from Hong Kong I cannot leave without saying a bit more about Li Li (or Lily), the girl with tuberculosis of the spine mentioned in the above letter of 7th May 1953. My mother writes of her thus:

When Cliff found the family, there was the father, mother and three children – two boys and one girl, Lily. Lily was lying on a bed – so-called – in a tiny shack, very ill with tuberculosis. There was practically nothing in the house.

He arranged with a local rice shop to supply the family each day with a small quantity of rice. He then set off to get Lily into hospital. He went to the various hospitals but they all said they could not take her. As Cliff described her condition they said it would be almost impossible to save her and they were too overcrowded to take in such a hopeless case. It was true, they were desperately overcrowded, with beds in the corridors and anywhere they could find space. Cliff, being Cliff, of course did not give up. On the second round a friend, a missionary doctor, said he would take her for Cliff's sake and 'To get rid of him!' Lily was then about ten years old.

Shortly after that Cliff returned to England. The next we heard of Lily was when we were living in Gloucester, about six years later. We received a letter from her. The doctor, Dr Moore, had taken care of her and she had recovered. Then he sent her to a school and paid her fees. She had just become a Christian and had been baptised. Her father and mother said that now she was able to write English and had become a Christian, she must write to Mr Cook and tell him. Dr Moore had returned to Australia, but somehow she got our address and here was a letter from her. Cliff replied, but heard nothing further for about another two years. Then came a letter and a parcel containing four pairs of gloves. Three pairs of black gloves for Cliff, Arthur and Ray, and one pair of white ones for me. The mother was knitting gloves for a living and wanted us to accept these with her thanks. Lily's letter informed us she had left school. She wanted to be a film star – an ambition she later fulfilled – and was already studying to that end. She hoped to get a scholarship to America.

There was another gap of two or three years, then

another letter, this time from America with an invitation to her wedding. She was marrying Sam Ng, a Christian. Soon afterwards there arrived a photo of the bride and bridegroom. After that, for several years at Christmas there came a card and a letter or a message of some sort.

Here is an extract from a letter written after she heard of Cliff's death.

'Rev Cook was very kind to me when I was a little girl, while I was so sick that time in Hong Kong. Without his help I wouldn't be that healthy and happy in life now...'

Unlike my parents' work in China, which was almost a life-time commitment, my father had gone out to Hong Kong on the understanding that he would remain there for only two years. The task the MMS had asked him to take on, that of assisting the flood of refugees from the mainland, was regarded as a short-term measure, to deal with a specific crisis. It had originally been hoped that a two year assignment would satisfy this problem, in the somewhat naïve belief that it would be sufficient time for the refugees to be absorbed into the life of colony, or dispersed to other countries. In the event it took many more years and when my father returned to England his former Hunan colleague, the Reverend Paul Jefferies replaced him and continued with this work.

Thus after two years my father returned to England with the hope of eventually returning to work in the overseas mission; but in the short term, while Arthur and I were at a crucial stage in our education, he decided to take up the offer of an appointment in the home circuit. Of the options offered to him he chose a circuit on the borders of Manchester and Salford, much of it being a severely deprived area. With Arthur and me going to boarding school they didn't need to worry about the quality of local schooling. Such a posting suited his talents and interests well and as always the pastoral or social side of his work was where he was able to make the most significant contribution. I can well recall a litany of battered wives, abused children, ex-offenders and others who had received less than their share of life's good fortunes taking up temporary abode in our home. The social problems were not the same as in China or Hong Kong, but social problems there were aplenty and helping people to face up to the unequal challenges of life was my father's forte.

Endnotes

1. Mr Cheung, a wealthy Methodist Chinese businessman, who owned a biscuit company and was a generous benefactor of the Church.

2. Wu Te-chen was indeed one of the most important political leaders in China during Chiang Kai-shek's period of ascendancy. He was Mayor of Shanghai and Garrision Commander 1932-37, and Governor of Kwangtung Province 1937-38. In 1939 he was appointed Secretary General of the Kuomintang and shortly afterwards made Foreign Secretary. While he was Foreign Secretary he was involved in US Secretary of State General George Marshall's unsuccessful attempt to brokerage a peace deal between the Kuomintang government and the Communists. On the fall of the Kuomintang government and the withdrawal of its leaders to Taiwan, he became Governor of Taiwan Province.

3. This refers to the plans to construct a village for some of the refugees. This was completed shortly after my father left Hong Kong. The village, known as Wesley Village, provided homes for

one hundred families.

4. My father's first home circuit after returning from Hong Kong was in Manchester. He specifically wanted a circuit in a poor area.

5. Meaning 'Hurry!', '*fai li*' being Cantonese and '*k'uai li*' the Mandarin equivalent.

Epilogue

跋

My father flew back to England just before Christmas 1953. After eight months of furlough, interspersed with deputations, conferences and meetings of various types, he took charge of his first English circuit, with a church in Manchester and one in Salford.

After four years in Manchester he and the family moved to the greener pastures of rural Gloucestershire, living in the then serene village of Hucclecote, in the years before the M5 cut a swathe through the surrounding fields. And six years later my father was appointed warden of Methodist International House (MIH), London, which delighted both my parents, who were always happiest when operating in an international environment.

When my parents left MIH in 1968 my father's health was not good and he was suffering from occasional black outs. Nevertheless he threw himself with his usual vigour into his new church in Kingston-upon-Hull. However, further health problems shortly emerged and in 1971 he was diagnosed as suffering from terminal cancer. He died in Hull on 8th February 1972, while still in service.

My mother, although seven years older than my father and having suffered poor health at times in China, having succumbed to typhoid, malaria and various other ailments, outlived him by twenty-seven years.

In 1985, after a mild stroke, she moved into a retirement home in Bath, where she lived until her death in 1999, just ten weeks short of her one hundredth birthday.

Something that gave her great pleasure during her later

years was receiving letters from old friends from their time in China, or their children, after so many years of silence. In the early 1980s, after having received no word from former Chinese friends or colleagues since the Communist takeover, letters suddenly started arriving in England, redirected by the Methodist Missionary Society. With increasing liberalisation the Chinese at last felt safe to re-establish contact with overseas friends. In many cases the principal characters, such as Li Chang Hsu, had long since died, but their children, widows, or other formerly less prominent people, started to write. On one occasion my mother even received a memorable visit from an old lady she had known in China, who was visiting her son in England, where he lived with his wife and children. A visit from three generations of a Chinese family was a wonderful reminder of the past for my mother.

However, the pleasure of renewing acquaintances after so many years was nothing compared with the knowledge, that slowly began to emerge, that after more than thirty years of religious suppression, especially during the years of the Cultural Revolution, the newly emerging Chinese Church was attracting far larger membership than it had before the Communist takeover and the expulsion of the European missionaries. This was an independent Church, happily embracing the 'Three Selfs' – self-support, self-propagation, self-government – required by the government. It no longer needed the help or support of overseas Churches.

Although both of my parents spent many years back in England after their final departure from China, their love and deep respect for the country they served with such dedication never waned; and if Queen Mary died with 'Calais' written on her heart my parents had 'China' written on theirs.

Bibliography

Blundred, Rev Frederick, *From Earthenware to China*, privately published in 1996.

Cook, Elsie M.*China As I Remember It*, privately published in 1994.

Hahn, E. *The Soong Sisters*, Robert Hale Ltd 1942

Hares, B. *Journeying into Openness*, Shoreline Books 1991.

Knowles, C. *Exploring China,* AA World Travel Guides 1999.

Lattimore, O. & E. *The Making of Modern China*, George Allen & Unwin 1945.

O'Donovan, P. *For Fear of Weeping*, MacGibbon & Kee 1950.

Outerbridge, T. *These Three,* Oxford Street Press 1990.

Pearson, Dr George H, *Get up and Go*, Epworth Press 1968.

Rattenbury, Rev H. B.

  Understanding China, Frederick Muller Ltd. 1942.

  China-Burma Vagabond, Frederick Muller Ltd. 1943.

  China My China, Frederick Muller Ltd. 1944.

  This is China, Frederick Muller Ltd. 1949.

Reason, J. *Chiang Kai-shek and the Unity of China*, Cargate Press 1943.

Rose, J. *A Church Born to Suffer,* Cargate Press 1951.

Simpson, B. *China Post*, Edinburgh House Press 1939.

Soothill, W. E. *A History of China*, Ernest Benn Ltd. 1950.

Stanfield, J. & M.*From Manchu to Mao*, Epworth Press 1980.

Thompson, Rev D. *A Mountain Road,* privately published 1994.

Tim Oi Li, F. *Much Beloved Daughter*, Dartman, Longman & Todd 1985.

Tong, H. K.*Chiang Kai-shek: Soldier & Statesman*, Hurst & Blackett 1938.

Webb, Sister M. *In Journeyings Oft,* privately published 1986

Wright, C. E. *Walking for Christ in Hunan (The story of Rev Earnest B. Wright)*, privately published 1999.

China Handbook 1937-1943, Macmillan 1943.

List of old and new place names

Provinces

Old name	New name
Hupeh	Hubei
Kiangsi	Jiangxi
Kwangsi	Guangxi
Kwangtung	Guangdong
Kweichow	Guizhou
Shensi	Shaanxi

Towns, rivers, lakes etc.

Old name	New name
Canton	Guangzhou
Chanchuin	Ch'ang ch'un
Darien	Dalian
Hangchow	Hangzhou
Hsiang River, or Siang River	Xiang Jiang
Hsiangtan, or Siangtan	Xiangtan
Hsiangyin	Xianggyin
Ichang	Yichang
Kiukiang	Jiujang
Kiyang	Qiyang
Kukong	Shaoguan
Kuling	Guling
Kweiyang	Guiyang
Lingling (Yungchow)	Yongzhou
Manchiuli	Man–chou–li
Mukden	Shenyang
Nanking	Nanjing
Nanyoh, or Nan Yo	Nanyue (one of the peaks of Hengshan)
Peking	Beijing

Pingkiang	Pingjiang
Shashih	Shashi
Sian	Xi'an

Index of people

Index of places and events